Innovation in Developing and Transition Countries

NEW HORIZONS IN REGIONAL SCIENCE

Series Editor: Philip McCann, *Professor of Urban and Regional Economics, University of Sheffield Management School, UK*

Regional science analyses important issues surrounding the growth and development of urban and regional systems and is emerging as a major social science discipline. This series provides an invaluable forum for the publication of high quality scholarly work on urban and regional studies, industrial location economics, transport systems, economic geography and networks.

New Horizons in Regional Science aims to publish the best work by economists, geographers, urban and regional planners and other researchers from throughout the world. It is intended to serve a wide readership including academics, students and policymakers.

Titles in the series include:

Agglomeration, Clusters and Entrepreneurship
Studies in Regional Economic Development
Edited by Charlie Karlsson, Börje Johansson and Roger R. Stough

Regional Development and Proximity Relations
Edited by André Torre and Frédéric Wallet

Knowledge, Innovation and Space
Edited by Charlie Karlsson, Börje Johansson, Kiyoshi Kobayashi and Roger R. Stough

The Regional and Urban Policy of the European Union
Cohesion, Results-Orientation and Smart Specialisation
Philip McCann

Innovation and Entrepreneurship in the Global Economy
Knowledge, Technology and Internationalization
Edited by Charlie Karlsson, Urban Gråsjö and Sofia Wixe

The Rise of the City
Spatial Dynamics in the Urban Century
Edited by Karima Kourtit, Peter Nijkamp and Roger R. Stough

Settlements at the Edge
Remote Human Settlements in Developed Nations
Edited by Andrew Taylor, Dean B. Carson, Prescott C. Ensign, Lee Huskey, Rasmus Ole Rasmussen and Gertrude Saxinger

Sustainable Innovation and Regional Development
Rethinking Innovative Milieus
Edited by Leïla Kebir, Olivier Crevoisier, Pedro Costa and Véronique Peyrache-Gadeau

Geographies of Growth
Innovations, Networks and Collaborations
Edited by Charlie Karlsson, Martin Andersson and Lina Bjerke

Knowledge Borders
Temporary Labor Mobility and the Canada–US Border Region
Kathrine E. Richardson

Graduate Migration and Regional Development
An International Perspective
Edited by Jonathan Corcoran and Alessandra Faggian

Innovation in Developing and Transition Countries
Edited by Alexandra Tsvetkova, Jana Schmutzler, Marcela Suarez and Alessandra Faggian

Innovation in Developing and Transition Countries

Edited by

Alexandra Tsvetkova

The Ohio State University, USA

Jana Schmutzler

Universidad del Norte, Colombia

Marcela Suarez

Freie Universität Berlin, Germany

Alessandra Faggian

Gran Sasso Science Institute, Italy

NEW HORIZONS IN REGIONAL SCIENCE

Edward Elgar
PUBLISHING

Cheltenham, UK • Northampton, MA, USA

Published by
Edward Elgar Publishing Limited
The Lypiatts
15 Lansdown Road
Cheltenham
Glos GL50 2JA
UK

Edward Elgar Publishing, Inc.
William Pratt House
9 Dewey Court
Northampton
Massachusetts 01060
USA

A catalogue record for this book
is available from the British Library

Library of Congress Control Number: 2017939806

This book is available electronically in the **Elgar**online
Economics subject collection
DOI 10.4337/9781785369667

ISBN 978 1 78536 965 0 (cased)
ISBN 978 1 78536 966 7 (eBook)

Typeset by Servis Filmsetting Ltd, Stockport, Cheshire
Printed and bound in Great Britain by TJ International Ltd, Padstow

Contents

List of editors   vii
List of contributors   viii
Preface   xii
Acknowledgements   xiii

1   Introduction. A context-specific two-way approach to the
    study of innovation systems in developing and transition
    countries   1
    Jana Schmutzler, Marcela Suarez, Alexandra Tsvetkova and
    Alessandra Faggian

PART I   THE ROLE OF PUBLIC POLICIES IN DEVELOPING
         AND TRANSFORMING NATIONAL AND
         SECTORAL INNOVATION SYSTEMS

2   From industrialization to innovation: building the Peruvian
    National System of Science, Technology and Innovation,
    1968–2015   15
    Miklos Lukacs de Pereny

3   The state of the National Innovation System of Armenia   49
    Tatevik Poghosyan

4   The role of public policies in building up a national
    pharmaceutical innovation system in Tunisia: challenges after
    the Jasmine Revolution   68
    Nejla Yacoub

5   Public policies to orient science, technology, and innovation in
    healthcare towards inclusive development: evidence from Brazil   86
    Cecilia Tomassini Urti

6   The role of public policies in promoting innovation and
    innovation complementarities in developing countries: the case
    of the Argentinian software industry   109
    Hernán Alejandro Morero

PART II   INNOVATION CHALLENGES AND RESPONSE
           STRATEGIES IN NATIONAL AND SECTORAL
           INNOVATION SYSTEMS: A FIRM-LEVEL
           PERSPECTIVE

  7   Health biotechnology in Malaysia: issues and challenges faced
      by the innovative biotechnology firms   131
      Gulifeiya Abuduxike and Syed Mohamed Aljunid

  8   Collaborating to innovate: the case of the Nigerian mining
      industry   156
      Oluseye Oladayo Jegede

  9   Collaboration among Hungarian SMEs in innovation   171
      László Csonka

 10   The developmental university in emerging innovation systems:
      the case of the Universidad Mayor de San Simón, Bolivia   190
      *Carlos Gonzalo Acevedo Peña, Walter Mauricio Hernán
      Céspedes Quiroga and José Eduardo Zambrana Montán*

 11   The lost tiger in technological catch-up: lessons learned and
      implications for latecomer strategic typology   206
      Xiao-Shan Yap and Rajah Rasiah

 12   Epilogue. Innovation systems in developing and transition
      countries: what is different, what is missing and what are the
      implications?   236
      Alexandra Tsvetkova, Jana Schmutzler and Marcela Suarez

 Index   245

Editors

Alessandra Faggian is a Professor of Applied Economics, the Director of Social Sciences and the Vice Provost for Research at the Gran Sasso Science Institute in L'Aquila, Italy. She is a co-editor of Papers in Regional Science and the President of the North American Regional Science Council. Dr. Faggian's research interests lie in the fields of Regional and Urban Economics, Demography, Labour Economics and Economics of Education. Her publications cover a wide range of topics including migration, human capital, labour markets, creativity and local innovation and growth. Dr. Faggian is ranked among the top 20 regional science scholars worldwide.

Jana Schmutzler is a Professor at the Business School at the Universidad del Norte in Barranquilla, Colombia. She holds a Ph.D. from the Bergische Universität Wuppertal, Germany. Her current research interests focus on the interplay between the socio-economic context and individual economic actors in shaping innovation processes and the entrepreneurial, networking and collaboration behaviour of innovators and entrepreneurs and its influence on success.

Marcela Suarez is a post-doctoral fellow at the International Research Training Group 'Between Spaces, Actors and Representations of Globalisation' at the Lateinamerika-Institut, Freie Universität Berlin, Germany. She specializes in topics on knowledge networks, the role of non-state actors in science and technology policy, digital qualitative research and the dynamics of new technologies such as nanotechnology and artificial intelligence, particularly drones.

Alexandra Tsvetkova is a post-doctoral researcher at the Department of Agricultural, Environmental, and Development Economics, The Ohio State University, USA, where she studies the effects of energy sector expansion, productivity growth and other processes on economic performance of urban and rural areas. Her broad research interests are in the determinants of regional economic growth with a specific focus on innovation and entrepreneurship.

Contributors

Gulifeiya Abuduxike is a lecturer at the institute of public health, Hacettepe University, Turkey. She has been teaching various public health courses and was involved in medical research projects in the areas of public health, with a particular focus on cancer screening, primary health care services and the public health surveillance system to control communicable diseases. Her research interests are related to women and child health, emerging and re-emerging diseases, disease epidemiology, innovative biotechnology applications and their impacts on healthcare systems and economic development.

Carlos Gonzalo Acevedo Peña is a Ph.D. student at the Universidad Mayor de San Simón (UMSS), Bolivia, and the Blekinge Institute of Technology, Sweden, within a collaboration programme Bolivia-Sweden promoted by the Swedish International Development Cooperation Agency. He holds a Swedish Licentiate degree in Technoscience Studies. His work at UMSS is focused on fostering inclusive innovation processes and co-evolutionary approaches in Bolivia. His experience as an independent consultant includes cluster facilitation for the Unit of Technology Transfer, UMSS, and studies of technological prospects for the Bolivian Vice-Ministry of Science and Technology within the Bolivian Innovation System framework.

Syed Mohamed Aljunid is a Professor of Public Health Medicine and Health Economics and Founding Head of the International Centre for Casemix and Clinical Coding at the National University of Malaysia (UKM). He currently serves as the Founding Professor and Chair of Health Policy and Management, Faculty of Public Health, Kuwait University. His main interest is in the strengthening of the health care system of developing countries through research and development in health policy, health economics and finance, with a specific focus on the development of social health insurance and provider payment methods.

Walter Mauricio Hernán Céspedes Quiroga is a Program Manager at the Bolivian Science and Technology Vice-Ministry where he concentrates on developing policies and mechanisms to strengthen the Bolivian science, technology and innovation system. He holds an MA degree in Public Management from the Nancy University (France), an MA degree in

Development Studies from the Catholic University of Louvain (Belgium) and more recently he became a Ph.D. fellow in Governance and Policy Analysis at Maastricht University (the Netherlands).

László Csonka is a researcher and the executive director of the IKU Innovation Research Centre at Financial Research Corp, Hungary. Science, technology and innovation policy constitute the main focus of activity at IKU and within that Dr. Csonka is specifically interested in the collaborative aspects of research and innovation processes, such as inter-firm and university–industry collaborations and networking.

Miklos Lukacs de Pereny holds a Ph.D. in Management from the Alliance Manchester Business School, University of Manchester, UK and is currently a Research-Professor at ESAN Graduate School of Business based in Lima, Peru. His research interests lie at the crossroads of innovation, development studies and political economy with a particular focus on Global Value Chains and Innovation Systems frameworks.

Oluseye Oladayo Jegede is a Research Fellow at the African Institute for Science Policy and Innovation, Obafemi Awolowo University in Ile-Ife, Nigeria. He holds a BSc degree in Geology, and MSc and Ph.D. degrees in Technology Management from Obafemi Awolowo University. From 2010 to March 2016, Dr. Jegede was a research officer at the Department of Science Policy and Innovation, National Centre for Technology Management (NACETEM), an agency of the Federal Ministry of Science and Technology, Nigeria. Dr. Jegede's main areas of research include science, policy and innovation.

Hernán Alejandro Morero is an Assistant Researcher at the Centro de Investigaciones y Estudios sobre Cultura y Sociedad (CIECS) at CONICET (National Scientific and Technical Research Council, Argentina) and Universidad Nacional de Cordoba where he studies innovation complementarities in the software sector. He is also an Assistant Professor of Industrial Economics and History of Economic Thought at the Faculty of Economics, Universidad Nacional de Cordoba. His research interests include innovation and learning processes at firm level in various industries, as well as industrial policy and technological strategies for developing economies.

Tatevik Poghosyan is finalizing her dissertation at the United Nations University-MERIT (Maastricht, the Netherlands). Currently she is working as a policy analyst and economist at the Federal Government of Canada (Ottawa, Canada). Her research interests cover a broad area of firm performance and innovation in the context of transition economies.

She is particularly interested in the ways personal networks substitute a lack of market-supporting institutions during radical societal changes. She is a recipient of a Research Award from the International Research Development Centre (Ottawa, Canada), where she spent a year working on different research projects.

Rajah Rasiah is a Professor of International Development at the Faculty of Economics and Administration, University of Malaya, Malaysia. He obtained his doctorate in Economics from Cambridge University in 1992, and was a Rajawali fellow at Harvard University in 2014. He has worked extensively on the conceptualization of technology, its link to development, and on methodologies designed to capture clustering, technological capabilities and industrial policies.

Cecilia Tomassini Urti is a researcher at the Research Commission (CSIC) of the Republic University, Uruguay, and a Ph.D. student in the Public Policies, Strategies and Development Program at the Economics Institute, Federal University of Rio de Janeiro, Brazil, where she is also a researcher of the REDESIST network. Her main research interests include the promotion of science, technology and innovation in healthcare and their relation to inclusive development, knowledge production and the social impact of knowledge as well as the sociology of science and gender.

Nejla Yacoub is an Associate Professor of Economics at the Faculty of Economics and Management of Mahdia, University of Monastir, Tunisia. She is a member of the research unit on Advanced Economics and Simulation (AES) at the same university. She obtained her Ph.D. in Economics of Innovation from the University of Tunis El Manar, Tunisia, and the University of Lille Nord de France, France. Her research interests lie in the area of intellectual property rights and their impact on technology transfer and innovation, with a special emphasis on the pharmaceutical industry and developing countries.

Xiao-Shan Yap is a post-doctoral researcher at Eawag, the Swiss Federal Institute of Aquatic Science and Technology in Zurich, Switzerland. Her research interest is technological innovations in the context of globalization, with a focus on catching up and leapfrogging of emerging economies. She obtained her Ph.D. in Development Economics from University of Malaya, Malaysia.

José Eduardo Zambrana Montán is a lecturer at Universidad Mayor de San Simón, Cochabamba, Bolivia. He is the founder of a Technology Transfer Unit at the university, a coordinator of an Innovation Program supported by the Swedish International Development Cooperation

Agency and is also in charge of the Research Office at the Sciences and Technology Faculty. He works to promote initiatives based on the Innovation System approach and studies the impacts of technology on productive sectors.

Preface

This book brings together recent interdisciplinary research of young and aspiring scholars from the developing and transition countries who are a part of the Global Network for Economics of Learning, Innovation and Competence Building Systems (Globelics). It is the first book of its kind but hopefully not the last. This particular volume seeks to answer the overall question of how National Innovation Systems (NIS) in developing and transition countries shape the activities of firms and industries and how firms and industries, in turn, influence the innovative systems of their host countries.

The reality of developing and transition nations calls for a stronger emphasis on mixed research methods in an attempt to understand innovation processes in these contexts. A highly heterogeneous and interdisciplinary body of the Globelics scholars is well positioned to offer a cutting-edge comprehensive perspective on the issue. Along those lines, the book presents a variety of methods including historical analysis, participatory action research, case studies, document analysis and survey-based quantitative research, as well as triangulation to study innovation and adaptation strategies in developing and transition countries. Based on these, we go beyond the question of whether the NIS concept is applicable to the context of developing and transition countries and try to answer a range of questions:

- What are the challenges for innovation at the system and firm levels, according to the experiences of developing and transition countries?
- What is the role of public policies in the transformation of national innovation systems?
- What innovation practices successfully overcome challenges to innovation?
- What is the role of collaboration and learning strategies in fostering innovation?

All in all, the edited volume offers fine-grained and nuanced insights into the innovation processes and innovative practices in the context of developing and transition nations. It is hoped that the material in the book will be instrumental in promoting engaged and well-informed dialogue on the issue of innovation systems consolidation in this group of countries.

Acknowledgements

Editors: Jana Schmutzler acknowledges financial support from the Universidad del Norte (Colombia) through the research project 'Sistemas de Innovación en Países en Desarrollo' (Innovation Systems in Developing Countries). Marcela Suarez acknowledges support from the International Research Training Group 'Between Spaces, Actors and Representations of Globalisation', funded by the Deutsche Forschungsgemeinschaft (German Research Foundation).

Chapter 3: Tatevik Poghosyan would like to thank Dr. Prof. Robin Cowan and Dr. David O'Brien for their valuable comments.

Chapter 5: Cecilia Tomassini Urti thanks Carlos Bianchi and Maria Clara Couto Soares for their reading of early versions of her chapter and for all their suggestions. She acknowledges the financial support of CAPES-UDELAR.

Chapter 6: Hernán Alejandro Morero thanks Jorge Motta, Diana Suárez, Carina Borrastero, José Miguel Natera and Mauricio Uriona for their careful reading of early versions of this manuscript, and all their remarks and warm support. He acknowledges financial support from the Science and Technological Secretary (Secyt), Universidad Nacional de Córdoba (UNC, Argentina), and CONICET (Argentina).

Chapter 7: Gulifeiya Abuduxike and Syed Mohamed Aljunid would like to acknowledge both University Kebangsaan Malaysia (UKM) and the United Nations University – International Institute for Global Health (UNU-IIGH) for their financial support.

Chapter 9: László Csonka gratefully acknowledges funding by the grants 'Chances of Hungarian SMEs in the globalizing knowledge economy' (KKVENT, INNOTARS-1-2009-0001, funded by NKTH, 2008–2011) and 'The role of networking in the innovation process' (PD101410, funded by OTKA, 2011–2014).

1. Introduction. A context-specific two-way approach to the study of innovation systems in developing and transition countries

Jana Schmutzler, Marcela Suarez, Alexandra Tsvetkova and Alessandra Faggian

Innovation is the cornerstone of success in the modern economy at firm, industry, regional, and national levels. An enormous body of academic literature documents how innovation and innovative practices flourish in the fertile environments of mature market economies, driving sustainable economic growth. A young strand of the literature, interdisciplinary in nature, investigates national innovation systems (Lundvall, 1992; Nelson, 1993) and, more recently, innovation systems at the regional (Asheim and Gertler, 2004; Uyarra, 2010), sectoral (Malerba, 2002), technological (Carlsson and Stankiewitz, 1991) and corporate (Granstrand, 2000) levels. This new strand argues that the innovation and learning of a nation or a region reflect the development of specific, systemic arrangements that include firms, institutions, and socioeconomic structures and relationships among them (Lundvall, 1992). Understanding innovative systems is therefore crucial to facilitate and enhance innovation in a more efficient, context-specific way. The significance of such an educated approach, which takes into account local factors and specificities, is especially important in the economic environment of developing and transition countries. Since innovation is a main driver of economic development (Malecki, 1997), it plays a fundamental role in achieving the goal – set by many less developed countries – of closing the economic gap with the developed world.

A study of innovative systems and their elements, however, is remarkably different in developing countries due to the (sometimes) elusive nature of their formal institutions, the prevalence of customs and traditions over laws, and the specific motivations of the agents involved in innovative activities at various levels (Altenburg, 2011). Acknowledging the importance of research on National Innovation Systems (NISs) in developing countries, recent scholarship has discussed the applicability of the NIS concept and whether it can serve successfully as an analytical tool and framework for decision-makers designing policy or firm strategies in such countries (e.g. Lundvall et al., 2011). Within this discourse, a specialized body of literature details the evidence on NISs in developing countries (e.g. Arocena and Sutz, 2000b; Cassiolato et al., 2003; Nour, 2016). A broad concept of an NIS which encompasses "relationships within and between organizations, institutions and socio-economic structures" (e.g. Lundvall et al., 2011, p. 6) has been the key for these analyses. However, it is clear that even this broad definition of an NIS is challenged by the realities of developing countries.

Arocena and Sutz (2000b), for example, argued that the NIS in the developing countries of Latin America has an ex-ante character, where micro-economic behaviour, aiming at generating innovation, remains rather isolated and does not integrate in a system-like manner. This may reflect the distinctive characteristics of developing countries with regard to their formal and informal institutions. Other authors have underlined the importance of economic development that is inclusive and proposed the articulation of the Science, Technology and Innovation (STI) policies that account for social needs (Lalics, 2014). As countries have shown increasing rates of economic growth that does not give rise to learning and collaboration processes, which benefit the broader society, the focus is shifting to an inclusive notion of development (Johnson and Andersen, 2012; Dutrénit and Sutz, 2014; Lalics, 2014). In this sense, developing countries face a constant tension between the need to follow a transnational scientific agenda in order to facilitate the technological catch-up process, and the pressing demand to implement local policies aimed at solving urgent social problems. These tensions become ever more important in the face of budgetary restrictions where elementary social needs and the support of innovation processes compete for limited public funding.

Another specific challenge highlighted in this book is the tensions related to the transition processes such as those in post-Soviet contexts (the case of Armenia in Chapter 3) or caused by political turmoil in the Middle East during the recent years (the case of Tunisia's Jasmine Revolution in Chapter 4). These tensions are rendered visible in the coexisting structures of old and new systems, institutions and practices that explain the fragmentation of policies and scarce interactions among actors. Weak institutions, together with the lack of transparency and accountability in policymaking, are fostering economic structures that promote the accumulation of knowledge, infrastructure and capacities in already well-positioned companies. As a result, STI activities are often concentrated in certain regions, sectors and companies (mostly large or multinational firms), which dominate policy agenda-setting.

In spite of all aforementioned challenges and debates, the study of NISs in developing and transition countries offers both theoretical and methodological opportunities to overcome some of the limitations of current academic debates and to offer a fresh perspective on the role that governments and private actors play in promoting innovative activities in developing and transition countries with a specific focus on policy approaches, collaboration and learning. The chapters in this book explicitly link these issues to cultural inheritance, economic structures and political contexts that are central to understanding innovation processes in this group of nations. By conveying the richness of the different experiences coming from nine developing and transition countries located on four continents, this book provides a detailed view documenting and analysing the diversity of challenges and adaptive strategies taken by firms, industries and governments in the less developed part of the world in order to succeed in global competition.

This book is divided into two parts, following the broad definition of an NIS. A broad perspective on NISs implies that the system level shapes the way competences are built, learning takes place and innovations are generated, while at the same time the interactions at the micro level are reflected in changes taking place at the system level (Lundvall et al., 2011). The first part of the book "The role of public policies in developing and transforming national and sectoral innovation systems" comprises five chapters that address a public policy (system level) perspective on NISs for developing and transition countries. The next five chapters in the second part of the book "Innovation challenges and response strategies in national and sectoral innovation systems: A firm-level perspective" bring in the micro perspective and document interactions both among individual firms and between firms and regional or national actors such as governmental bodies or universities. Taken as a whole, the book offers a balanced and rounded empirical perspective on the two levels of the NIS concept.

As shown by numerous chapters in this book (with Chapters 2–6 offering a more detailed discussion), government actions contribute tremendously to the establishment of innovation capabilities, a point emphasized by the NIS literature. However, state intervention *per se* is only a part of the picture. Within the broad NIS definition, the macro level is linked to the micro behaviour in a two-way manner (Lundvall et al., 2011). Changes at the macro level induced by the government should be aimed towards shaping the learning and competence-building processes at the micro level within firms, universities and the like, while at the same time public policies should reflect the feedback received from the micro level. Chapters 2–6 provide ample material for discussion especially on the latter point.

In most general terms, Chapters 2 through 6 present a discussion of whether the NIS framework can serve as an analytical and/or a normative tool in these contexts. All chapters recognize the need to adopt a broad NIS definition (Lundvall et al., 2011). In other words, an explicit focus on sociocultural institutions, macroeconomic conditions and various infrastructures that potentially impact learning and competence-building processes, as well as interactions among different actors at various levels, appears crucial for a deeper understanding of actual and potential challenges faced by NISs in these countries. Such a deeper understanding enables scholars to advance research and, most importantly, may offer insights necessary for policymakers and practitioners to design policies aimed at the development and consolidation of NISs. As such, the analyses presented in the book chapters make a strong point in favour of context-dependent NIS development that builds on and takes advantage of the uniqueness of local milieu.

Additionally, the book stresses the importance of the often-overlooked informal institutions. Informal institutions are not necessarily made explicit or even communicated among social actors and they are – unlike formal institutions – self-enforcing. Informal institutions include conventions, codes of conduct, norms and moral values, which constrain the behaviour and actions of economic actors (North, 1990). With informal institutions being difficult to measure, research (including the research focused on the NIS concept) has been strongly biased towards formal institutions. Drawing on in-depth case studies, the first part of this book is able to show that informal institutions matter in the context of developing and transition countries where formal institutions are weak and under-developed. It appears that informal elements such as trust among various economic actors within an NIS directly interact with public policies in determining the success of an NIS.

Chapter 2, by Miklos Lukacs de Pereny, analyses Peru's public policies in the transition from industrialization to innovation-based development during the 1968–2015 period. The author provides a detailed overview of the Peruvian NIS-building throughout this period. More importantly, the chapter relates this transformation to economic, political and institutional changes, pointing out barriers, which have limited the success of the Peruvian NIS. This historical analysis enables the reader not only to scrutinize the influence of sociocultural and economic structures on the NIS formation, but also to observe path dependencies in the development of public policies within Peruvian NISs, which have been significant. The author highlights coordination problems among economic actors within the NIS and stresses the importance of the NIS's informal dimensions, such as willingness to cooperate or a lack of trust in state agents by Peruvian firms.

In a similar vein, Tatevik Poghosyan in Chapter 3 analyses the Armenian NIS, highlighting the country's experiences in the transition from a socialist system to a market economy. The chapter shows that, even though Armenia was a highly industrialized country, the "Soviet culture", understood as the historical heritage, technological specialization and prevailing innovation practices, has shaped the challenges faced by the country in its innovation-led development and the barriers that still hinder economic growth. The chapter demonstrates that a broad definition of an NIS coupled with the analysis of socio-economic and cultural traditions contributes to understanding of current economic processes in Armenia. Since the Soviet legacy is very unique, the chapter is able to validate another important point that many chapters in this book make, that is, the influence of the past is very persistent and may last many decades. For policymakers this points to the fact that the real change is likely to be slow, whereas short-term measures that are not ingrained in local culture are unlikely to have lasting effects.

Chapter 3 and Chapter 4 are a testimony to the importance of the sociopolitical environment in determining the way Innovation Systems (IS) are structured, built and how they evolve. In Chapter 4, Nejla Yacoub describes the Tunisia's pharmaceutical innovation system before the Jasmine Revolution and explores to what extent a more democratic environment, brought about by the revolution, enhances learning and competence-building in the context of a sectoral innovation system (SIS). Based on a detailed description and analysis of the macro environment, combined with a survey of pharmaceutical companies, the author shows the threats and opportunities presented to the pharmaceutical industry by the Jasmine Revolution in Tunisia. In contrast to the previous chapter, the eventual effect of the political turnaround on the SIS development is yet to be seen. A close comparison of the NIS in transition countries such as that described in Chapter 3 might be useful in understanding the possible trajectories of development, post-revolution. Such comparisons, though appropriate and requested (Lundvall et al., 2011), should be undertaken with education purposes rather than as a basis for specific policy approaches. This book shows that the sociocultural contexts of transition countries in Europe and of some Arabic countries, which tried to incorporate democratic elements in their political systems, differ considerably. Based on the observation that the evolution of an NIS is path-dependent, shaped by history and institutional composition, public policies successful in one context may not necessarily lead to the same result elsewhere.

The next chapter (Chapter 5) by Cecilia Tomassini Urti tackles a different but extremely important question of social impacts of technology-led economic growth. Even when considerable resources are allocated to support the key NIS actors and to promote competence-building, society as a whole may not necessarily benefit. In fact, advanced technological development often leads to negative distributional consequences (Altenburg, 2011). For developing – and to a lesser extent transition – countries this issue is of utmost importance given their prevalent high levels of poverty. It is a common practice that the STI policies and the Millennium Development Goals[1]-based policies are competing for limited public resources. As a result, the concept of inclusive innovation has received increasing attention. The idea of inclusive innovation is based on an assumption that innovation/technology and social policies can and should be developed in such a way as to promote the same outcomes reinforcing the impacts on each other (Paunov, 2013). The case of the Brazilian healthcare sector, analysed by Cecilia Tomassini Urti in Chapter 5, shows that the allocation of resources and the generation of capacities linked to NISs are not enough. Through document analysis and semi-structured interviews with policymakers and healthcare scholars, the author details the trajectory of public policies that support science, technology and innovation in this industrial sector. In particular, the analysis shows how the promotion of healthcare – as an example of a social inclusion goal to be attained – has been incorporated into STI policies. Whereas Chapter 2 provides evidence for the need to integrate the micro and the macro levels within an NIS, Chapter 5 draws attention to another important requirement for a harmonious and successful NIS development, the synchronization of the end policy targets and of policy actors' actions across all governmental bodies and programmes. When the traditional aim of an NIS to generate competence-building and learning as a means to promote innovation and to stimulate economic growth is supplemented with the aim to generate social inclusion, a mix of effective policy instruments has to be expanded to centrally include mechanisms of policy coordination, such as political agreements, national conferences, public and private partnerships in addition to special programmes that articulate specific roles of policy actors involved in the process.

Hernán Alejandro Morero in Chapter 6 provides further evidence on the importance of coordination between the different actors and levels of an NIS. Through a case study of the software industry in Argentina, this chapter provides empirical evidence for complementarities between the use of internal and external innovation sources for firms' innovative activities in this sector. Unlike other empirical studies that evaluate whether internal and external innovation sources have complementarity or substitution effects, the author emphasizes the role public policies play in encouraging software companies to invest in innovations internally in addition to collaborating externally for the innovation process. As such, this chapter contributes to the discussion of the role the system level plays in shaping the behaviour of economic actors at the micro level.

With this, Chapter 6 builds a bridge to the second part of the book. Lundvall and colleagues argued that within the broad definition of an NIS, "learning will reflect the prevailing institutions and the socio-economic structure" (Lundvall et al., 2011 p. 6). After a public policy perspective adopted by the chapters in the first part of the book, the second part evaluates challenges to national and sectoral innovation systems and presents strategies to overcome these challenges from the perspective of a firm. The contributions in the second part of the book link the firm-level learning and collaboration strategies to the context-dependent systemic level.

In Chapter 7, Gulifeiya Abuduxike and Syed Mohamed Aljunid identify the main challenges that the Malaysian firms face in the health biotechnology knowledge field and suggest potential strategies, which – according to the private firms in this sectoral innovation system – should be implemented. Through a mixed-method approach that consists of semi-structured interviews, a survey and focus groups combined with secondary data triangulation, the authors nicely complement the discussion of Chapters 2 through 5, showing that a lack of trust among economic actors in this sector hampers cooperation and coordination not only among firms but also among governmental institutions, leading to uncoordinated, and thus ineffective, sectoral innovation system public policies.

The following chapters (Chapters 8–11) focus on the challenge of enabling sustainable interactions, cooperation and coordination. While collaboration strategies driving the processes of competence-building and learning are a central component of any NIS, much of the current research, including most of the chapters contained in this volume, shows a lack of strong linkages between various actors within an NIS. Parting from the underlying premise that innovation is an interactive process (Lundvall, 1992), the concept of an NIS is relational (Arocena and Sutz, 2000a). A close interaction and connection between various actors within an NIS is key, especially in less developed parts of the world (Arocena and Sutz, 2000a). At the same time, formal and informal collaborations are a central aspect of firms' innovation strategies (Srholec and Verspagen, 2008). In the context of developing and transition countries, it is argued that firms rely on collaborations as an essential tool for overcoming the numerous barriers they face (McCormick and Atieno, 2002), including underdeveloped, highly volatile and unreliable formal institutions as well as small, fragmented and imperfect markets. Another distinguishing feature of developing countries is a weak coordination between actors comprising an NIS coupled with infrequent collaborations at the firm level (Arocena and Sutz, 2000a; de Melo et al., 2001).

The potential for learning opportunities, which have opened up in the new global landscape – characterized by economic globalization, new business strategies and the enabling technological developments – is large (Archibugi and Pietrobelli, 2003). Some developing countries were particularly successful in exploiting these opportunities via active collaboration and networking. However, many other countries have failed to benefit from collaboration and learning (Chaminade and Vang, 2008). Thus, a deeper understanding of how firms in developing and transition countries may successfully tap into information flows, through collaboration in general and through collaboration with international economic partners in particular, is important. Chapters 8 and 9 explore the link between the collaboration and networking strategies of firms and their innovation processes. Oluseye Oladayo Jegede in Chapter 8 focuses on collaboration strategies of firms in the Nigerian mining sector. Through questionnaires, structured interviews, and field observations of 150 mining companies, the author shows the impact that these strategies had on the process of innovation. Despite a very different socio-economic context, Chapter 8 accounts, just as Chapters 2 and 3, for similar barriers for the consolidation of the IS: weak interactions between private firms and public or governmental institutions. In Chapter 9, László Csonka presents comparable evidence from a survey of Hungarian small and medium enterprises (SMEs), offering insights into the motivation to collaborate both domestically and internationally, together with other important factors that shape collaboration and networking strategies of SMEs in this transition country.

Extending the discussion on interactions among various actors of an NIS, Carlos Gonzalo Acevedo Peña, Walter Mauricio Hernán Céspedes Quiroga and José Eduardo Zambrana Montán discuss in Chapter 10 the role of public Bolivian university Universidad Mayor de San Simón in promoting an innovation system by acting as a bridge-builder. Through a participatory research at the university's technology transfer office, the authors contend that at least two factors are at the core of competence-building and learning processes. In addition to the central role played by social relations among NIS participants, the alignment of goals among participating actors is equally or even more important. Only when each actor involved comprehends the necessities and capabilities of the other, may effective coordination and cooperation take place. As a result, the authors highlight how the concept of a developmental university exemplifies a new societal role that a university can play in developing countries contributing to a range of desirable social and economic ends.

In the last chapter (Chapter 11), Xiao-Shan Yap and Rajah Rasiah evaluate collaboration from a very different angle. Based on four case studies in the Malaysian wafer fabrication and semiconductor sector, the authors document how indigenous firms employ learning strategies to catch up by incorporating into global value chains (GVC). The inflow of knowledge and technology from foreign sources has long been considered crucial for developing countries' catching-up process, and participation in GVC may be an effective way to achieve this goal (Pietrobelli and Rabellotti, 2011). The chapter expands our knowledge on the determinants of successful participation in GVC by developing a taxonomy of latecomer business strategies that relates strategic choices to their promise for success.

It has been our aim to provide evidence for the applicability of the NIS concept (perhaps with some adjustments) in developing and transition countries through this book. The chapters of this volume demonstrate that a broad definition supplemented by the explicit focus on the influence of the sociocultural context, macroeconomic structures and institutions is the only way to ensure a deep understanding of innovation processes in these contexts. At the same time, it is the systemic element of this definition that the various chapters of this handbook provide plentiful evidence for. Taken as a whole, the book shows how the system level influences the way firms and other actors build up competences and learn, while demonstrating that the outcomes of interactions among actors at the micro level shape the NIS environment. It is crucial for the governments to account for this environment when devising innovation-focused strategies and approaches. We have attempted to provide detailed descriptions and analyses of some specific challenges faced by policymakers, firms and other economic actors who are engaged in the development and consolidation of an NIS. We believe that the book offers abundant material for learning and further discussions to both students of the NIS and practitioners working to build successful and efficient Innovation Systems in their countries and hope it will be instrumental in promoting engaged and well-informed dialogue on the issue.

NOTE

1. Millennium Development Goals were defined by the United Nations with the target date 2015 (http://www.un.org/millenniumgoals/).

REFERENCES

Altenburg, T. (2011). Building inclusive innovation systems in developing countries: Challenges for IS research. In B.-Å. Lundvall, K. Joseph, C. Chaminade and J. Vang (eds.), *Handbook of innovation systems and developing countries: Building domestic capabilities in a global setting* (pp. 33–56). Cheltenham, UK and Northhampton, MA: Edward Elgar Publishing.

Archibugi, D., and Pietrobelli, C. (2003). The globalisation of technology and its implications for developing countries: Windows of opportunity or further burden? *Technological Forecasting and Social Change, 70*(9), 861–883.

Arocena, R., and Sutz, J. (2000a). Looking at national systems of innovation from the South. *Industry and Innovation, 7*(1), 55–75.

Arocena, R., and Sutz, J. (2000b). *Interactive learning spaces and development policies in Latin America.* Copenhagen: Department of Industrial Economics and Strategy, Copenhagen Business School.

Asheim, B., and Gertler, M. (2004). The geography of innovation: Regional innovation systems. In J. Fagerberg, D. C. Mowery and R. R. Nelson (eds.), *The Oxford handbook of innovation* (pp. 291–217). Oxford: Oxford University Press.

Carlsson, B., and Stankiewicz, R. (1991). On the nature, function and composition of technological systems. *Journal of Evolutionary Economics, 1*(2), 93–118.

Cassiolato, J. E., Lastres, H. M. M., and Maciel, L. (2003). *Systems of innovation and development: Evidence from Brazil.* Cheltenham, UK and Northampton, MA: Edward Elgar Publishing.

Chaminade, C., and Vang, J. (2008). Globalisation of knowledge production and regional innovation policy: Supporting specialized hubs in the Bangalore software industry. *Research Policy, 37*(10), 1684–1696.

de Melo, M., Denizer, C., Gelb, A., and Tenev, S. (2001). Circumstance and choice: The role of initial conditions and policies in transition economies. *The World Bank Economic Review, 15*(1), 1–31.

Dutrénit, G., and Sutz, J. (2014). Sistemas de Innovación para un Desarrollo Inclusivo. La experiencia latinoamericana. Ciudad de México: FCCyT.

Granstrand, O. (2000). The shift towards intellectual capitalism – the role of infocom technologies. *Research Policy, 29*(9), 1061–1080.

Johnson, B. H., and Andersen, A. D. (2012). *Learning, innovation and inclusive development: New perspectives on economic development strategy and development aid* (Globelics Thematic Report, Vol. 2011/2012). Aalborg: Aalborg Universitetsforlag.

Lalics (2014). *Declaración LALICS: Aportes desde la Ciencia, la Tecnología y la Innovación a la Inclusión Social,* accessed 13 November 2016 at http://lalics.org/index.php?option=com_content&view=article&id=180:declaracion-lalics&catid=2:uncategorised&Itemid=108&lang=es.

Lundvall, B.-Å. (1992). *National systems of innovation: An analytical framework.* London: Pinter.

Lundvall, B.-Å., Joseph, K., Chaminade, C., and Vang, J. (2011). *Handbook of innovation systems and developing countries: Building domestic capabilities in a global setting.* Cheltenham, UK and Northampton, MA: Edward Elgar Publishing.

Malecki, E. (1997). *Technology and economic development: The dynamics of local, regional, and national change,* accessed 13 November 2016 at https://ssrn.com/abstract=1496226.

Malerba, F. (2002). Sectoral systems of innovation and introduction. *Research Policy*, *31*, 247–264.

McCormick, D., and Atieno, R. (2002). Linkages between small and large firms in the Kenyan food processing sector. In M. En van Dijk and H. Sandee (eds.), *Innovation and small enterprises in the Third World* (pp. 223–248). Cheltenham, UK and Northampton, MA: Edward Elgar Publishing.

Nelson, R. R. (1993). *National innovation systems: A comparative analysis.* Oxford: Oxford University Press.

North, D. C. (1990). *Institutions, institutional change and economic performance.* Cambridge: Cambridge University Press.

Nour, S. S. O. M. (2016). *Economic systems of innovation in the Arab region.* New York: Palgrave Macmillan.

Paunov, C. (2013). *Innovation and inclusive development: A discussion of the main policy issues* (OECD Science, Technology and Industry Working Papers, No. 2013/01). Paris: OECD.

Pietrobelli, C., and Rabellotti, R. (2011). Global Value Chains meet innovation systems: Are there learning opportunities for developing countries? *World Development*, *39*(7), 1261–1269.

Srholec, M., and Verspagen, B. (2008). *The voyage of the Beagle in innovation systems land: Explorations on sectors, innovation, heterogeneity and selection* (Working Paper 2008–008). Maastricht: UNU-MERIT.

Uyarra, E. (2010). What is evolutionary about "regional systems of innovation"? Implications for regional policy. *Journal of Evolutionary Economics*, *20*(1), 115–137.

PART I

The role of public policies in developing and transforming national and sectoral innovation systems

2. From industrialization to innovation: building the Peruvian National System of Science, Technology and Innovation, 1968–2015

Miklos Lukacs de Pereny

2.1 INTRODUCTION

Theoretical contributions and empirical evidence provided by economic history have shown the importance of industrial emulation for national economic development (Hamilton, 1791; List, 1841; Veblen, 1915; Rosenstein-Rodan, 1943; Nurkse, 1953; Hirschmann, 1958; Gerschenkron, 1962; Lall, 1987; Reinert, 1995; Chang, 2002; Cimoli et al., 2009). Following Britain's Industrial Revolution, during the second half of the nineteenth century laggard countries such as the US, Germany and Japan shifted from agricultural to manufacturing activities and consolidated modern economies based on increasing returns. A similar path to industrialization was followed a century later by South Korea and Taiwan, which diversified their productive structures and upgraded their technological and organizational capabilities (Amsden, 1992; Wade, 1992). More recently, under the guidance of state capitalism, China has also reduced the technological gap through learning and acquisition of innovation-driven research and development (R&D) skills.

Yet, as global production and trade systems increase in size and complexity, power asymmetries between developed and developing countries continue to widen, thus questioning the feasibility of industrialization as an economic development strategy. In response to these concerns Whittaker et al. (2008) introduced the concept of compressed development to highlight the merits of industrialization in a multilayered and highly interconnected international economic system. The first notion contained in this concept refers to shorter periods incurred by nation-states for catching-up; while Germany, the US and Japan roughly needed between 60 and 100 years to industrialize, South Korea, Taiwan and China did so faster. Beyond context-specific organizations, institutions and policies, knowledge, learning and innovation have been common drivers for successful economic transition. The second notion of compressed development refers to tensions between inward industry-led growth and outward engagement into geographically and functionally fragmented Global Value Chains (GVCs)[1] (Gereffi, 1994; Kaplinsky, 2000; Gereffi et al., 2005).

Born from industrial policy and organization studies, as well as evolutionary economics, the National Innovation System (NIS) framework (Freeman, 1987; Lundvall, 1992; Nelson, 1993) identifies and describes the array of organizations – the actors of the system – and institutions – its rules – involved in the generation, diffusion, transfer and adoption of innovations.[2] Although 'national' shares the inward orientation of industrialization, it is knowledge and learning – the core concepts of the NIS framework – that are crucial drivers for outward engagement and upgrading in global trade (Humphrey and Schmitz, 2002). In spite of the relative academic novelty of NIS, functional innovation systems based on economic agglomeration, integration and diversification already existed in Delft, The Netherlands and Venice, Italy in the 1650s (Reinert, 2007).[3] In this regard, while England decided to emulate the Dutch model and pave its way to the Industrial Revolution, bullion-hungry Spain chose to accumulate capital rather than develop manufacturing skills ending with inflation and severe economic crises.

After 300 years of Spanish colonization since the sixteenth century and throughout its Republican history, the Peruvian economy has remained primary-based and export-dependent. From silver to cotton and *guano* to copper, the country's productive base has been characterized by concentrated ownership of factors of production, poor infrastructure and marginal technological progress. The resulting supply of low value-added goods has exposed Peru's deficient capabilities for industrial upgrading and innovation-driven development. This paradox of plenty has been exacerbated by the extractive political and economic institutions[4] inherited during colonization, which have configured highly informal, uncoordinated and non-transparent domestic markets. Furthermore, unequal access and distribution of rents has frequently led to internal political conflicts and shaped the country's local, regional and national productive structures as well as its capacity to take full advantage of international trade networks.

Peru's failed attempts to industrialize date from the late 1950s but more recently the government has embraced the policy dimensions of NIS to achieve compressed development. However, as noted by Arocena and Sutz (2000) innovation systems is an *ex ante* concept in Latin American countries in the sense that these have very few of the innovation determinants that are found in developed ones. Second, the normative character of the concept collides with the organizational and institutional deficiencies inherited by Peru during Spanish colonial rule. Finally, although innovation systems are policy-oriented constructs, developing countries' capabilities to purposefully design functional NISs are questioned. Nevertheless, Cassiolato et al. (2005) believe that in spite of structural weaknesses the NIS framework is flexible enough to accommodate sectoral policies and interests. As systems with political and economic qualities, this observation is particularly relevant given that negotiation and compromise between state and non-state actors are crucial elements for NIS-building.

This chapter traces, describes and explains Peru's policy transitions from industrialization to innovation during the 1968–2015 period. The organizational and institutional trajectories leading to the construction of the current National System of Science, Technology and Technological Innovation (SINACYT) are analysed in historical perspective to leverage the influence of political and socio-economic contexts and determinants into its development process. Following this introduction, Section 2.2 covers these historical developments proper through further division into four sub-sections: (i) 1968–80; (ii) 1980–90; (iii) 1990–2000; and (iv) 2001–15. Each sub-section addresses the country's main organizational, institutional and policy trajectories and shifts from inward-looking and industry-led to outward and innovation-driven national economic development. Section 2.3 discusses the main structural weaknesses and limitations of SINACYT as well as its main strengths and opportunities for overcoming them while Section 2.4 concludes.

2.2 BUILDING THE PERUVIAN NATIONAL SYSTEM OF SCIENCE AND TECHNOLOGY

During the past 25 years Peru has achieved remarkable macroeconomic progress. Successful free-market reforms introduced during the 1990s saw poverty decrease from 58 per cent in 1990 to 31 per cent in 2010 and Gross Domestic Product (GDP) experienced a seven-fold expansion with an average growth rate of 5.7 per cent during the 2000–10 decade (see Table 2.1). Sustained growth led many international business and policy circles to praise the country's performance in the Latin American region although not without caution.[5] Nevertheless, recent economic slowdown has reminded Peruvians of the frail political and economic orders underpinning its primary resource-based and export-dependent economy.

Table 2.1   Basic social, economic and S&T indicators of Peru, 1970–2010

	1970	1980	1990	2000	2010
GDP (current US$ billion)[a]	7.3	17.6	19.3	51	128.5
Average GDP growth of previous decade (%)	5.9	3.5	−1.0	4.0	5.7
Inflation (%)	4.9	58.5	7 481.7	3.8	1.5
Exports (% of GDP)	14.4	16.0	16.1	16.8	26.6
Imports (% of GDP)	9.7	13.5	14.1	18.8	23.5
Agriculture, value added (% of GDP)	14.2	9.9	13.3	9.0	7.2
Industry, value added (% of GDP)	30.2	29.3	28	31.6	38.4
Services, value added (% of GDP)	55.6	60.8	58.7	59.4	54.4
Expenditure on S&T (% of GDP)	NA	0.3	0.76[2]	1.29	0.08[5]
Expenditure on R&D (% of GDP)	0.42[1]	NA	0.08[3]	0.1	0.15[4]
Population (million)	13.3	17.3	21.8	25.9	29.3
Poverty rate (% of population)	50	46	58	54	31

Notes:
[a] GNI from 1990 onwards.
[1] 1975 data; [2] 1993 data; [3] 1997 data; [4] 2004 data; [5] 2011 data.

Source: Author's elaboration based on BCRP (1999), INEI (2016), World Bank (2016) and Sagasti (1989).

According to the 2015–16 Global Competitiveness Index (GCI), Peru ranks 69th among 140 economies – 7th out of 30 in Latin America and the Caribbean region – and 23rd in the macroeconomic environment, earning the label of an efficiency-driven economy (WEF, 2015). Yet, it is far from achieving innovation-driven status as CGIs innovation indicators show: 105th in capacity to innovate, 117th in quality of R&D institutions, 115th in company spending on R&D, 108th in university–industry collaboration and 117th in availability of scientists and engineers (ibid.). Furthermore, the country invests only 0.14 per cent of its GDP on STI activities in comparison to 0.7 per cent in Latin America and 2.2 per cent by OECD members (PRODUCE, 2014). While R&D investment totalled US$239 million in 2010 it was 52 times smaller than in Brazil, 21 than Mexico and 5 than Chile in PPP terms (RICYT, 2016), firmly placing Peru at the regional bottom. With structural deficiencies deeply rooted in Peru's political and socio-economic history, the country's attempts to reverse them through industrialization and, more recently, through Science, Technology and Innovation (STI) policy, are described and analysed next.

2.2.1 Failed Industrialization and the Limits of State Interventionism, 1968–80

Initial industrialization efforts can be traced back to 1959 with the promulgation of Law of Industrial Promotion aimed at fostering industrial development and diversification across all export-oriented sectors. Heavily dependent on agriculture (e.g. sugar and cotton), mining (e.g. copper, silver and iron), fishmeal and oil, between 1960 and 1968 the Peruvian economy saw its industrial share of national GDP raise from 17 to 20 per cent with agriculture decreasing from 21 to 15 per cent and fishing and mining remaining stable at a combined 8 per cent (Thorp and Bertram, 1985, p. 395). However, for De Althaus (2008) industrial performance was artificial and costly due to heavy subsidies, marginal value addition and the small size of the country's domestic market. As public investment contracted and foreign private firms overtook strategic sectors – most notably oil and mining – Peruvian capitalism under 'creole liberalism' rapidly deteriorated in 1967 and ended in a military state coup the following year (Thorp and Bertram, 1985).

The military government criticized Peru's submission to foreign and private interests and justified state interventionism. Ideologically underpinned by Dependency Theory,[6] a large-scale Import-Substituting Industrialization (ISI) programme was rapidly implemented, beginning with expropriation of foreign-owned companies and nationalization of key industries and services.[7] Additional measures aimed at infant industry protection included prohibitions to import industrial goods produced locally and the imposition of high tariffs – as high as 66 per cent – applicable to nearly 3000 foreign products. Barring of all private capital – foreign and domestic – extended to the agricultural sector through the implementation of the Agrarian Reform in 1969 where private farms were expropriated and distributed among 325,000 peasants (Flindell-Klaren, 2000). Interventionism was deepened in 1970 with the Law of Industrial Community, which ordered the formation of agricultural and industrial community enterprises under collective ownership.

Early attention was also paid to scientific and technological development. During the first half of the 1960s, a series of technical missions were sent by the United Nations Educational, Scientific and Cultural Organization (UNESCO) throughout Latin America to spread the importance of Science and Technology (S&T) for social and economic progress. Two additional meetings between representatives of the American and Peruvian Academies of Science in 1966 and 1968 ended in Peru's first S&T operational framework (Sagasti, 1989). Among its main recommendations were the creation of a national S&T policy and funding organization, applied research institutes and a broad platform of national universities and laboratories devoted to basic research (Academy of Sciences, 1967, quoted by Díaz and Kuramoto, 2010). In November 1968 – one month after the state coup – the National Research Council (CONI), Peru's first S&T organization, was founded.

Under direct supervision by the Presidency of the Republic, CONI counted with strong political support but the national S&T funding agency never came to existence. Unfortunately, political enthusiasm quickly faded away, limiting CONI's activities to the elaboration of base studies. Yet, a number of Sectoral Public Research Institutes (SPRI) funded by special taxes was created throughout the 1970s in the telecommunications, mining, defence and fisheries sectors (see Table 2.2). The Institute for Industrial Technology and Technical Norms (ITINTEC) acquired a leading role and became the *de facto* S&T steering and funding agency in the country. It is estimated that until its deactivation in 1992, ITINTEC provided US$30 million to 740 enterprise projects with mixed results (Flit, 1994, quoted by Díaz and Kuramoto, 2010). Research output and impact of SPRIs was limited due to a shortage of qualified staff, excessive red tape, weak inter-organizational linkages and low domestic demand (OECD, 2011). Moreover, although state funding for SPRIs increased from US$30 million in 1970 to US$120 million in 1978, drastic fund cuts afterwards worsened research performance (Kuramoto and Sagasti, 2002).

In spite of the state's erratic political and financial support, the idea behind the creation of CONI and SPRIs was the formation of a National System of Science and Technology (NSST), serving the needs of industrialization. It was a far-sighted aspiration, which explicitly rejected what the military government perceived as an incompetent, selfish and rent-seeking private sector. Links with the business community were severed and implementation of the Law of Industrial Community furthered the damage by empowering labour unions politically managed by the government. Moreover, within the Andean Pact[8] framework, imports of foreign equipment and technology were restricted, increasing fixed costs and limiting technological upgrading opportunities. Outright hostility towards the private sector forced many firms to transfer net utilities abroad. The purposeful abolition of domestic competition and primacy of winner industries[9] over private firms consolidated supply-side policies in detriment of domestic demand. Announcement of the Plan Inca in 1974 – a government strategy for achieving economic and political self-dependence – summarized the government's long-term vision of a socialist state.

Like private firms, universities also stood among the losers of S&T policy under military rule. Regionally competitive until the late 1960s,

Table 2.2 Operational SPRIs of SYNACYT

Institute	Created	Sector	Main research areas
National Institute of Health (INS)	1936	Health	Public health; diagnosis methods; food health; quality control of drugs
National Cancer Institute of Peru (INEN)	1939	Health	Cancer diagnosis, treatment and prevention methods; drug testing
National Geographical Institute (IGN)	1944	Defense	Cartography; geodesy; photogrammetry
Peruvian Geophysical Institute (IGP)	1947	Environment	Seismology; climatology; volcanology
Peruvian Institute of the Sea (IMARPE)	1964	Production	Oceanography; aquaculture; fishing extraction methods; marine biodiversity
National Meteorology and Hydrology Service of Peru (SENAMHI)	1969	Environment	Climate change; technological and information services
National Telecommunications Research and Training Institute (INICTEL-UNI)[1]	1971	ICT	Satellite communications; network and broadband technologies
National Commission for Aerospace Research and Development (CONIDA)	1974	Defense	Astrophysics; geomatics; scientific instrumentation
Peruvian Nuclear Energy Institute (IPEN)	1975	Energy and Mines	Biomaterials; radiopharmaceuticals; functional composite materials
National Institute of Statistics and Computer Science (INEI)	1975	Presidency of the Council of Ministers	Statistical tools; social and economic information
National Training Service for the Construction Industry (SENCICO)	1976	Housing, Construction and Sanitation	Construction materials and planning; housing standards
Tourism Training Center (CENFOTUR)	1977	Foreign Trade and Tourism	Applied research in tourism services
Geological, Mining and Metallurgical Institute (INGEMMET)[2]	1978	Energy and Mines	Granting and monitoring of mining concessions; water certifications

Table 2.2 (continued)

Institute	Created	Sector	Main research areas
National Council of Science and Technology (CONCYTEC)[3]	1981	Presidency of the Republic	Multidisciplinary
National Institute of Mental Health (INSM)	1981	Health	Mental health research, epidemiology of mental diseases
Peruvian Amazon Region Research Institute (IIAP)	1981	Environment	Amazonian biodiversity; forest management; water resources
National Institute of Ophthalmology (INO)	1987	Health	Ocular health, blindness prevention research
National Institute of Agricultural Innovation (INIA)	1992*	Agriculture	Genetic resources and biotechnology (livestock/plants); irrigation systems
National Agricultural Health Service (SENASA)	1992	Agriculture	Agricultural health and safety; food safety; organic products
Technological Institute of Production (ITP)	2013**	Production	Fishery resources processing; fishery resources sustainability
National Institute for Glacier and Mountain Ecosystem Research (INAIGEM)	2014	Environment	Climate change; water resources; physical geography

Notes:
[1] Management transferred by the Ministry of Transport and Communications to the National University of Engineering (UNI).
[2] From the fusion of the Institute of Geology and Mining (IGEOMIN) and the Scientific and Technological Mining Institute (INCITEMI).
[3] Successor to the National Research Council (CONI) created in 1968.
* As National Institute of Agricultural Research and Promotion (INIPA) created in 1980.
** As Technological Institute of Fisheries (ITP) created in 1979.

Source: Author's elaboration based on Mullin (2002) and OECD (2011).

public universities saw applications increase from 64,312 in 1970 to 239,000 in 1980 (see Table 2.3). Yet, with most financial resources devoted to land reform and industrialization, infrastructure and equipment gradually deteriorated and disincentives such as low salaries and poor research facilities led to a shortage of qualified academic staff. Further funding cuts after 1975 accelerated quality downgrading and saw the proliferation of social science programmes in detriment of science and engineering ones, which strongly politicized university life. Civil society organizations such as professional associations and colleges displayed isolated efforts through the organization of small S&T workshops and training programmes but their role in the NSST was also downplayed by the government.

Industrialization stimulated public investment but industrial imports continuously exceeded exports, leading to trade deficits of US$0.4 billion in 1970 and US$0.7 billion in 1979 (Sheahan, 1999, p. 85). Funding for national industries came mostly from foreign loans generating financial dependency with tariffs and restricted import of supplies limiting efficiency and technical progress (ibid.). Heavy borrowing increased external debt as domestic demand could not finance industrial expansion. With rising fiscal deficit, backing-off of foreign lenders and unsatisfied social demands, the economy contracted, triggering a second military state coup in 1975. Although less radical than the previous one, protectionism and interventionism remained, increasing the share of industrial exports from 2 per cent in 1970–74 to 11 per cent in 1975–79 (Carranza, 2015). Nevertheless, a decade of military rule eroded public support, forcing the government to negotiate a transition to democracy with formerly proscribed political parties. Negotiations resulted in a new Constitution in 1979 and presidential elections the following year.

In S&T policy terms, the military government failed to articulate a minimally functional NSST. From its conception, the highly centralized and poorly resourced CONI was surpassed in its financial and technical capabilities by ITINTEC and was unable to foster linkages and interactions among ministries, national industries, SPRIs and collective enterprises. Disputes for funding among SPRIs were common and replaced state collaboration with competition. Domestic markets were deliberately abolished excluding the private sector and subsidies to national industries increased dependency on foreign money. Incapable of absorbing demand, universities experienced a steady decline and civil society actors were completely ignored, thus depriving the NSST from knowledge generation and transfer organizations and institutions. Lastly, failed industrialization and land reform aggravated fiscal deficit, fostered inflation and marked the return to economic development based on comparative advantage.

Table 2.3 Total population and demand for university education in Peru, 1970–2010

Year	Total population (million)	Total number of universities		Number of applicants	Percentage of total population	Number of entrants	Percentage of total population
		Public	Private				
1970	13.3	20	30 10	64 000	0.48%	24 000	0.18%
1980	17.3	25	35 10	239 000	1.38%	59 000	0.34%
1990	21.8	27	49 22	263 000	1.21%	73 000	0.33%
2000	25.9	29	73 44	381 000	1.47%	101 000	0.39%
2010	29.3	39	89 50	548 000	1.87%	258 000	0.88%

Source: Author's elaboration based on ANR (2012).

24

2.2.2 The Lost Decade, 1981–90

In May 1980, 6.5 million Peruvians cast their votes to signal the transition from military to civilian rule. Unfortunately, return to democracy was stained by the first terrorist act of the Shining Path (Sendero Luminoso, SL)[10] – in a remote Andean village on the same day the election took place. To understand Peru's recent history, including its efforts to build a national S&T system, without pondering the actions of this organization would be an incomplete and misleading undertaking. Initially confined in the southern region of Ayacucho, terrorism was fuelled by a radical anti-imperialist and class struggle discourse, which rapidly expanded throughout the country. Systematic destruction of communications, transportation and public services infrastructure as well as daily killings of peasants, policemen, local authorities and judges paralysed political and economic life (Degregori, 1990). Gradual territorial control was achieved by SL through the establishment of 'liberated zones' and 'armed strikes' aimed at eroding state authority (Kay, 1999). Until 1990, the threat of terrorism was downplayed by the government, allowing violence to escalate and leading the country to the worst political, economic and social crisis of its Republican history.

Science and technology activities were also affected by growing political and socio-economic instability. According to Sagasti (1989), in 1980 Peru had 370 research institutions and 4858 researchers, similar in number to Chile and Colombia but between four and six times less than Argentina, Brazil and Mexico. Low S&T development conditioned by government incompetence ended with CONI's deactivation and promulgation of Legislative Decree No 112 in 1981, which created the National Council of Science and Technology (CONCYTEC) and its funding branch, the National Fund of Science and Technology (FONDECYT), both under supervision by the Presidency of the Council of Ministers (PCM).[11] Until 1985 CONCYTEC's budget increased eightfold, allowing the agency to hire qualified staff, establish a basic operational framework and set-up a small funding programme for individual researchers (ibid.). Yet, like CONI, CONCYTEC was quickly marginalized in the political agenda, thus weakening its guiding, coordinating and articulating mission.

Considered by the new administration as remnants of militarism and failed industrialization, until 1985 public funds for SPRIs decreased 57 per cent from US$60 million in 1981 (Sagasti, 1989, p. 21). The dismantling of SPRIs began in 1981 with only three inaugurated during the 1980–85 period. Public universities continued to be ignored with their 1985 national budget 50 per cent lower than their 1967 peak. Government failure was expressed by accumulated and unsatisfied educational demand although a more welcoming market environment prompted the creation of 12 new private universities during the decade. On the other hand, public universities continued their steady decline, leading to a stall in applications and their transformation into SL indoctrination camps.

On the economic front, timid market liberalization reforms partially rolled back state interventionism and protectionism. Yet, public investment – mostly devoted to reparation of damaged infrastructure – food imports and internal defence were financed with international loans increasing Peru's external debt from US$6 billion in 1980 to US$10.9 billion in 1985 (MEF, 2016). A friendlier approach to private firms did not translate into stronger domestic demand due to decreasing stocks of social capital and market uncertainty stemming from terrorist violence. Private investment decreased from 21.2 per cent in 1982 to 12.2 per cent of GDP in 1985 (Crabtree, 2005). In terms of S&T promotion and development, private sector involvement was encouraged but links with the state were restricted to personal contact between a few businessmen and S&T bureaucrats. Funding for private firms from CONCYTEC decreased from US$9.7 million in 1981 to US$2.5 million four years later (Sagasti, 1989). Lastly, articulation with universities and civil society organizations was almost non-existent, thus configuring a highly uncoordinated and dysfunctional NSST.

The new government in 1985 confronted a stagnated economy and mounting violence. However, implementation of 'all-out-populism' in exchange for liberal structuralism further deepened Peru's socio-economic and political crisis (Sheahan, 1999). Until 1987, state subsidies ranging from basic products to gasoline brought relative stability and an artificial betterment of the economy but exhaustion of public funds and the declaration of credit ineligibility by multilateral organizations[12] unleashed an inflationary spiral that was tackled with money emissions. Resulting currency devaluation triggered an attempt by the state to nationalize the private banking system but citizen outrage forced a retreat. Nevertheless, government support plunged and private investment vanished. As the country entered into recession, price, wage and exchange rate controls further distorted the domestic market and small economic shocks were applied to stabilize prices. Yet, as shown in Table 2.1, medication proved worse than the disease with inflation reaching 1722 per cent in 1988 and 7481.7 per cent in 1990 (BCRP, 1999).

On the political front, although the peasantry had initially volunteered to join SL, active recruitment was needed to cope with rapid terrorist territorial expansion. Forced conscriptions were enforced and 'traitors' unwilling to join invariably faced execution. In response to indiscriminate violence and absence of the rule of law, the peasantry organized self-defence committees but offered little resistance to the better-armed terrorist organizations (Kay, 1999). By 1990, Lima was under siege with 50 per cent of the country's territory under *de facto* terrorist control (Biglione, 2008). As a consequence of political violence, Altamirano (2006, p. 23) estimates that between 1985 and 1990, 270,000 Peruvians fled the country – 75,000 in 1990 alone – among them Peru's most qualified scientists and professionals, the consequences of this brain drain can still be felt.

On the verge of national collapse, S&T activities became irrelevant in the public agenda. Devoid of qualified human and financial resources, CONCYTEC implemented a small research programme offering sums of US$3000 to US$10,000 for research enthusiasts across the country (Carranza, 2015). Funding was allocated without any clear criteria in terms of applicants' qualifications and aims, objectives and purpose of research efforts (ibid.). Unsurprisingly, S&T populism was also a failure but at least it stimulated research activity in Peru's provinces. Although no reliable statistics are available, Sagasti (1995, p. 34) estimates that CONCYTEC's budget plunged 50–60 per cent in real terms between 1985 and 1990 hardly covering essential administrative costs. Due to hyperinflation, the real value of SPRIs funding also decreased 90 per cent during this period, continuing their steady decline.

Hyperinflation and underemployment, widespread violence, negative net reserves, international financial isolation, extended informality, decreasing productivity and brain drain all contributed to explaining Peru's average GDP rate of -1 per cent during this lost decade (see Table 2.1). It is hard to agree with Sagasti's (1995) conclusion that the state kept its role as main articulator and promoter of the NSST. The critical condition of CONCYTEC and SPRIs – most of them operating via international charity – alongside disarticulated and languishing universities, fragmented third sector organizations and financially devastated private firms configured a non-existent NSST. Furthermore, two decades of radical economic policy shifts exacerbated by the exclusion of non-state actors from NSST-building contributed to marginal generation and accumulation of knowledge, weakened learning capabilities and limited opportunities for technology transfer. Lastly, the rationale of competition in a highly contracted, informal and failure-plagued domestic market was replaced by clientelism and survival, driving demand to historical lows and increasing poverty to historical highs.

2.2.3 Resetting the Organizational and Institutional Foundations, 1991–2000

The national crisis reached its zenith in July 1990 with salaries holding 33 per cent of their 1985 real value and formal employment decreasing from

47 to 17 per cent (Villarán, 2010). Accumulated inflation of 2,178,482 per cent since 1985 also turned any economic initiative into a hopeless endeavour. Moreover, according to Sheahan (1999) during the 1980s nearly 21,000 Peruvians were killed and 200,000 forced to migrate within a context of extreme violence and risk.[13] Both terrorism and hyperinflation 'created enormous concern among the population and led to a widespread demand for the restoration of economic and political order' (Wyeland, 2000, p. 484). Aware of the country's critical condition, the newly elected government implemented an emergency plan towards national reconstruction and pacification. Free market reforms including the end of price controls and a drastic economic shock were adopted alongside active promotion of Foreign Direct Investment (FDI) and privatization of inefficient state companies inherited from the import-substitution industrialization (ISI) period. In addition, negotiations with the IMF and WB were carried out to regain access to international financial circuits. On the political front, the government authorized the fully-fledged intervention of the army and empowered peasant self-defence committees to combat terrorism and recover territorial control (Kay, 1999).

Public universities were hotspots of propaganda, indoctrination and recruitment by SL including the National University of San Marcos (UNMSM), the oldest on the American continent.[14] Political violence prompted the military occupation of UNMSM's campus in 1991 and similar interventions were carried out at educational institutions throughout the country. Strengthened national morale urged the presidency to petition legislative faculties for counterinsurgency measures and liberal economic reforms but political opposition in Congress denied them jeopardizing the executive power's plans. Under these circumstances, a self-coup took place on 5 April 1992, ending in closure of the Congress and intervention of the judiciary power. Although anti-constitutional, given the state of emergency a substantial majority of Peruvians supported these measures[15] and turned their backs on the highly discredited political parties and their lost decade legacy. Civilian support for the presidency was strengthened with the capture of SL's leadership on 12 September 1992. Following international pressure, democracy was restored *via* legislative elections and the instalment of a new Congress in November 1992.

Structural reforms were quickly passed and implemented with a legitimate government majority in Congress. Economic reconstruction required basic organizations and institutions aimed at increasing market stability and predictability through regulation, supervision and formalization. To this end, the government created a number of technocratic and professionally staffed agencies[16] in contrast to party-affiliated appointments, which had configured an incompetent and expensive bureaucracy. Drastic reduction of public wages was also accompanied by destitution of nearly 300,000 bureaucrats whose salaries sliced a third of the national budget in 1992 but only 15 per cent three years later (Alfageme and Guabloche, 1998). These measures provided the organizational and institutional backbone of Peru's domestic market but were mostly oriented towards urban areas. However, similar attention was provided to the rural sector, badly hit by the impact of terrorism. Social programmes such as the Cooperation Fund for Social Development (FONCODES) and the National Programme for the Administration of Hydrographic Basins and Soil (PRONAMACHCS) were successfully implemented with assistance from multilateral and international cooperation agencies to increase productivity and diversify rural economies.

Full reversal of state interventionism and protectionism was signalled by the Constitution of 1993 – Peru's 13th since national independence in 1821 – which stressed free private enterprise and defined a subsidiary role of the state in a new social market economy.[17] National S&T duties were also outlined in Article 14 through state promotion and the coordination of scientific and technological research, the formulation of S&T policy and the integration of non-state actors under CONCYTEC's guidance. Ministries assumed a more active role in S&T activities, in particular the Ministry of Agriculture, which was politically empowered through the creation of four new SPRIs to improve peasant welfare[18] (see Table 2.2). On the verge of extinction due to lack of financial resources, agricultural experimental stations were passed to private firms for administrative and financial management and private–public alliances were formed to stimulate applied research. After two decades of neglect, the private sector finally began to play an active role in the country's S&T agenda and the first functional linkages of the NSST were established.

Results of economic reform and national pacification became tangible from 1993 onwards with GDP growing 12.3 per cent in 1994 and inflation under control at 6.5 per cent in 1997 (BCRP, 1999). A more welcoming environment for private investment saw FDI flows total US$16.5 billion during the 1991–2000 period in contrast to US$300 million between 1981 and 1990 (MEF, 2016). The end of fixed exchange rates also meant the surge of a better operating and regulated market. Formalization also translated into higher tax revenues from 4.9 per cent of GDP in 1989 – the world's third lowest, only ahead of Zaire and Uganda – to 14.1 per cent in 1997 (Sagasti, 1995, p. 35). Private investment in telecommunications and energy infrastructure alongside significant public spending in transportation infrastructure and public services articulated the national territory and supported the formation of competitive agro-industrial clusters in the coastal regions of Ica and La Libertad. Peruvian asparagus, avocado, lemon, mango and grapes finally reached international markets and allowed private firms to engage in GVCs. On the other hand, the end of terrorist 'liberated zones' allowed civil society organizations, especially national and international NGOs, to access isolated rural areas and forge links with local governments for the provision of technical assistance and training programmes to the peasantry. Overall – although mostly need-driven – entrepreneurial activity also blossomed nationwide.

A better economic situation and safer university campuses triggered applications for tertiary education. Yet, unable to absorb demand, the government authorized the creation of private for-profit universities in 1996[19] doubling their number from 22 to 44 during the 1990s (see Table 2.3). A year later CONCYTEC called private firms, universities, foreign aid agencies and independent S&T communities to participate in the first 'Systemic Study of the National Reality of Science and Technology'. The study was elaborated by multidisciplinary teams and its recommendations were leveraged into the government's national development strategy becoming the state's first real attempt to integrate and build the NSST (CONCYTEC, 1999). Additionally, the first National S&T Census was organized and conducted between 1997 and 1999 to create basic S&T indicators for the elaboration of sectoral studies. Its first recorded results offered no space for optimism as R&D expenditure in 1997 reached only 0.08 per cent of GDP while the regional average was 0.53 per cent (RICyT, 2016).

Unexpected natural disasters such as El Niño phenomenon and the Asian, Mexican, Brazilian and Russian financial crises between 1997 and 1998 lowered economic expectations with negative GDP growth of −0.4 per cent in 1998 (INEI, 2016). Full membership in the Asia-Pacific Economic Forum (APEC) brought some hope to exporters by broadening commercial destinations and opening the door for future bilateral and multilateral trade agreements. In 1999 the Ministry of Agriculture (MINAG) created the Programme for Promotion of Technological Innovation and Competitiveness of Peruvian Agriculture with financial and technical support from the WB.[20] It became the building block of the Innovation and Competitiveness Programme for Peruvian Agriculture (INCAGRO), Peru's first functional STI funding programme. Inspired by the success of its first S&T systemic study, CONCYTEC called S&T stakeholders again to elaborate the National Strategic Plan for Scientific and Technological Development. The plan focused on technology transfer activities and refinement of S&T indicators to measure NSST performance but political turmoil at the end of the decade prevented completion. Allegations of government corruption and a questioned electoral process in 2000 led to social instability resulting in the resignation of the presidency and new elections in 2001.

According to Sagasti (1989) and Carranza (2015), low investment in S&T during the 1990s was due to a lack of interest by the government. However, based on the national economic and S&T indicators available, this was hardly the case. More important was the strengthened national context during the 1990s, underpinned by durable institutional and organizational foundations laid for future national S&T promotion and development. A more secure and stable country saw economic activity flourish as small and medium enterprises (SMEs) increasingly engaged in national and international trade. Competitiveness was fostered through compliance of private firms with international standards and regulations, learning by doing, technology imports and broader educational opportunities available at universities and technical institutes. Without these foundational economic and political achievements, no NSST could ever be possible.

2.2.4 Sectoral Within National Innovation Systems and Public Funding Bonanza, 2001–15

In contrast to previous economic policy discontinuities, the free market model, established in the early 1990s, was preserved by successive governments. A six-fold increase in exports, poverty reduction from 54.8 to 22.7 per cent and an average GDP growth rate of 5.3 per cent between 2001 and 2015 are evidence of the benefits brought by economic liberalization (World Bank, 2016). However, although market institutions hardened to provide more stability and predictability, the 2008–2009 Global Financial Crisis exposed the structural limitations of Peru's primary-based economy with GDP growth plunging from 9.8 per cent in 2008 to 1 per cent a year later. Positive trade balances have been regularly achieved since 2002, but as in the 1970s, natural resources still constitute 75 per cent of exports. Moreover, the political system remains fragmented and highly polarized.

A more affluent economy meant more attention and financial support for national STI development. Yet, findings from an independent study commissioned by the state in 2002 confirmed CONCYTEC's limited technical and financial capabilities to steer an NIS (Mullin Consulting, 2002). Shortage of S&T public funding led to negotiations with the WB and the creation of INCAGRO under the management of the National Institute of Agricultural Innovation (INIA) to finance sectoral innovations (See Table 2.4). Additionally, a national STI emergency plan was elaborated in 2002 under CONCYTEC's leadership, with contributions from state agencies, private firms, universities, research institutions and professional colleges. Participation of non-state actors was extended to international organizations for the elaboration of performance indicators and a new STI legal framework.[21] Although these initiatives were built on the technical

Table 2.4 National funding programmes for science, technology and technological innovation

Programme/source	Since	Sector	Steering agency	Funds (US$ million)	Targeted activities	Current status
FONDEPES	1992	Production	PRODUCE	NA	• Loans for artisan fisheries and aquaculture sector • Technology transfer, technical training and service innovations • Fisheries and aquaculture infrastructure	Operational
INCAGRO	2001*	Agriculture	INIA	65 55% from WB loan 45% from executing agencies	• Agricultural research and technology transfer • Innovation in agricultural services • Technical training programmes towards agricultural competitiveness	Deactivated in 2010
FINCYT I	2007	PCM	PCM	36 25 (IADB loan) 11 (State funds)	• Technological innovation projects focused on resource-based sectors • Scholarships for S&T training • Improving R&D capabilities in universities and research institutes	FINCYT II
FIDECOM	2007	Production	InnovatePe	65	• Applied technological research and productive innovation in firms • Technical training and technology transfer for SMEs • Knowledge generation and transfer	Operational
AGROIDEAS	2011**	Agriculture	MINAG	100[a]	• Association of small producers (agriculture, livestock and forestry) • Adoption of agricultural technologies • Small enterprise management	Operational

Programme	Year	Sector	Agency	Amount (US$ million)	Objectives	Status
FINCYT II	2013	Production	InnovatePe	100 35 (IADB loan) 65 (State funds)	• Technological innovation projects focused on value addition • Scholarships for S&T training • Improving R&D capabilities in universities and research institutes	Operational
Start-Up Peru	2013	Production	InnovatePe	15 Funded by FOMITEC	• Seed capital for business entrepreneurs • Promotion and support for business incubators • Technological innovation in products and services	Operational
FOMITEC	2013	Production	CONCYTEC InnovatePe	80	• US$65 million for CONCYTEC (Cienciactiva programme) • US$15 million for PRODUCE (Start-Up Peru programme)	Operational
Cienciactiva[1]	2013	PCM	CONCYTEC	65 Funded by FOMITEC	• Scholarships for S&T training • Promotion of basic and applied R&D • Promotion of S&T partnerships among non-state actors	Operational
PNIA	2014	Agriculture	INIA	165.5 40 (IADB loan) + 40 (WB loan) 85.5 (State funds)	• US$55.5 million for applied research and seed capital for small producers • US$26.5 million for basic and applied agro-research and scholarships	Operational
MIPYME	2015	Production	InnovatePe COFIDE	180	• US$150 million for financial instruments • US$30 million as non-financial instruments	Operational

Notes:
1 Current denomination of FONDECYT.
a Amount disbursed up to October 2015.
* Created in 1999 as the Programme for Promotion of Technological Innovation and Competitiveness of Peruvian Agriculture.
** Created in 2009 as the Programme of Compensations for Competitiveness (PCC).

Source: Author's elaboration.

and organizational foundations laid during the late 1990s, their importance rests in the formal introduction of innovation as a concept into national policy discourse.

Within the new STI institutional framework CONCYTEC elaborated a National Strategic Plan of Science, Technology and Innovation for the 2006–21 period (PENCTI), which was formally approved by the government in 2006. The plan's goal was to reach 0.52 per cent of GDP expenditure on STI by 2011 – so far not achieved – by stimulating private demand for national STI goods and services, promoting linkages between academia and private firms and supporting sectors with comparative advantage, mainly in the agriculture, aquaculture, mining and metallurgy, forestry and tourism sectors. Most importantly, PENCTI sealed the fate of state-led industrialization by placing private firms – not industries – as key actors of the newly launched National System of Science, Technology and Technological Innovation (SINACYT) and by focusing on the promotion of private returns and social spillovers instead of subsidized social returns (CONCYTEC, 2006). The state also adopted, at least in its rhetoric, a market pull rationale and redefined its role as an innovation enabler for non-state actors.

Inspired by the success of INCAGRO and with a US$25 million loan from the IADB, the government implemented the Fund for Innovation, Science and Technology (FINCYT) in 2007 to finance technological innovation projects in primary-based sectors. Under the initiative of the Ministry of Production (PRODUCE), a Fund for Research and Development for Competitiveness (FIDECOM) was also created to increase SMEs productivity. However, these initiatives were exclusively targeted to urban areas in detriment of the rural hinterland. The Andes mountain range stands as a formidable geographical barrier for Peru's STI development. During the last 45 years, with the exception of the 1968–75 and 1990–2000 periods, state presence in backward rural areas has been limited as evidenced by lesser infrastructure and widespread market informality and fragmentation. The Ministry of Agriculture has been the government's most active agency in the provision of training and technology transfer to rural communities disarticulated from SINACYT. To amend this historical absence, in 2008 the government created the National System of Agricultural Innovation (SNIA) and the Programme of Compensations for Competitiveness (PCC) as its funding branch,[22] entrusting INIA as the steering and coordination agency of the new agricultural innovation system within SINACYT.

Between 2003 and 2009, public spending in STI increased 66 per cent in absolute terms (Díaz and Kuramoto, 2010). Innovation became a widely diffused and adopted concept among STI stakeholders and the government expressed genuine commitment to leverage S&T and R&D initiatives into national economic development. However, in spite of some minor achievements,[23] SINACYT remained a weak and highly disarticulated system, composed of myriad fragmented actors with different capabilities and needs. Among them, private firms and producers' associations, particularly in the mining, agro-export and textile sectors, seized opportunities offered by Free Trade Agreements (FTAs)[24] but low productivity and marginal value addition kept them confined at the bottom end of GVCs. Nevertheless, at the core of SINACYT's institutional and organizational limitations was a marginalized CONCYTEC whose steering capabilities were further eroded by political, financial and technical empowerment of PRODUCE and INIA.

Strong macroeconomic recovery was experienced after the Global Financial Crisis and continued despite a polarized presidential race in 2011. The newly elected government was ideologically sympathetic towards 1968–75 social and economic policies but market pressures tempered attempts for state interventionism and protectionism. Public expenditure on STI continued at a low 0.1 per cent of GDP (see Table 2.1) but a public STI funding system began to emerge founded on INCAGRO and FINCYT. Although the former was discontinued in 2010 to consolidate SNIA's PCC – now branded Agroideas – FINCYT was extended in 2011 through a US$35 million loan from the IADB and US$65 million from the state.[25] Diversification of state funding sources continued in 2013 and 2014 with the creation of Startup Peru, targeted at innovation-driven entrepreneurs and FONDECYT's conversion into the Cienciactiva programme, aimed at both S&T and R&D promotion and training and partially financed by the STI Framework Fund (FOMITEC) (see Table 2.4). Yet, the proliferation of funding schemes led to the duplication of functions and objectives, prompting PRODUCE to establish the National Programme of Innovation for Competitiveness and Productivity (InnovatePe) in 2014, towards financial harmonization.[26]

State STI funds can be potentially accessed by 1,883,531 firms in the country – 99.64 per cent of them private – of which 94.92 per cent are micro, 4.11 per cent small and 0.6 per cent medium and large (INEI, 2014). However, 70 per cent are informal, posing serious challenges to contract enforcement, transactional transparency and IPR protection (CONCYTEC, 2013). Although regulatory and supervisory state agencies such as INDECOPI and COFOPRI have strongly supported market formalization, low stocks of social capital inherited from the lost decade restrict interactions among SINACYT actors, leading to low quality, low productivity and limited diversification. In an attempt to reverse these limitations, in 2014 PRODUCE launched the National Plan for Productive

Diversification (PNDP) to break dependency on natural resources and increase firms' competitiveness through product and process upgrading. The plan considered the creation of Industrial Eco-Technological Parks (PITEs) to act as export-oriented clusters (PRODUCE, 2014). Nevertheless, PITEs run the risk of following a failed supply-side industrial policy rationale where industrialization would be simply replaced by the more fashionable concept of innovation. Beyond these considerations, through executive political power and STI funding management, PRODUCE has consolidated its position as the *de facto* steering agency of SINACYT in detriment of CONCYTEC.

In terms of non-state actors, the number of universities skyrocketed reaching a total of 139 in 2015. Since 1960 Peru's tertiary education system was supervised by the autonomous National Assembly of Vice-Chancellors (ANR). However, taking advantage of public financial incentives provided to universities in 1996, the ANR became a space for the promotion of private interests in detriment of educational quality. As a result, no Peruvian university but one is featured among the top 500 in world rankings and regional performance is also poor (QS, 2015; THE; 2015; ARWU, 2015).[27] In response to this situation, Law 30 220 or University Law was promulgated in 2014 to improve national teaching and research standards. The law ordered deactivation of the ANR and its replacement by the National Superintendency of Education (SUNEDU) responsible for setting and enforcing quality standards on academic staff, degree programmes and R&D activities. The law also withdraws tax incentives for profit-oriented institutions, which do not reinvest 30 per cent of utilities to fulfil their educational mission. Although opponents of the law – mainly former ANR members and associated groups of interests – argue against potential state interventionism through SUNEDU, the need to reverse educational mercantilism and improve overall educational quality justifies its promulgation.

Disarticulation has been one of SINACYT's major problems, which state actors like Technological Innovation Centers (CITEs) are attempting to reverse. The first CITEs were created by the state in 2000 to provide technical training and facilitate technology transfer to SMEs. Demand for CITE services increased steadily – especially in rural areas – and coverage was extended to petty industries[28] prompting the government to authorize the creation of private CITEs in 2014. Services have expanded from training to product and process upgrading in productive sectors where the country has comparative advantages, thus transforming CITEs into important enablers of SME engagement with GVCs. Payment for services by customers contributes to financial sustainability and nationwide presence fosters STI decentralization. Supervised by the Peruvian Technological

Institute (ITP), there are currently 32 public and 23 private CITEs promoting and supporting grassroots innovations throughout the country.

Overall, in spite of the broader participation of non-state actors, increased funding options and a more predictable domestic market, disarticulation and poor governance of SINACYT remain unresolved. Keeping the economy in 'automatic pilot' and failing to introduce political reforms have hampered STI development. Furthermore, the overlapping of STI functions and red tape continues to limit collaboration among state agencies, firms, universities and civil society actors. Lastly, structural problems, namely a US$130 billion deficit in public infrastructure, low quality primary and secondary education, low productivity, limited economic diversification and a rigid labour market constitute major obstacles which require immediate attention if Peru aims to achieve compressed development by becoming an innovation-driven economy.

2.3   DISCUSSION

During the past 45 years Peru has shifted from inward state-led industrialization to outward export-driven economic development. During the 1968–80 period national industries became core actors of the economy at the expense of private firms, universities and civil society organizations. However, although the first national S&T organizations were established, exclusion of non-state actors, deliberate abolition of market competition and political disempowerment of CONI impeded the configuration and articulation of a minimally functional and integrated NIS. This situation worsened during the 1980s when timid reversal of state interventionism followed by all-out populism led to the worst economic and political crisis in Peru's republican history. Hyperinflation and terrorism resulted in physical and institutional destruction of markets and organizations, severe erosion of social capital and absence of the rule of law. Moreover, international isolation, the widening of a historically rooted urban–rural divide and massive brain-drain evaporated any hopes for scientific and technological advancement.

Structural economic reforms and national pacification achieved during the 1990s laid out the institutional and organizational foundations of SINACYT. Market liberalization alongside the creation of regulatory and supervisory state agencies still constituted the backbone of a stable and predictable macroeconomic environment. Although mostly need-driven, entrepreneurial activity flourished throughout the decade, leading to a more dynamic and competitive domestic market. The benefits of economic and political stability were also capitalized on by universities, which increased in number to satisfy national demand, although at the expense of teaching and research quality. Following political turmoil in 2000–01, the free market model has been kept in 'automatic pilot' mode at the expense of second-generation reforms. Consequently, the problems of informality, lack of incentives for private investment and red tape remain unsolved. Yet, government commitment to STI development expressed in increased and harmonized public funding as well as grassroots articulation through CITEs are commendable initiatives waiting for replication and escalation. Promulgation of the University Law in 2014 aimed at reversing educational mercantilism and PRODUCE's national economic diversification strategy also constituted solid building blocks for Peru's NIS construction.

A current representation of SINACYT is provided in Figure 2.1. The system is composed of five main groups of actors: (i) State agencies represented by CONCYTEC, ministries, SPRIs and STI funding programmes; (ii) private firms and industries; (iii) public and private universities; (iv) state regulators and supervisors; and (v) civil society organizations. Arrows represent dominant interactions and linkages among groups of actors rather than specific actors. Despite the organizational, financial and legal efforts displayed by the state, SINACYT remains more a concept than a reality. Displaced by PRODUCE's executive power and financial resources and weakened by the existence of an independent agricultural innovation system within SINACYT, CONCYTECs steering and coordination duties have been eroded, posing serious challenges to NIS governance. Moreover, duplication of functions and continued dominance of supply-side policies in relation to demand configure a highly disarticulated, uncoordinated and centralized NIS.

With the release of PENCTI in 2006, private enterprises have replaced industries as the most important innovation partners for the state. Yet, only large private firms – less than 10,000 nationwide – can tap into global learning and technological networks while the rest – mostly need-driven, informal and labour-intensive SMEs – have limited access to knowledge, technology and financial resources. Weak articulation and coordination with government agencies is conditioned by excessive red tape, limited information and mistrust in a massive bureaucracy while no guarantees exist to capture rents from innovation. As a result, low productivity and value-addition underpin grassroots innovation – mainly in petty industries – where opportunities for product and process upgrading are exclusively provided by CITEs and a handful civil society organizations (for example NGOs) acting as facilitators. Universities face similar problems in terms of access to funding sources and integration into SINACYT. Besides a few islands of educational excellence in the natural sciences and management studies, most universities have a weak enterprising spirit and are incapable of tapping

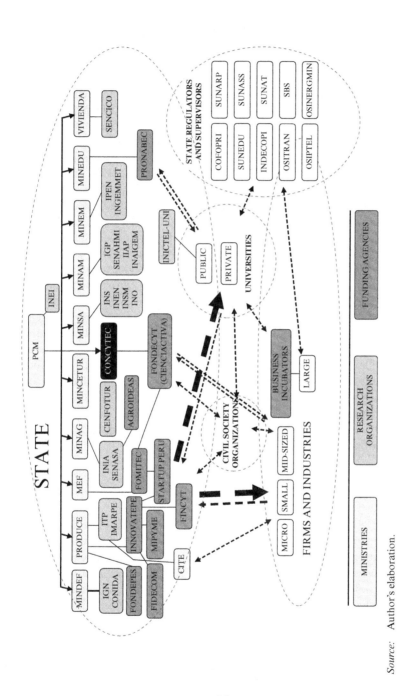

Source: Author's elaboration.

Figure 2.1 Structure and interactions of SINACYT, 2015

into commercial opportunities. Additionally, educational mercantilism has severely undermined teaching and research quality, limiting endogenous knowledge generation, diffusion and application, making universities unattractive business partners.

While Peru has achieved the highest poverty reduction, lowest inflation, second highest economic growth and third lowest public debt in Latin America during the past 15 years, fragmentation of STI actors, weak linkages among them and duplication of functions among state agencies continue to undermine governance of SINACYT. The main lesson offered by Peru to other developing countries is that macroeconomic progress alone is a necessary but insufficient condition to set up an NIS. Past proposals to improve SINACYT's governance structure have included the creation of a Ministry of Science and Technology, an empowered and decentralized STI agency and an inter-ministerial steering body, but none have generated consensus (OECD, 2011). However, based on the current configuration and dynamics of SINACYT, incorporating CONCYTEC as a Vice-Ministry of Innovation within PRODUCE and preserving SNIA under MINAG's aegis, stand as more feasible options. Both systems can be independently managed at ministerial level by PRODUCE and MINAG respectively, ensuring political support with remaining ministries responding to specific sectoral STI demands (for example through SPRIs and CITEs). Rather than forcing inter and intra-systemic coordination – an expression of supply-side STI policy – building organizational, institutional, technical and financial capabilities through learning by planning, implementing and interacting with non-state actors offers better prospects for a two-pronged NIS building process. Lastly, scarcity and unreliability of STI data and information demands immediate attention as no performance-driven STI interventions will succeed in their absence.

2.4   CONCLUSIONS

Through a historical account of Peru's economic and political processes and transitions this chapter has traced, described and explained the organizational and institutional trajectories shaping the construction of the country's NIS between 1968 and 2015. Failed industrialization due to politically motivated state interventionism and protectionism followed by acute political and economic crises throughout the 1980s led the country to the verge of national collapse. Yet, initial state efforts to develop endogenous S&T and R&D capabilities must be commended but it is hard to find any positive legacies from the lost decade. On the other hand, recovery of the political order and free-market reforms introduced during the 1990s laid the institutional and organizational foundations of the current NIS. Economic policy continuity since 2001 has resulted in significant macroeconomic progress but at the expense of second-generation reforms which, since 2013–14 have exposed the structural limitations of a primary-based and export-dependent economy. However, strong political commitment as well as increased technical and financial support for innovation-driven STI development – notably since 2011 – also deserve recognition.

Among the major strengths of the country's NIS is the predictable and stable, albeit stagnated, macroeconomic environment in which it is embedded; a substantially endowed and harmonized public STI funding portfolio managed by InnovatePe; successful grassroots innovation promoters and articulators represented by CITEs; pockets of educational excellence in scientific and management research; and political consensus on the importance of innovation for national economic development. Increased engagement of non-state actors in STI policy planning and implementation; active participation of private firms in national and international learning and technology networks; tertiary education reform triggered by the recent promulgation of University Law; continued financial support from multilateral organizations; sustained demand of SMEs for CITE services; and government awareness of the distinct needs and capabilities of urban and rural STI stakeholders offer opportunities for systemic and sub-systemic replication and escalation.

Unfortunately, structural limitations hamper the consolidation of a fully functional, integrated and coordinated NIS. Continuous reliance on comparative advantage, widespread informality, deficit of infrastructure, a largely unskilled labour force, labour market rigidity, scarce and unreliable STI data and few incentives for private STI investment pose serious challenges to increased productivity, value addition and economic diversification. Excessive red tape, historically rooted mistrust in national bureaucracy and limited law enforcement capabilities by the state also deter non-state actors from engaging more actively in STI activities. Moreover, political and financial predominance of PRODUCE and INIA-MINAG over CONCYTEC have displaced the latter from its STI steering mandate. Overlapping functions and political competition among state agencies exacerbate supply-side policies without paying proper attention to domestic demand for STI, leading to inefficient allocation of human, technological and financial resources. The emergence of SNIA within SINACYT and the dynamic innovation sub-system generated around PRODUCE both call for alternative institutional and organizational arrangements. The transformation of CONCYTEC into a Vice-Ministry of Innovation within PRODUCE and the full operational and financial independence of SNIA from SINACYT would lead to a two-pronged NIS-building effort where less top-to-bottom interventions would contribute to better governance. Last but not least, organizational simplification expressed by lesser public acronyms would also be much appreciated.

NOTES

1. GVCs are empirically based, theoretical constructs used to study processes of transformation from raw materials to value-added end products. As global production and trade systems undergo structural transformations, production and exchange activities throughout their input–output structures, as well as market and non-market coordination mechanisms among chain actors, suffer alterations which influence the generation and distribution of rents. Actors' capabilities to generate and control these rents at the local, regional, national and international level are a major research concern for GVC scholars.
2. In light of further taxonomies, namely regional, technological and sectoral, Edquist (1997) introduced the theoretically oriented umbrella concept of Innovation Systems and defined its variables, determinants, functions and boundaries.
3. These European cities were capable of developing thriving manufacturing economies underpinned by learning and innovation. Cursed – or blessed? – by scarcity of natural resources, by 1650 Delft developed a complex but well interconnected innovation system where the local arts and sciences' communities, industries (for example textiles, pottery and tiles) and the Dutch navy exchanged value added goods and provided mutually beneficial services which fostered virtuous cycles of economic development (Reinert, 2007).
4. According to Acemoglu and Robinson (2012, p. 76) extractive institutions are those 'designed to extract incomes and wealth from one subset of society to benefit a different subset'.
5. See http://www.economist.com/news/americas/21571162-biggest-threats-latin-americas-economic-star-are-overconfidence-and-complacency-hold.
6. The theoretical and ideological foundations of industrial policy in Latin America can be found in Structuralism (Prebisch, 1949) and Dependency Theory (Frank, 1966; Furtado, 1964; Santos, 1970). Developed by a group of economists working at the Economic Commission for Latin America and the Caribbean's (ECLAC), Dependency Theory conceived a world divided by developed countries located at an industrial centre, and developing countries at the agricultural periphery, which configured uneven terms of trade. As a means of breaking this dual structure, a transition from primary and export-led economies to industrial and technologically based ones was advocated through the application of the import-substitution industrialization (ISI) model. According to Saad-Fihlo (2005), in spite of its close theoretical and historical relationships with Dependency Theory, Structuralism does not propose socialism as the only alternative for successful industrialization.
7. The oil industry controlled by the US-based International Petroleum Company – widely acknowledged as the triggering factor of the military state coup – was expropriated without compensation and led to the creation of Petro Peru. State-owned companies followed in the iron (Hierro Peru), fisheries (Pesca Peru), non-ferrous minerals (Centromin Peru), electricity (ElectroPeru) and telecommunications (Entel Peru) sectors.
8. Currently named Andean Community of Nations (CAN) and headquartered in Lima, the Andean Pact was founded in 1969 by the Cartagena Agreement with the participation of the governments of Bolivia, Chile, Colombia, Ecuador, Peru and Venezuela. Its initial objective was to promote sub-regional integration through joint

market and industrial development. The Chilean government resigned membership in 1976 but became associate member 30 years later while Venezuela withdrew from the pact in 2006.

9. Industrial policy literature refers to 'picking winners' as a strategy in which governments target and benefit certain sectors or particular industries through subsidies, tax incentives or higher tariffs on foreign competitors. However, problems such as lack or diminished competition and clientelistic networks usually arise, transferring costs to consumers, producers and the economy at large (Bianchi and Labory, 2006).

10. Sendero Luminoso is a terrorist organization created in the late 1960s by Abimael Guzman Reynoso, a former Professor of Philosophy at Universidad Nacional San Cristobal de Huamanga in Ayacucho. Its violent activities peaked during the 1980s but were significantly reduced during the 1990s after the capture of Guzman in September 1992. Its extreme brutality has been condemned by the governments of the US, Canada and the European Union, which still list it as a terrorist organization. At present, according to the Peruvian government, less than 100 militants are active in the south-eastern Apurimac and Ene valleys, operating in alliance with local drug lords.

11. In 1983, alongside the approval of the National Science and Technology Strategy, Supreme Decree No 27-83-ED ordered the transfer of CONCYTEC to the Ministry of Education but two years later, under the new government, CONCYTEC was transferred back to the Ministry of the Presidency by Supreme Decree No 357 which assumed S&T policy in the country.

12. The entering government adopted the unilateral decision to limit external debt payments to 10 per cent of total national exports until 1990. As a result, the International Monetary Fund (IMF) and the World Bank (WB) declared the country ineligible for credit assistance.

13. According to the Truth and Reconciliation Commission (CVR) formed in 2001, the number of victims stemming from political violence totalled 69,000 between 1980 and 2000. However, validity and reliability of this figure have been questioned by independent experts, given the flawed methodology used for calculations with more accurate estimations standing at 30,000 deaths (Ideele, 2013).

14. Founded in 1551, the Universidad Nacional Mayor de San Marcos is the oldest university in the Americas. Its foundation was followed by San Antonio Abad National University in Cusco in 1692, National University of Trujillo in 1824 and the National University of San Agustin in Arequipa in 1827.

15. According to national pollster CPI, a few days after these events, 87.9 per cent of Peruvians were in favour of Congress closure and 94.3 per cent approved the intervention and restructuration of the judiciary power (Prieto, 2010, p. 330).

16. By December 1992, the following organizations had been created to regulate and supervise free market competition and the privatization of public services: (i) National Institute for the Defence of Free Competition and Intellectual Property (INDECOPI); (ii) Supervisory Agency for Private Investment in Telecommunications (OSIPTEL); (iii) Supervisory Agency for Private Investment in Energy and Mining (OSINERGMIN); (iv) Supervisory Agency for Private Investment in Public Transportation (OSITRAN); (v) National Superintendency of Sanitation Services (SUNASS); (vi) National Superintendency of Tax Administration (SUNAT); and (vii) Superintendency of Banking, Insurance and Private Pension Funds Administrators (SBS). The Commission for the Official Registration of Informal Property (COFOPRI) and the National Superintendency of Public Registries (SUNARP) were now responsible for formalization efforts. All these agencies operate to the present time.

17. Additional S&T state responsibilities are incorporated in Articles 24–30.

18. The National Council of South American Camelids was in charge of promoting llama and alpaca meat and fibre production but was deactivated in 2007, while the National Institute of Natural Resources (INRENA) ceased functions in 2008 and was replaced by the National Service of Natural Protected Areas (SERNANP), which does not conduct S&T and R&D activities.

19. Legislative Decree No 882 also provided tax exemptions and incentives for educational institutions which invested over 30 per cent of net utilities.
20. The three main goals of the programme were: (i) generation of a favourable environment for private investment in agriculture; (ii) tackling structural problems in rural areas; and (iii) poverty alleviation (Dias et al., 2010).
21. Among participating agencies were the Network on Science and Technology Indicators – Ibero-American and Inter-American (RICYT), Organization of Ibero-American States (OEI), UNESCO, National Assembly of University Vice-Chancellors (ANR), National Institute of Statistics and Informatics (INEI), Ministry of Education (MINEDU), Ministry of Economy and Finance (MEF) and INDECOPI.
22. The Programme of Compensations for Competitiveness (PCC), renamed Agroideas in 2011, and the Integrated System of Agricultural Statistics (SIEA) were formally approved in 2008 by Legislative Decrees 1077 and 1082 respectively. Both agencies of SNIA operate under the leadership of INIA, which also incorporates MINEDU, regional and local governments, public and private universities, producers' organizations and INDECOPI into the system's STI and R&D promotion and development mission.
23. Scientific publications by Peruvian authors in indexed journals increased 71 per cent between 2001 and 2006 and formal agreements were reached by CONCYTEC, with international databases such as HINARI, EBSCO and PROQUEST and British Royal Society archives available for free access.
24. After three years of negotiations carried out by the Ministry of Foreign Trade and Tourism (MINCETUR), Peru signed its first FTA with the US in 2006 and soon followed other bilateral and multilateral trade agreements with China, Chile, Canada, Singapore, Mexico, South Korea, Thailand, Japan, Panama, Costa Rica, Venezuela, CAN, the World Trade Organization (WTO), APEC, the Common Market of the South (MERCOSUR) and the Pacific Alliance, all of which cover 95 per cent of the country's export destinations. Additional FTAs are currently being discussed with India, Turkey and the Doha Development Round.
25. Negotiations between IADB and government officers are currently being held to extend FINCYT for a third period, starting in late 2016 or early 2017. So far the state has committed US$100 million for this purpose and it remains to be seen what amount is loaned by the IADB.
26. InnovatePe currently manages five funding programmes, which have financed a total of 1793 projects while Cienciactiva remains under CONCYTEC's management.
27. With the exception of the Pontifical Catholic University of Peru (PUCP), ranked at 491 in the 2015/2016 QS World University Rankings, no other Peruvian university is placed among the top 500 in major international university rankings such as the Academic Ranking of World Universities (ARWU) by Shanghai Jiao Tong University and World University Rankings by Times Higher Education (THE). The highest ranked Latin American institution is Brazil's University of Sao Paulo, which ranks 101–50 by ARWU ranking but is placed at 251–300 in THE ranking and 143 in QS (second only to University of Buenos Aires, Argentina at 124). In the QS regional rankings, only three Peruvian universities feature in the top 100, namely PUCP at 19, National University of San Marcos at 60 and Cayetano Heredia University at 64.
28. Besides grape producing and shoe-making SMEs, new small industries serviced by CITEs are leather, meat, wool and fibre, software, fashion and textiles, mining and jewellery, tropical fruits and herbs, and aquaculture.

REFERENCES

Acemoglu, D., and Robinson, J. (2012). *Why nations fail: The origins of power, prosperity and poverty*. London: Profile Books.

Alfageme, M. A., and Guabloche, M. K. (1998). Estado, gasto público y desarrollo de las capacidades: una aproximación. *Revista de Estudios Económicos, 2*, accessed 25 March 2016 at http://www.bcrp.gob.pe/docs/Publicaciones/Revista-Estudios-Economicos/02/Estudios-Economicos-2-4.pdf.

Altamirano, T. (2006). *Remesas y nueva 'fuga de cerebros': Impactos transnacionales.* Lima: Fondo Editorial Pontificia Universidad Católica del Perú.

Amsden, A. (1992). *Asia's next giant: South Korea and late industrialization.* Oxford: Oxford University Press.

ANR. (2012). *Datos Estadísticos Universitarios*, accessed 11 January 2016 at http://www.academia.edu/9011627/DATOS_ESTAD%C3%8DSTICOS_UNIVERSIT ARIOS.

Arocena, R., and Sutz, J. (2000). Looking at national systems of innovation from the South. *Industry and Innovation, 7*(1), 55–80.

ARWU. (2015). *Shanghai Academic Ranking of World Universities 2015*, accessed 26 March 2016 at http://www.shanghairanking.com/.

BCRP. (1999). *Memoria Anual Banco Central de Reserva del Perú*, accessed 26 March 2016 at http://www.bcrp.gob.pe/docs/Publicaciones/Memoria/1999/Memoria-BCRP-1999-1.pdf.

Bianchi, P., and Labory, S. (2006). *International handbook on industrial policy.* Cheltenham, UK and Northampton, MA: Edward Elgar Publishing.

Biglione, E. (2008). Sendero Luminoso, fragilidad institucional y socialismo del siglo XXI en el Perú. In G. Lazzari and H. Ñaupari (eds.), *Políticas Liberales Exitosas II Soluciones para superar la pobreza* (pp. 13–34). México: Red Liberal de América Latina Fundación Friedrich Naumann para la Libertad.

Carranza, V. (2015). *Perú: Ciencia, tecnología e innovación social – hechos, redes de poder y discursos.* Lima: Universidad Nacional de Ingeniería, Editorial Universitaria.

Cassiolato, J., Guimarães, V., Peixoto, F., and Lastres, H. (2005). *Innovation systems and development: What can we learn from the Latin American experience.* Paper presented at the 3rd Globelics Conference. Pretoria, South Africa.

Chang, H. J. (2002). *Kicking away the ladder: Development strategy in historical perspective.* London: Anthem Press.

Cimoli, M., Dosi, G., and Stiglitz, J. (2009). The future of industrial policies in the new millennium: Toward a knowledge-centred development agenda. In M. Cimoli, G. Dosi and J. Stiglitz (eds.), *Industrial policy and development: The political economy of capabilities accumulation* (pp. 541–560). Oxford: Oxford University Press.

CONCYTEC. (1999). *Estudio Sistémico de la Realidad Nacional en Ciencia y Tecnología*, accessed 4 November 2015 at http://dspace2.conicyt.cl/bitstream/handle/10533/90154/ESTUDIO%20SISTEMICO%20DE%20LA%20REALID AD%20NACIONAL%20EN%20CIENCIA%20Y%20TECNOLOGIA.pdf?seq uence=1.

CONCYTEC. (2006). *Plan Nacional Estratégico de Ciencia, Tecnología e Innovación para la Competitividad y el Desarrollo Humano*, accessed 31 October 2015 at https://portal.concytec.gob.pe/images/stories/images2012/portal/areas-institucion/pyp/plan_nac_ctei/plan_nac_ctei_2006_2021.pdf.

CONCYTEC. (2013). *La Innovación Tecnológica en el Sector Manufacturero: Esfuerzos y resultados de la pequeña, mediana y gran empresa*, accessed 31 October 2015 at https://portal.concytec.gob.pe/index.php/publicaciones/documentos-de-trabajo/item/download/48_2a42545ecd674d3c318e06f5b0e20e74.

Crabtree, J. (2005). *Alan García en el poder*. Lima: Ediciones Peisa.
De Althaus, J. (2008). *La revolución capitalista en el Perú*. Lima: Fondo de Cultura Económica.
Degregori, I. (1990). *El surgimiento de Sendero Luminoso: del movimiento de la gratitud por la enseñanza al inicio de la lucha armada*. Lima: Instituto de Estudios Peruanos.
Dias, F. A., Salles-Filho, S., and Alonso, J. E. (2010). *Impacto de la I&D+i Agraria en el Perú: la Experiencia de Incagro*, accessed 23 October 2015 at https://www.alice.cnptia.embrapa.br/alice/bitstream/doc/901069/1/Impactodela.pdf.
Díaz, J., and Kuramoto, J. (2010). *Evaluación de políticas de apoyo a la innovación en el Perú: Informe Final*. Grupo de Análisis para el Desarrollo GRADE. Lima: Perú, accessed 21 October 2015 at https://www.mef.gob.pe/contenidos/pol_econ/documentos/Estudio_Background_Spanish_version13072010.pdf.
Edquist, C. (1997). *Systems of innovation: Technologies, institutions and organizations*. London: Pinter.
Flindell-Klaren, P. (2000). *Peru: Society and nationhood in the Andes*. Oxford: Oxford University Press.
Frank, A. G. (1966). The underdevelopment of development. *Monthly Review*, *18*(4), 17–31.
Freeman, C. (1987). *Technology policy and economic performance: Lessons from Japan*. London: Pinter.
Furtado, C. (1964). *Desarrollo y subdesarrollo*. Buenos Aires: EUDEBA.
Gereffi, G. (1994). The organization of buyer-driven global commodity chains: How U.S. retailers shape overseas production networks. In G. Gereffi and M. Korzeniewicz (eds.), *Commodity chains and global capitalism* (pp. 95–122). London: Praeger.
Gereffi, G., Humphrey, J., and Sturgeon, T. (2005). The governance of global value chains. *Review of International Political Economy*, *12*(1), 78–104.
Gerschenkron, A. (1962). *Economic backwardness in historical perspective – A book of essays*. Cambridge, MA: Belknap Press, Harvard University.
Hamilton, A. (1791). *Report on the Subject of Manufactures*, accessed 31 October 2015 at http://www.constitution.org/ah/rpt_manufactures.pdf.
Hirschmann, A. O. (1958). *The strategy of economic development*. New Haven, CT: Yale University Press.
Humphrey, J., and Schmitz, A. (2002). How does insertion in global value chains affect upgrading in industrial clusters? *Regional Studies*, *36*(9), 1017–1027.
Ideele. (2013). *La Polémica sobre las Cifras: las Sobreestimaciones de la CVR*, accessed 7 March 2016 at http://revistaideele.com/ideele/content/la-pol%C3%A9mica-sobre-las-cifras-las-sobreestimaciones-de-la-cvr.
INEI. (2014). *Encuesta Nacional de Innovación en la Industria Manufacturera 2014*. Lima: Instituto Nacional de Estadística e Informática.
INEI. (2016). *Portal de Estadísticas*, accessed 10 January 2016 at https://www.inei.gob.pe/#url.
Kaplinsky, R. (2000). Globalisation and unequalisation: What can be learned from value chain analysis? *Journal of Development Studies*, *37*(2), 117–146.
Kay, C. (1999 November). *Conflict and violence in rural Latin America*. Annual conference of ADLAF (Asociación Alemana de Investigación sobre América Latina), Hamburg, Germany.
Kuramoto, J., and Sagasti, F. (2002). Integrating local and global knowledge, technology and production systems: Challenges for technical cooperation. *Science, Technology and Society*, *7*(2), 215–247.

Lall, S. (1987). *Learning to industrialize.* London: Macmillan.

List, F. (1841). *The national system of political economy.* London: Longmans, Green and Co.

Lundvall, B.-Å. (1992). *National systems of innovation: Towards a Theory of Innovation and Interactive Learning.* London: Pinter.

MEF. (2016). *Ministerio de Economía y Finanzas – Estadísticas,* accessed 13 January 2015 at http://www.mef.gob.pe/index.php?option=com_content&view=section &id=49&Itemid=100358.

Mullin Consulting. (2002). *Un Análisis del Sistema Peruano de Innovación.* Inter-American Development Bank, Mullin Consulting, Canada.

Nelson, R. R. (1993). *National innovation systems: A comparative analysis.* Oxford: Oxford University Press.

Nurkse, R. (1953). *Problems of capital formation in underdeveloped countries.* Oxford: Basil Blackwell.

OECD. (2011). *OECD Reviews of Innovation Policy: Peru.* Paris: OECD Publishing.

Prebisch, R. (1949). El desarrollo económico de la América Latina y algunos de sus principales problemas, *El Trimestre Económico, 16*(63(3)), 347–471.

Prieto, F. (2010). *Así se hizo el Perú: crónica política de 1939 a 2009.* Lima: Editorial Norma.

PRODUCE. (2014). *Plan Nacional de Diversificación Productiva: nuevos motores para el desarrollo del país,* accessed 22 January 2016 at http://www.produce. gob.pe/images/stories/Repositorio/publicaciones/plan-nacional-de-diversificac ion-productiva.pdf.

QS. (2015). *QS World University Rankings 2015/2016,* accessed 26 March 2015 at http://www.topuniversities.com/university-rankings/world-university-rankings/2 015#sorting=rank+region=+country=+faculty=+stars=false+search=.

Reinert, E. (1995). Competitiveness and its predecessors: A 500-year cross-national perspective. *Structural Change and Economic Dynamics, 6*(1), 23–42.

Reinert, E. (2007). *Why rich countries got rich and why poor countries stay poor.* London: Constable & Robinson Ltd.

RICyT. (2016). *Red de Indicadores de Ciencia y Tecnología – Iberoamericana e Interamericana.* Indicadores por país: *Perú,* accessed 26 November 2015 at http://db.ricyt.org/query/PE/1990,2012/calculados.

Rosenstein-Rodan, P. N. (1943). Problems of industrialization of Eastern and South-Eastern Europe. *The Economic Journal, 53*(210–211), 202–211.

Saad-Filho, A. (2005). The rise and decline of Latin American structuralism and dependency theory. In K. S. Jomo and E. Reinert (eds.), *Development economics: How schools of thought have addressed development* (pp. 128–145). London: Zed Books.

Sagasti, F. (1989). Vulnerabilidad y crisis: ciencia y tecnología en el Perú de los ochenta. *Interciencia, 14*(1), 18–27.

Sagasti, F. (1995). Política científica y tecnológica en el Perú en los últimos 30 años. *Tecnología y Sociedad, 3,* 31–38.

Santos, T. (1970). The structure of dependence. *American Economic Review, 60*(2), 231–236.

Sheahan, J. (1999). *Searching for a better society: The Peruvian economy since 1950.* University Park, PA: The Pennsylvania State University Press.

THE. (2015). *Times Higher Education World University Rankings 2015–2016,* accessed 26 March 2016 at https://www.timeshighereducation.com/world-univer

sity-rankings/2016/world-ranking#!/page/0/length/25/sort_by/rank_label/sort_or der/asc/cols/rank_only.

Thorp, R., and Bertram, G. (1985). *Perú 1890–1977: Crecimiento y políticas en una economía abierta.* Lima: Mosca Azul Editores.

Veblen, T. (1915). *Imperial Germany and the Industrial Revolution.* Kitchener: Batoche Books.

Villarán, F. (2010). *Emergencia de la Ciencia, Tecnología e Innovación en el Perú.* Lima: Organización de Estados Iberoamericanos para la Educación, la Ciencia y la Cultura.

Wade, R. (1992). *Governing the market – Economic theory and the role of government in East Asian industrialization.* Princeton, NJ: Princeton University Press.

WEF. (2015). *World Economic Forum Global Competitiveness Index 2015– 2016,* accessed 29 November 2015 at http://reports.weforum.org/global-com petitiveness-report-2015-2016/competitiveness-rankings/.

Whittaker, H., Zhu, T., Sturgeon, T. J., Tsai, M. H., and Okita, T. (2008). Compressed development. *Studies in Comparative International Development,* *45*(4), 439–467.

World Bank. (2016). *World Bank Open Data.* accessed 29 November 2015 at http:// data.worldbank.org/.

Wyeland, K. (2000). A paradox of success? Determinants of political support for president Fujimori. *International Studies Quarterly, 44*(3), 481–502.

3. The state of the National Innovation System of Armenia

Tatevik Poghosyan

3.1 INTRODUCTION

A successful management of an innovation system can drive the growth of both companies and national economies. At the national level, governments develop instruments and policies to foster science and technology as well as the innovative activities of the private sector. Many developing countries face challenges of technological upgrading. To this end, they employ strategies for catching-up with the countries at the technological frontier. The post-Soviet transition countries, too, are among those that face significant barriers to upgrading their science and technology. These countries, however, differ from others in the developing world by their common historical experiences and production system heritage together with a shared set of difficulties brought about by the collapse of the Union of Soviet Socialist Republics (USSR).

Years of operating under a central planning system and the corresponding lack of economic incentives for innovativeness left deep marks on business behavior, with companies being slow and rigid in dealing with market challenges. It took time for firms to alter their mindsets and develop an understanding of how capitalist markets operate and how to generate higher economic returns under a new post-Soviet system. Inability of the early transition period to provide satisfactory work opportunities for highly skilled workers and scientists, coupled with high demand for relatively cheap highly skilled specialists in developed countries, led to a substantial brain drain.

Armenia's transition, which began in the 1990s, started with an ethnic conflict that ended in 1995. After 1995, the country embarked on its post-war recovery by developing economic and social policies, which came into effect mostly after 2000. Macroeconomic data confirm that the main transformation processes were in effect after 2000, and the majority of innovation policies were developed in the 2000s (UNECE, 2014). After the war (1991–1995), Armenia faced a problem common to all transition countries: how to integrate into the world economy with an "old fashioned" production system, poor technology and a lack of financial resources for education and science. However, Armenia inherited some advantages from its "Soviet" past: high-quality human capital, well developed laboratories and universities for natural sciences, and a diaspora that was willing to invest in the country's economy.

This chapter aims to deepen our understanding of National Innovation System (NIS) characteristics in transition countries and, in particular, discuss the conditions in which Armenian NIS is transforming. It reviews the key historical path dependencies that are particularly important to explain the interplay between the development level of the NIS and the economic development of Armenia. Several stylized research questions are addressed in this context: How can transition countries exploit current opportunities and resolve the weaknesses of the inherited state planning system to construct an effective NIS? What are the major drivers of the change in Armenian NIS? What opportunities do firms have for learning and innovation in Armenia?

To answer these questions, the chapter starts with a discussion of the NIS approach in transition countries from an evolutionary perspective. It points out how the initial transition reforms and common historical path dependencies steer the development of NIS in transition countries and continue to affect them. It furthers the analysis by introducing the determinants and actors in Armenia's NIS by highlighting the macroeconomic environment, past industrial development and the challenges that Armenia faced during the transformation of its Regional Innovation System (RIS) as a republic within the USSR into a small country's NIS. The chapter also discusses the innovation governance system in Armenia, which is seen as an integral part of the NIS. Section 3.4 presents learning and networks as an important aspect of the NIS approach. They also play a crucial role in explaining innovation and economic development in transition countries. Finally, in Section 3.5, the major research questions are reviewed and some suggestions are put forward with the possible avenues of analyzing firm's innovation in Armenia.

3.2   NATIONAL INNOVATION SYSTEMS IN TRANSITION COUNTRIES

The NIS is an important factor for accelerating national growth and competitiveness. The NIS research tradition goes back to List (1841) who introduced it as a national system of political economy; later, Schumpeter (1934), and Abramovitz (1986) presented it as a science and technology change that explains economic growth. More recent views on the NIS specify the role of innovation rooted in the production system, first discussed by Lundvall (1985), and innovation based on the science and technology system (Freeman, 2004) bridging the macro and micro perspectives of the innovation systems. Another important aspect of the recent NIS approach is the consideration of socioeconomic features of national institutions in knowledge generation and innovation. In the 1980s, the Organisation for Economic Co-operation and Development (OECD) adopted a comprehensive framework of NIS, which emphasizes the role of government, firms and research institutions and their interaction in a country's innovative performance. In this framework, the innovation process includes a set of actors such as government, public and private research organizations, and firms and their interactions, where actors are influenced by country-specific characteristics – existing institutions, socioeconomic context, history and so forth.

Most of the early research on the NIS focused on developed countries. Since 2000, however, researchers have turned their attention to the specific nature of NIS in developing (Arocena and Sutz, 2002; Intarakumnerd et al., 2002), and transition contexts (Kitanovic, 2007; Krammer, 2009). Arocena and Sutz (2002) note that the NIS was conceptualized based on empirical evidence from the developed world, and was exposed to the developing country as an "ex-ante" concept; therefore, some aspects of the NIS in the southern context are underestimated. These include, for example, knowledge production and knowledge transfer, where interactive learning is a key concept, or collective attitudes, as defined by Putnam's social capital concept, which emphasizes the crucial roles of institutions. If the NIS approach is applied in the context of the less developed countries, it should incorporate specific characteristics of developing, and perhaps even more so, of transition economies (Arocena and Sutz, 2000; Kitanovic, 2007).

The post-Soviet transition economies historically possess a number of unique characteristics. First, these countries inherited completely different innovation and production systems compared to market economies. In the planned economy, the production system was wholly integrated into political and social systems. After the dissolution of the Soviet Union, market actors who, for decades operated within a planned system, were not ready to accept changes forced by market-oriented transformations. These changes were so quick that people and firms were unable to adapt. Second, the post-Soviet transition countries adopted different policies to introduce a market economy and to build institutional frameworks based on historical experience. As a result, each transition country followed its own path-dependency of technological change (Kitanovic, 2007). Finally, even after implementing radical market reforms, those countries preserved certain features of socialistic system and old values. One of the fundamental changes implemented in post-Soviet countries was a mass privatization of the national property. The underlying logic of the fast and large-scale privatization was the assumption that the market itself will redefine the property relations and will regulate further restructuring of the state-owned enterprises. During that time and beyond, the presence of widespread market imperfections and a lack of the knowledge and experience among local actors has led to the situation where short-term profit opportunities were prioritized over investments in long-term enterprise restructuring and innovation.

In the transition economies, primary attention was paid to establishing new political and economic environments via economy liberalization and privatization. Restructuring of enterprises did not receive much consideration (Baković et al., 2013) because it was assumed that economic agents would intensify innovation in order to adjust to a competitive environment. Overall, the course of economic transformation in transition countries proved to be harder and longer than anybody could imagine, partly because the "Soviet heritage" was rooted very deep in the economy and the minds of people.

Building up an innovation system was even more challenging for a number of reasons. First, there were no institutions in place to facilitate innovation (e.g. the financial sector and regulations). Second, reforms primarily focused on privatization of industry and on education and did not attempt to build a new innovation system or to restructure the existing one. Third, reliance on strong personal linkages was a dominant strategy of doing business in the Soviet era. After the USSR collapsed, highly ranked officials found themselves better connected and able to use their status to navigate the changing environment. This often meant that business leaders tried to enrich themselves, whereas developing a successful and innovative business was much less a priority. As a result, the dominance of strong and inflexible networks in the business sector of transition countries slowed the speed of liberalization and derailed the originally conceived direction of changes.

The "learning economy" is a crucial concept within the NIS framework. It refers to the ability of a country to absorb new knowledge introduced in the economy. The successful "learning," however, is not entirely based on absorptive capabilities, but also on the quality of political and social institutions (Lundvall et al., 2002). Post-Soviet countries have a high level of educational attainment and enjoy a strong base in fundamental research. They nevertheless suffer from low productivity and lag behind many countries on the frontier of technology. Overcoming this gap requires substantial efforts. Gu (1999), for example, argues that transition economies (compared to developing countries) are more likely to require a direct policy intervention to restructure the countries' innovation systems.

Knowledge exchange is particularly important for catching up with technological leaders. Unfortunately, opportunities for knowledge spillovers and knowledge exchange in transition countries are limited. Even when former Soviet republics passed large-scale privatization, new owners were still mostly locally based. The lack of foreign ownership prevented local companies from recognition and the adoption of new strategies. Indeed, "learning by exploring" was the most dominant way of learning and knowledge accumulation in the Soviet system (Kitanovic, 2007).[1] During the Soviet times, companies in the USSR had no incentives to innovate in order to improve their production because higher returns were collected by the state. After the Soviet Union collapsed, poor innovative outcomes in transition countries were, at least partially, determined by the persistence of such attitudes and a lack of initiative.

The Lundvall and Johnson (1994) learning model is a highly appropriate depiction of the learning process in the context of transition. According to the model, the learning process includes "creative forgetting" and "low-end forgetting." The difference between "low-end forgetting" and "creative forgetting" is that the former refers to a type of knowledge, which is destroyed without serving a purpose of technological progress, while the latter serves as a ladder for the creation of new knowledge. To create new knowledge, transition countries first needed to destruct the old knowledge, old habits and routines, and at the same time provide appropriate regulatory frameworks and institutions to support these changes (Kitanovic, 2007). Some of the old knowledge, nevertheless, needs to be retained so that the introduction of new knowledge is successful. "Creative forgetting" requires special institutions that could be created or adapted from the existing ones. Ironically, the path of radical reforms followed by many post-Soviet countries did not facilitate the creation of legitimate institutions that could support organizational learning. As a result, learning in the transition economies mostly proceeded through the "low-end forgetting" path. The destruction of economic linkages and existing structures happened haphazardly, without control or direction by the governmental or other institutions. A massive brain drain that characterized most transition countries is, perhaps, the most vivid example of "low-end forgetting process"-related negative consequences. As a result, a significant endowment of the transition countries with the knowledge stock in the beginning of the market liberalization was often irreversibly lost.

The transition process characterized by the replacement of the old planned system with liberalized market and open trade initiated the disruption of the production chains that existed in the USSR and dealt a blow to the research and development (R&D) system. Because goods produced in the Soviet Union were, in general, less technologically advanced, they were not competitive in foreign markets. Additionally, rapidly expanding imports made local production unviable and many factories were shut down, leaving thousands of scientists and engineers unemployed. As large factories that were a part of the Soviet R&D system lost their old markets and production, the national R&D systems were destroyed. To survive, high-tech industries often shifted their productions to low-tech sectors. For example, Armenian electronic factory Sirius was a leading producer of electronic chips in the USSR; unable to survive the transition as a high-tech enterprise, it switched to making shoes, souvenirs and other irrelevant products, while thousands of engineers had to find jobs as low-skilled labor in other sectors of the economy.

To sum up, the privatization and market liberalization did not facilitate firms' adaptation of new and efficient strategies, and created rather unfavorable conditions such as hard budget constraints, a weak regulatory framework and a lack of innovation policies. Left by themselves, firms were not able to modernize their production and provide necessary training for scientific personnel in order to stay up to date on recent technological developments. Yet, despite reducing the stock of R&D spending and employment, early transition countries maintained their relative competitive position, and did not drop into the less-developed countries category; however, in terms of the transformation of this stock into assets and sources for economic growth, transition countries failed (Radosevic, 2002).

It appears that exiting gradually from the old economic and innovation systems inherited from the USSR is crucial for preserving local human capital and R&D infrastructure in a well-functioning shape until it can be modernized. In this case, learning would follow "creative forgetting" rather than "low-end-forgetting." Unfortunately, fast reforms provided blurry vision on potential opportunities both at state, firm and individual levels. As a result of wrong policy choices throughout the transition, many transition countries lost their R&D potential.

3.3 NATIONAL INNOVATION SYSTEM IN ARMENIA: DETERMINANTS, ACTORS AND NETWORKS

Armenian NIS strongly relied on the planning system legacy where the dominant linkages were between the central government in Moscow and

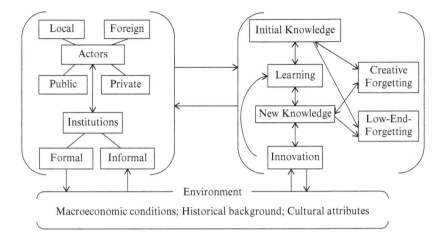

Source: Adapted from Kitanovic (2007).

Figure 3.1   National Innovation System in transition contexts

large *combinates* (factories) across the USSR (Radosevic, 2002). The strong dependence of individual republics on the central government during the USSR became a major barrier to transforming planned economies into market-oriented national innovation systems once those republics gained their independence. This situation was common to all former Soviet countries, which faced similar challenges (Radosevic, 2002), but applied different policies and enjoyed different economic opportunities.

The point of departure for the analysis of the factors that influence the NIS in Armenia presented in this section is the NIS model developed by Kitanovic (2007) to explain the specification of an NIS in a transition context. Figure 3.1 presents the conceptual framework in a graphic form, which illustrates the role of actors, linkages, learning and the external environment in the formation of the NIS in Armenia and is a slightly modified version of Kitanovic's model.

The important features of this model include interactions among all components of the innovation system that shape the emergence of an NIS, and the centrality of the learning process in explaining the innovation system. Literature on innovation systems shows that the macroeconomic environment plays a crucial role in determining the innovative performance of a country (Arocena and Sutz, 2002; Lundvall et al., 2002). State policies can hinder or boost innovation, whereas global market conditions and the historical background are as important as the role of national policies. In the context of transition economies, it was privatization and Soviet innovation infrastructure that nurtured innovation processes. Different patterns of privatization determined the presence of foreign actors and the formation of informal networks in a country (Radosevic, 2002). Compared to other socialist countries, Armenia and other nations within the Commonwealth of Independent States (CIS) mostly adopted the insider privatization model, where ownership of privatized enterprises went to locals (usually employees), thereby minimizing the presence of foreign owners.[2] Foreign actors in general were positively associated with the efficient restructuring of the economy in transition countries, providing enterprises with rich financial support as well as playing a notable role in the learning process. The dominance of local enterprise networks and weak national policies characterizing CIS countries were considered high-risk markets for foreign direct investments (FDIs) and foreign involvement, compared to Central and Eastern European countries, where the national frameworks and local owners had relatively less power in controlling the markets and economic restructuring.

Large firms (factories) were a part of Armenia's R&D network during the Soviet period, but unfortunately, for a number of reasons, they were often not capable of engaging in R&D activities in the post-Soviet period. The loss of the market for their product and of Soviet production chains as well as a shift in ownership from state-owned to private were among the most prominent ones. It was hoped that private firms would be more efficient than state-owned enterprises (SOEs), but early transition reforms overestimated the new opportunities for the privatized firms. All the changes that occurred in the transition period did not enhance the country's innovativeness, and large corporations were too rigid to implement the restructuring necessary for successful transition. Creativity and research activities were seen as serious barriers rather than avenues for productivity growth. In this way, transition countries suffered from a lack of state intervention to boost innovation, in contrast to many capitalist countries, which had public policies that were an integral part of innovation processes (Baković et al., 2013).

3.3.1 Macro Environment

Armenia's severe transition experience started with the war with Azerbaijan over the Nagorno-Karabakh region. The consequences were devastating; Armenian economy lost about half of its GDP. After the war was over in 1995, the country's GDP grew by around 12 percent per year until 2009. The global financial crisis in 2008 forced the Armenian economy to contract and when the growth resumed, it stayed at 4 percent only.

Armenia is a small and open economy with a consolidated ownership structure and a strong Soviet legacy, which means that highly developed R&D stock is not well related to local industries. After independence, Armenia, like other CIS countries, was paralyzed because Moscow did not provide direction. Lack of experience in the collaboration between R&D institutes and industries hindered efficient learning and knowledge exchange between these two actors of the NIS during the early independence period.

According to the Soviet principles that guided industrial development in the USSR regions, economic activity was diffused uniformly across all USSR republics, with republics interdependent on inputs. The primary production was often located geographically far from raw materials, resources and markets (Anderson, 2006). The economic development strategies were highly politicized, and, therefore, did not comply with economic theory.

In Soviet Armenia, military and defense manufacturing, heavily dependent on inputs from other republics, accounted for 40 percent of the economy (Anderson, 2006). Another important feature of the Armenian economy was its diversity, which was an advantage during the Soviet period that determined the important role Armenia played in the USSR industrial chain (relative to its size), and allowed an average Armenian citizen to enjoy higher standards of living. However, industrial diversity and dependence on production inputs from other countries made Armenia highly vulnerable to the changes after the USSR collapse (Anderson, 2006). Resources, including skilled labor and scientists, were widely spread across various industries and scientific fields. As a small country, Armenia was able to sustain this type of diversity because of the "Big USSR R&D laboratory"[3] approach, where each republic could contribute but also benefit. After the USSR collapsed and its production chains disintegrated, Armenia lost most of its R&D and production resources precisely because it was very diversified for its small size; supporting a wide range of research and production activities whose products were not in demand appeared to be an impossible task.

The transition period also affected the allocation of public resources to R&D. In almost all CIS countries, including Armenia, the early transition was a survival period, and public policies were not directed toward the formation and development of science and innovation policies. Only after 2000 did Armenia experience some positive changes in terms of governmental acts and decisions, and an increase in spending on research and science. Before 2000, Armenia spent 0.22 percent of its GDP on innovations; this number increased to 0.3 percent of GDP after 2008 but the share of high technology exports in total export remains under 5 percent.

The 2013 EBRD[4] transition report shows that post-Soviet countries generally had low factor productivity, caused by inefficient allocation of resources before the 1990s, but after 1990 restructuring of their economies provided the basis for the rapid total factor productivity growth. The growth in factor productivity has slowed down over time, suggesting that the opportunities of efficiency improvement within the given economic structure were exhausted and new structural and policy changes were needed to keep productivity growing.

At the macro level, productivity depends on the availability of capital, labor, skills and endowment with natural resources, while available technology determines how efficiently these resources are utilized. Policies play an important role in creating and supporting favorable environments for productivity growth. For Armenia, with its limited natural resource endowment, human capital appears to be the main competitive advantage (Gevorkyan, 2015). According to the 2013 Human Capital Report (World Economic Forum, 2013), Armenia ranks 60th in terms of education, which places the country above its neighbors. The Armenian business climate, however, is not as favorable as some of its neighbors (World Bank, 2013) but the country enjoys the highest Global Innovation Index rank among its regional peers and is ahead of its many neighbors (including Russia, which is a larger economy and cannot be directly compared to that of Armenia) in terms of innovation linkages. Armenia is also a regional leader in knowledge absorption (WIPO, Cornell University, and INSEAD, 2014).

Another important factor for the process of the Armenian transition to market economy is the role of diaspora in economic development. Armenia has a sizable diaspora, which exceeds the country's population. The diaspora factor was critical in some areas. For example, during the early transition diaspora investors led the way in establishing new businesses based on foreign direct investment (FDI); links between diaspora and motherland stimulated scientific and cultural exchange, whereas sizable remittances stimulate domestic demand, boosting the economy in general. Some authors, such as Gevorkyan (2015), however, believe that the diaspora effect is not as positive as one might think. According to the researcher, the Armenian diaspora lacks political unity, and a lack of systematic interactions between the Armenian government, society and the diaspora leads to haphazard, albeit short-lived, effects on the country's economic development.

3.3.2   Components of the Innovation System of Armenia

Since 2000, Armenia has introduced several legislative changes to support the formation of a NIS. Starting from the early 2000s, the Armenian economy moved from a survival-oriented phase to a development and innovation-oriented phase. Among important policy initiatives in this direction were: the Law on Scientific and Technological Activity, adopted in 2000, outlining the main principles for science and technology (S&T) policies (Khnkoyan, 2011); the Law on State Support to Innovation adopted in 2006; the strategy on the Development of Sciences for 2011–20 in 2010; the government resolution on the Strategy of Export-Led Industrial policies in 2011; and the government resolution on intellectual property rights (IPR) in 2011 (see full list in UNECE report, 2014). The strategic vision of all these policies was based on a more narrow view of innovation systems, paying the most attention to the internationalization of Armenian high-tech companies and serving as a laboratory for large multinationals. The strategic objectives of export-led policies were to diversify the export portfolio and to shift the economy from resource-based to knowledge-incentive industries. This strategic view, however, left out the importance of academia–industry linkages and the role of small firm innovation.

The current innovation governance system in Armenia is based on three main strategies: Development of Science, Development of Innovation Economy and Export-lead Policy (UNECE report, 2014). The Ministry of Education and partially independent Science Councils are responsible for science and education policies, and industrial development is a priority of the Ministry of Economy. Despite the presence of several important components that should drive the development of the Armenian NIS, the system in place is highly fragmented and lacks systematic collaborations. As a result, industry and academia follow their own strategies without taking into account a holistic view on innovation systems (UNECE, 2014).

In 2011, the Ministry of Economy introduced a concept paper titled "Innovative Economy Development: An Initial Strategy," which presented a plan to develop and promote innovation strategies in Armenia across three time horizons. In the short term, a legal framework and innovation-supporting financial and other types of infrastructure should be developed in order to boost the business sector; in the midterm, international business standards, engineering education and a modernization of companies should be implemented; and in the long term the objective is to establish internationally recognized science laboratories (UNECE, 2014). At the same time, the concept of science development in Armenia for the period of 2011–2020 solely focuses on the development and modernization of the educational system and science and does not attend to the needs of the business sector. Since 2011, however, the government passed the legislature that allowed the National Academy of Science (NAS) to establish spin-offs as a mechanism to commercialize their R&D outputs.

Although these two main concepts are related to the country's innovation system, they do not target common goals; rather, they seem to stretch the Innovation System into different directions (market push from the Ministry of Economy and technological push from NAS) without developing the same vision on NIS. As a result, high-tech companies, most notably in the information technology (IT) sector, often have to retrain newly hired university graduates, as the university education system has not upgraded its curricula to match the knowledge requirements of IT firms.[5]

Another fact that influences Armenian innovation governance is that the industrial and innovation policies highly depend on external funding, and instruments are developed to attract public and private donors, which potentially may further their own interests (UNECE, 2014). Additionally, reliance on external funding is increasing the gap between science and industrial policies, instead of establishing the linkages between industry and science, which could facilitate the transformation of research results into innovative products and their commercialization.

The UNECE report (2014) presents important statistics on industry–university linkages in Armenia. Table 3.1 shows a collaboration category for each type of industrial R&D. The R&D capacity in Armenia is concentrated in research institutions. Most of them either belong to the National Academy of Science or the Ministry of Economy, and they are predominantly financed from the national budget. The Armenian export market is dominated by low technological products such as raw materials and food and beverages. In general, local businesses have a low innovative capability and lack incentives to establish collaboration

Table 3.1   Cooperation by type of industrial R&D

	Exploratory	Exploitative	Imitative
Modalities of collaboration	Research grants, R&D Contracts, Joint R&D, Licensing	Customer–Supplier Technology exchange agreements, R&D Contracts, Joint R&D, Licensing	Complementarities of partners
Technology exchange	More tacit, embodied in people	Coded, embodied in artifacts	Coded, embodied in artifacts
Linkages with universities	Many and stronger	Few and weaker	Negligible

Source: Based on UNECE report (2014).

with universities. According to the "National Competitiveness Report," Armenia consistently ranks low for university–business research collaboration, which also suggests that firms in Armenia perceive the quality of research institutions and universities in the country as quite low (EV Consulting, 2012). The only significant actors that are effective in establishing links between universities and industry are multinational enterprises. In the IT sector, the presence of multinationals makes for favorable changes in the university–business collaboration sphere. For instance, Synopsys, a US-based IT company, established several R&D centers in Armenia in close collaboration with universities. A few research organizations have links with foreign firms and export their production to the US, the EU or Russia. Despite the increasing presence of multinationals, the linkages between industry and universities are not prevalent in Armenia. Research institutes and the government focus on strategies more relevant to the "science push" innovation, while undermining the importance of R&D results for commercialization. Firms, on the other hand, are predominantly small and are confined to a local market and have limited opportunities to search for more innovative ways to increase their productivity.

During the last decade, Armenia has seen an establishment of innovation centers, S&T parks and free economic zones. However, the efficiency gains from these new institutional arrangements seem to be low[6] for a number of reasons. First, these projects fail to facilitate networking with local firms or to match their production interests and learning goals. Besides which there is a mismatch between the services the S&T parks provide and the needs of local firms. Overall, the ambitious policy initiatives implemented in Armenia post-2000 appear to be fragmented and poorly aligned to the needs of domestic firms and universities. Perhaps most importantly, the policies did not establish close and well-integrated networks between research centers and the industry, which should be the backbone of an efficient innovation system and would respond to the challenges and the needs of Armenia with its unique heritage as a post-Soviet republic.

3.4 LEARNING AND INNOVATION

Networks, collaborations and their effects on learning are central concepts of the NIS. Since Armenia is a small country, the perspective on innovative systems (IS) presented by Roolaht (2012) appears to be particularly relevant. According to this perspective, inward FDI and knowledge flows, extensive international collaboration, clear development goals, human and social capital and higher flexibility in policy schemes are the factors crucial for NIS success in small countries. Perry (2001) shows that in the case of small

Nordic countries, shared trust and collective learning stimulate innovation in industries. This study argues that institutions and political environments should address the importance of changing business habits in creating more open and trustful interactions between economic actors. Another important determinant is knowledge production and absorptive capacity (Roolaht, 2012; Yalcinkaya et al., 2007). This is particularly the case with small countries that are not endowed with rich natural resources, as they can find a niche in Global Value Chains by providing knowledge skills. Empirical evidence suggests that in small economies, innovation policies have limited impact on growth, as they cannot provide a large contribution to global technology development, and have to rely on the absorption of an external global knowledge base (Bye et al., 2009; Roolaht, 2012). Bye et al. (2009) also highlight that in a small open economy, the promotion of technological export strategies has proven to be the most efficient, and knowledge transfer and spillovers from abroad enhance country's productivity growth.

The brief literature review above suggests that Armenia, with a small economy, poorly endowed with natural resources, has to purposefully develop its innovation policies, taking these characteristics into account. As an important step, export stimulation and the attraction of foreign actors in general should be central to the developmental strategy. Unfortunately, the peculiarities of transition, such as the exclusion of foreigners in the early privatization process, complicate the development and implementation of successful innovation-based development policies in the country. National patterns of privatization undermined the role of foreign actors in the economy, creating mostly local networks that were not conducive to the promotion of innovations.

3.4.1   Learning Through Local Networks

Radosevic (2002) shows that in the early transition the industrial networks had a complementary production base. Whereas companies in Central and Eastern Europe integrated into international industrial networks through foreign actors, trade and production linkages, companies in post-Soviet countries were more embedded in local networks. In many post-Soviet economies, researchers document "thick" networks of enterprises and less developed formal institutional settings, which in some cases lock out foreign actors (McDermott, 2002; Radosevic, 2002). With the limited role of the formal institutional set-up in countrywide innovation and learning facilitation, informal institutions and local networks become essential factors. Compared to the Central European countries, firms in former Soviet countries, including Armenia, relied heavily on domestic networks, which constrained their further integration into global networks

(Radosevic and Sadowski, 2004). This means that firms in Armenia had limited access to foreign markets, foreign assets, knowledge and resources; hence, learning and economic transformation in this setting was based mostly on local experimentation and learning through local connections.

Given the challenges typical to the transition context, cohesive local networks function as mechanisms to cope with uncertainties, to learn from each other, and to ensure trust and reciprocity. In this context, learning is a result of social cooperation, where "know-who" becomes an important factor for the access to information and knowledge (Lundvall and Johnson, 1994). Kitanovic (2007) distinguishes four types of learning through social networks. First is the individual learning, without any social interaction. The second is the knowledge acquired through interaction, but with limited understanding, which will not facilitate the further development of the new technology. The third type includes more interactions, but based on feedback rather than commonly created knowledge; and the fourth type is an organized interaction directed toward the creation of new knowledge, such as collaborations with universities and collaborative R&D activities.

In transition countries, firms are challenged to shift toward learning types three and four, however they still need to change their routines, habits and structures to better adapt to a new market economy. The drawback of a slow shift is losing a stock of initial knowledge, for example, in the case of strong engineering knowledge inherited by Armenia from its past as a Soviet republic, which was not employed fully during the transition. As a result, the country followed the "low-end forgetting" path that further complicates successful and rapid development of an integrated and efficient NIS.

3.4.2 Learning Through Foreign Actors

Studies of socialist economies show that integration of local networks into global networks takes place because of the presence of foreign actors, even in the cases when governments are not able to reinforce innovation policies (Radosevic, 2002). Among transition countries, the post-Soviet nations are the least successful in the integration of their local networks into international ones. In the case of Armenia, a major lack of foreign actors within the national economy slowed down the process of integration of the local firms into the global networks, and the embeddedness of the networks inherited from the Soviet era further inhibited the search for new opportunities. One should keep in mind, nevertheless, that foreign actors may be more helpful in specific areas, such as in the utilization of new technologies as opposed to new technological developments (Wignaraja,

2003), or other actors may have a more pronounced positive effect (Ca, 1999; Mytelka, 1992).

In the case of Armenia, learning from foreign actors and local R&D stems mostly from collaborations with multinational companies, which primarily help in the adaptation of foreign technology rather than developing new technologies and by using cheap skilled labor for outsourcing innovative ideas. The multinationals are viewed in the transition context with some suspicion. Their propensity to expand and the intentions to use local resources are readily related in public conscience to the fears of merciless exploitation that would enrich the international firms and leave domestic actors impoverished. The evidence from developing countries suggests, to the contrary, that it is typical for local firms to learn and upgrade their knowledge and to adopt new technologies, although foreign presence does not stimulate the development of independent domestic R&D competence (Ca, 1999; Mytelka, 1992; Wignaraja, 2003). The latter should be the focus of governmental innovation policies with the goal to stimulate research and to improve mechanisms for FDI-driven knowledge spillovers (Klochikhin, 2013).

3.5 CONCLUSION

This chapter describes the state of the Armenian National System of Innovation. Based on the literature on NIS in transition countries, it systematizes unique features of innovation systems in this context. It explores the system-level changes through identifying innovation determinants in terms of historical heritage, macroeconomic conditions, and the role of main actors and networks. It illustrates how the Soviet legacy and different patterns of privatization policies affected the transformation of the National Systems of Innovation. Three main periods of the NIS transformation are observed in recent Armenian history: before 1990, early transition (before 2000) and after 2000. Before 1990, all post-Soviet countries were coordinated by a central planning system and were a part of the USSR innovation system. Early transition was dominated by restructuring strategies and survival. Only after 2000 did Armenia develop policies and strategies to shape specifically its National Innovation System. Yet, new innovation policies could not erase the past, and even the establishment of new institutions needs time and further changes to work efficiently.

Inherited from the Soviet innovation system, the innovation governance system in Armenia is quite fragmented, which creates additional challenges for industry–academia linkages. Although statistics report that Armenia is a regional leader in terms of the Global Innovation Index, it still falls behind other transition countries, especially those in Central and Eastern Europe.

Industry–academia linkages that are vital for efficient NIS are the weakest component in the Armenian innovation system. Firms in this case seek access to external knowledge sources through their personal networks or foreign firms. However, the potential for FDI's contribution in Armenian IS is very small.

Current public institutions and policies do not support firms in their attempts to overcome shortages in skilled labor and financial resources, and fail to promote a strong innovative culture among organizations. Radosevic (2002) argues that the establishment of new institutions that were mostly initiated and supported by western actors did little to deal with the complexities of preexisting institutions. Additionally, those new institutions failed to address the requirements and needs of the local actors. In the short run, the consequences were profound, as they did not operate efficiently.

Overall, the efforts to build an efficient and knowledge-driven market economy in Armenia are still in their infancy. So far the results of the previous two decades include the destruction of the initial knowledge stock and poor integration of domestic firms into S&T knowledge networks. The major challenges are seen in the lack of collaboration between NIS actors, especially between firms and universities, with firms that have little interest in knowledge acquisition and universities that have little interest in promoting private sector innovation.

NOTES

1. The author divides knowledge-searching activities into two types: first, when new knowledge-searching activities are very closely connected to production, while the second way is "the less profit-oriented" basic research activities of universities and similar organizations, where knowledge search is not influenced by the market or the needs of producers.
2. Mass privatization in Armenia went in two phases: first, the state distributed vouchers to all eligible citizens, citizens could use their vouchers to participate in privatization of the state property; and second, a major portion of the shares of enterprises were distributed among employees, so that employees became shareholders of the enterprise they worked for. Such a model is usually referred to as an insider model (Arakelyan, 2005; International Monetary Fund, 1998).
3. This refers to highly centralized Science and Technology policies, where all decisions were made in Moscow.
4. European Bank for Reconstruction and Development (2013).
5. Source: interviews with more than 20 Armenian firms in the IT sector.
6. This conclusion is based on interviews with firms, policy advisors and representatives of industrial unions.

REFERENCES

Abramovitz, M. (1986). Catching up, forging ahead, and falling behind. *Journal of Economic History*, *46*(2), 385–406.

Anderson, R. J. (2006). Industrial firm linkages in a post-Soviet urban economy: Implications for development policy and programmes. *Progress in Development Studies*, *6*(3), 224–241.

Arakelyan, V. (2005). *Privatization as a means of property redistribution in the Republic of Armenia and in the Russian Federation* (Doctoral dissertation), accessed March 24, 2016 at https://tampub.uta.fi/bitstream/handle/10024/67491/951-44-6319-6.pdf?sequence=1.

Arocena, R., and Sutz, J. (2000). Looking at national systems of innovation from the South. *Industry and Innovation*, *7*(1), 55–75.

Arocena, R., and Sutz, J. (2002). *Innovation systems and developing countries* (Working Paper 02-05). Copenhagen: Copenhagen Business School, Department of Industrial Economics and Strategy.

Baković, T., Lazibat, T., and Sutić, I. (2013). Radical innovation culture in Croatian manufacturing industry. *Journal of Enterprising Communities: People and Places in the Global Economy*, *7*(1), 74–80.

Bye, B., Fæhn, T., and Heggedal, T. R. (2009). Welfare and growth impacts of innovation policies in a small, open economy: An applied general equilibrium analysis. *Economic Modelling*, *26*(5), 1075–1088.

Ca, T. N. (1999). *Technological capability and learning in firms*. Aldershot: Ashgate.

European Bank for Reconstruction and Development (EBRD). (2013). *Transition report 2013*. London, accessed January 10, 2016 at http://www.ebrd.com/downloads/loans/16b.pdf.

EV Consulting. (2012). *National competitiveness report of Armenia*. Annual Report. Yerevan, accessed March 24, 2016 at http://ev.am/sites/default/files/attachments/pdf/ACR%202011-2012_eng.pdf.

Freeman, L. C. (2004). Technological infrastructure and international competitiveness. *Industrial and Corporate Change*, *13*(3), 541–569.

Gevorkyan, A. V. (2015). The legends of the Caucasus: Economic transformation of Armenia and Georgia. *International Business Review*, *24*(6), 1009–1024.

Gu, Sh. (1999). *Implications of national innovation systems for developing countries: Managing change and complexity* (UNU-INTECH Discussion Paper Series 9903), accessed March 24, 2016 at https://ideas.repec.org/p/unm/unuint/199903.html.

Intarakumnerd, P., Chairatana, P., and Tangchitpiboon, T. (2002). National innovation system in less successful developing countries: The case of Thailand. *Research Policy*, *31*(8–9), 1445–1457.

International Monetary Fund. (1998). *Armenia: recent economic developments*, accessed March 24, 2016 at https://www.imf.org/external/pubs/ft/scr/1998/cr9822.pdf.

Khnkoyan, A. (2011 September). *Development of scientific and innovation policy in Armenia in 2000s*. Paper presented at the 4th Atlanta Conference on Science and Innovation Policy, Georgia Institute of Technology, Atlanta, USA.

Kitanovic, J. (2007). The applicability of the concept of national innovation systems to transition economies. *Innovation*, *9*(1), 28–45.

Klochikhin, E. A. (2013). Innovation system in transition: Opportunities for policy learning between China and Russia. *Science and Public Policy*, *40*(5), 657–673.

Krammer, S. M. (2009). Drivers of national innovation in transition: Evidence from a panel of Eastern European countries. *Research Policy*, *38*(5), 845–60.

List, F. (1841). *The national system of political economy*. London: Longman.

Lundvall, B.-Å. (1985). *Product innovation and user–producer interaction*. Aalborg: Aalborg University Press.

Lundvall, B.-Å., and Johnson, B. (1994). The learning economy. *Journal of Industry Studies*, *1*(2), 23–42.

Lundvall, B.-Å., Johnson, B., Andersen, E. S., and Dalum, B. (2002). National systems of production, innovation and competence building. *Research Policy*, *31*(2), 213–231.

McDermott, G. A. (2002). *Embedded politics: Industrial networks and institutional change in postcommunism*. Michigan: University of Michigan Press.

Mytelka, L. K. (1992). Ivorian industry at the cross-roads. In F. Stewart, S. Lall and S. Wangwe (eds.), *Alternative development strategies in SubSaharan Africa* (pp. 243–264). Palgrave Macmillan: London.

Perry, M. (2001). Shared trust in small industrial countries? An evaluation from New Zealand. *Norsk Geografisk Tidsskrift – Norwegian Journal of Geography*, *55*(1), 1–8.

Radosevic, S. (2002). Regional innovation systems in Central and Eastern Europe: Determinants, organizers and alignments. *The Journal of Technology Transfer*, *27*(1), 87–96.

Radosevic, S., and Sadowski, B. M. (2004). *International industrial networks and industrial restructuring in Central and Eastern Europe*. Dordrecht: Kluwer Academic Publishers.

Roolaht, T. (2012). The characteristics of small country national innovation systems. In E. G. Carayannis et al. (eds.), *Innovation systems in small catching-up economies* (pp. 21–37). Springer: New York.

Schumpeter, J. A. (1934). *The theory of economic development: An inquiry into profits, capital, credit, interest, and the business cycle*. London: Transaction Publishers.

United Nations Economic Commission for Europe (UNECE). (2014). *Innovation performance review of Armenia* (UNECE. Country Report). New York and Geneva. Retrieved from http://www.unece.org/index.php?id=35916.

Wignaraja, G. (2003). *Competitiveness strategy in developing countries: A manual for policy analysis*. New York and London: Routledge.

WIPO, Cornell University, and INSEAD. (2014). *Global innovation index*. Geneva, accessed January 10, 2016 at http://www.wipo.int/publications/en/details.jsp?id=3254.

World Bank. (2013). *Doing Business Report 2013*. Washington, accessed January 10, 2016 at https://openknowledge.worldbank.org/bitstream/handle/10986/11857/DB13_Full%20report.pdf.

World Economic Forum. (2013). *The human capital report 2013*. Geneva, accessed March 24, 2016 at http://reports.weforum.org/human-capital-index-2013/.

Yalcinkaya, G., Calantone, R. J., and Griffith, D. A. (2007). An examination of exploration and exploitation capabilities: Implications for product innovation and market performance. *Journal of International Marketing*, *15*(4), 63–93.

4. The role of public policies in building up a national pharmaceutical innovation system in Tunisia: challenges after the Jasmine Revolution

Nejla Yacoub

4.1 THE BACKGROUND OF THE STUDY

In the conditions of globalization and technological change enhancing competitiveness is the main objective of firms and countries. The economic literature emphasizes the important role of technological innovation as a determinant of structural competitiveness (March, 1991; N. Yacoub and Laperche, 2010; N. Yacoub, 2012) mostly in the context of developed countries. In the last two decades, however, several developing countries such as Tunisia have increasingly worked on setting-up innovation systems (IS) to strengthen their structural competitiveness in many sectors.

In the early 1990s, Tunisia introduced a public policy aiming to enhance research and development (R&D) and innovation. The aim of the set of public policies defined by the Tunisian government was to drive economic growth via promoting foreign direct investments (FDI), exports and innovation with the ultimate goal to increase per capita income, promote education and to enhance social welfare via lower unemployment, poverty and inflation rates. The main policy instruments included establishing technopoles in several regions of the country, investing in information and communication technologies (ICT) and carrying out programmes to improve the national education system (Aubert et al., 2012). The innovation policy specifically targeted promising and high value-added sectors, such as pharmaceuticals.

The Tunisian pharmaceutical industry emerged in the late 1980s and has been growing on average at about 19 per cent per year between 1989 and 2013. According to the Ministry of Public Health (MPH), local production covers about half of the Tunisian market. Exports represent 9 per cent of the local production (MPH, 2016). Main exports destinations are the Maghreb region, sub-Saharan Africa and a few European countries.

By the beginning of the 2010s, the government was unable to fulfil the objectives set by the innovation policy. Despite the stated goals, the economic and social situation in Tunisia was deteriorating with unemployment reaching 18 per cent in early 2011, against 13.3 per cent in 2009 (Index-mundi, 2016). The economic and social tensions in the society, combined with corruption, lack of transparency and democracy, have generated a general frustration, mostly among young people. In December 2010, numerous participants of strikes and rallies held across the country and lasting longer than a month demanded a change. On 14 January 2011 the former president left the country; this date marks the Jasmine Revolution and the beginning of a new era in Tunisian history.

This chapter attempts to evaluate the effectiveness of the innovation policy in strengthening the pharmaceutical innovation process in Tunisia and the impact of the Jasmine Revolution on pharmaceutical innovation. Answering these questions requires a comparative assessment of the Tunisian pharmaceutical innovation system (TPIS) *pre* and *post* revolution, although a short period of time that has passed after the Revolution introduces certain challenges into the assessment. For this reason the *post*-revolution analysis is presented mostly in terms of future perspectives based on the objectives of the post-revolution public innovation policy and their applicability in the current political and economic context.

The remainder of this chapter is organized as follows: the next section describes the national sectoral innovation system (NSIS) in Tunisia before the Jasmine Revolution. The following section explores the public policy reforms implemented after the revolution and the challenges in their enforcement. On the basis of this analysis, the last section summarizes the strengths and weaknesses of TPIS and discusses the likelihood of its future success.

4.2   THE TUNISIAN PHARMACEUTICAL INNOVATION SYSTEM BEFORE THE JASMINE REVOLUTION

Innovation is a dynamic process that involves multiple actors and heavily relies on their interaction. The innovation system can be delineated by national (Lundvall, 1992), regional (Agrawal et al., 2014; Nour, 2014), sectoral (Malerba, 2002) or technological (Wieczorek et al., 2015) boundaries. The broad definition of innovation systems includes all formal and informal institutions that are directly or indirectly related to the process of new technology creation (Casadella and Benlahcen-Tlemceni, 2006). The narrow definition focuses only on institutions directly involved in knowledge exchange (KE). As illustrated in Figure 4.1, this chapter uses the broad approach to analyse the TPIS, since KE interactions are still rare in developing countries (Djeflat, 2012; N. Yacoub, 2013).

The originally implemented public policies supported an *infant* pharmaceutical industry at that time. The initial goal of these policies was to develop production. To this end the government has set up a two-pronged (supply–demand) support policy for pharmaceutical laboratories established in the country. The policy relied on two sets of instruments, short-run and long-run ones. The short-run instruments, termed here conjunctural policy instruments, aim to increase production volume and to enhance the cost competitiveness of Tunisian pharmaceutical firms. The long-run instruments, called structural policy instruments in this chapter, include policy measures that aim to strengthen the structural competitiveness of pharmaceutical firms in Tunisia via bolstering their innovation capabilities, since innovation is the key determinant of structural competitiveness (N. Yacoub, 2012).

4.2.1   The Conjunctural Support Policy

The supply-side policies provided several fiscal advantages to the Tunisian pharmaceutical companies. According to the Tunisian Investment Incentive Code (IIC)[1] and the Decree 94-1191 of 30 May 1994, the Tunisian, as well as the Greenfield[2] foreign pharmaceutical firms, are exempt from customs duties on imports of packaging items, raw materials and R&D equipment. They also enjoy a value-added tax rate of 6 per cent instead of the 12 per cent applied to other sectors.

Local market opportunities for the pharmaceutical companies were promoted via demand-side measures. The Tunisian pharmaceutical market is rather small; it is only about 5 per cent of the French market (N. Yacoub, 2013), for example. Nevertheless, the Tunisian market has a high growth potential in terms of demand solvency. In 2013, the annual healthcare expenditures per capita grew up to 200 Euros against 126.7 Euros in 2009 and to 34 Euros in the early 1990s. The 2007 reform of the Tunisian social security system was behind such substantial growth. It encouraged patients to buy domestically produced pharmaceutical products instead of imports. For instance, when patients buy an imported drug, social security refunds them only the difference between the paid price and the price of a domestic produced equivalent, which is always cheaper. In contrast, the cost of domestic drugs is reimbursed by social security, making patients' out-of-pocket expenses equal to zero, which

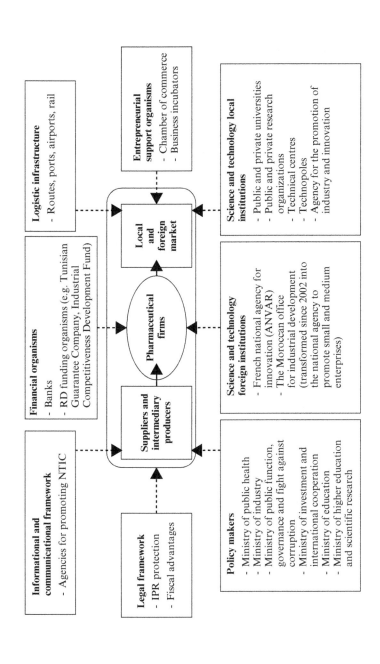

Source: Author's own elaboration.

Figure 4.1 Illustration of the Tunisian pharmaceutical innovation system

71

serves as a strong incentive to switch to domestically produced drugs (MPH, 2016).

In addition to the local demand, Tunisia has recently become a major medical destination for neighbouring countries such as Libya and Algeria, and to a lesser extent for European countries. This comes as a result of the improved medical expertise of the local doctors, expanding tourism, as well as a cost advantage. Since the early 2000s, Tunisia has implemented a health tourism policy that has been successful in attracting healthcare tourists further boosting demand for pharmaceutical products in the country.

4.2.2   The Structural Support Policy

In 1995, Tunisia introduced an upgrade programme for industrial firms and an industrial modernization programme. Both programmes aim to reduce the gap in industrial standards between Tunisia and developed countries in terms of human capital skills, new technology use and diffusion, patents exploitation and so on (L. Yacoub, 2008). The programmes were active in establishing specialized institutions with the aim to promote innovation and knowledge exchange, developing human capital training and streamlining the legal framework.

4.2.2.1   Innovation centres and collaborative incentives
In order to improve the linkages between the actors within an innovation system and to make them more targeted on knowledge exchange, the Tunisian government has established several public institutions such as technical centres, technological parks and consulting bureaus. The mission of these institutions is to guide and assist industrial firms throughout the innovation process, in line with the agenda of the national consulting bureau for scientific and technological research established in 2002.

Twenty-six entrepreneurial nurseries have been set up within research organizations and universities across the country. Their mission is to guide and support young researchers, engineers and graduate students in carrying out their own investment projects and becoming entrepreneurs. The entrepreneurial nursery programme has played a considerable role in the increased applications of academic research in the market.

The government has also created eight technical centres focused on specific industries. The centres upgrade local industrial capability by implementing professional continuing education programmes, and offering consulting services based on the evaluation of the strengths and weaknesses of industrial firms. In this same context, nine technological parks focusing on specific sectors have been established across the country.

The host locations for these technopoles were chosen based on the specific characteristics of each region, such as the concentration of related investments, the presence of universities and the abundance of natural resources. Technological parks are expected to promote cluster formation in R&D intensive industries that should accelerate innovation dynamics. Technopoles encourage industrial and public–private cooperation in the area of research and development, utilize the local highly trained labour force and improve the attractiveness of a territory to high-tech foreign direct investments (FDI). The 'biotechpole of Sidi Thabet', established in 2002, specializes in healthcare and pharmaceutical biotechnological research. Industrial pharmaceutical firms, biotechnology public and private research institutions and universities in related fields populate this technopole.

Despite the promotional efforts, overall Tunisia lacks sufficient human and technological assets and financial resources necessary to carry out the whole technological innovation process. In such circumstances international cooperation is particularly important. Tunisia is party to a number of R&D cooperation agreements at the regional and international levels, such as the multilateral cooperation agreement signed on 30 October 2001 with the French national agency for innovation (ANVAR) and the Moroccan office for industrial development (transformed since 2002 into the national agency to promote small and medium enterprises (SMEs)). This agreement intends to improve cooperation between SMEs within the three partner countries and to stimulate the development of innovation-based start-ups.

Patents and other intellectual property rights (IPR) are central to the ability of companies from other countries to bring new technologies and to engage in research and development. As a member of the World Trade Organization, Tunisia signed the Trade-Related Intellectual Property Rights (TRIPS) agreements in 1995. According to the TRIPS, patents have been recognized in most technology fields since 2000, whereas patents in pharmaceuticals have been recognized since 2006. Patent protection is a measure meant to attract innovative FDI and to promote collaborative innovation (Laperche et al., 2013).

4.2.2.2 Financial mechanisms to support R&D

Tunisia has created several financial mechanisms to respond to funding needs, especially those of innovative SMEs. The Tunisian Guarantee Company (TGC) has a mission to provide coaching and technical assistance to firms and to facilitate their access to financial resources to fund R&D activities. Financial subsidies for R&D investment (better known in Tunisia by the French abbreviation PIRD) are available to industrial firms upon the presentation of an innovative and original project. The subsidy covers 5 per cent of the project study costs and up to 50 per cent of expenses on experiments. To qualify for this subsidy an applicant firm must cover at least 20 per cent of costs and the project must involve three partners: the firm, a technical centre and a research laboratory in the same sector with the applicant company. An additional funding opportunity is provided by the Industrial Competitiveness Development Fund (ICDF), which covers up to 70 per cent of investments in intellectual assets carried out within the upgrade programme. Another widely used incentive provided by the government is covering half of the salary of newly hired employees with graduate degrees from public sources. It is hoped that this assistance programme would contribute to financial solvency and advanced expertise of Tunisian SMEs.

4.2.2.3   A human capital policy targeted on KE

Human capital is the driving force of innovation. The experience of the developed countries shows that the high level of human capital is crucial for the development of a well-structured and mature innovation system. Tunisia has steadily increased its public expenditures on education, reaching 4.8 per cent of GDP in 2009, which is close to the share spent on education by some other developed countries such as France.

To close the gap between the university education and the technical skills required in the market, Tunisia adopted the MANFORME programme in 2002, which created 140 training centres especially targeted on pharmaceuticals and biotechnologies. The aim of this programme is to improve the preparedness of graduates by teaching the skills required by industrial employers. In 2002, the Decree 2002-1573 of the IIC was passed with the goal to promote partnerships between universities, firms and public institutions by encouraging academic researchers in public universities to carry out tripartite research projects in collaboration with technological parks and industrial firms. As a result, the Tunisian education system was ranked nineteenth in the world in terms of the quality of the academic formation programmes and ninth in terms of the availability of engineers and scientific researchers (WEF, 2014–2015).

4.2.3   The Efficiency of the TPIS: A Firm-Level Analysis

Since the early 1990s, Tunisia has striven to catch up with the more innovative countries. To this end, it has implemented several policies that aim to stimulate R&D capabilities together with technology use and diffusion in various sectors, including pharmaceuticals. This section describes how the following goals and methods of the policy measures are translated and felt at the firm level: interaction between its actors, enforcement of the public policies and their efficiency in stimulating innovation capabilities and performance.

4.2.3.1 The firm-level innovation survey

The analysis is based on a firm-level innovation survey conducted by Nejla Yacoub over six months[3] (2012, 2013). It uses a qualitative approach to assess the innovation potential and performance of pharmaceutical firms in Tunisia. All 32 drug-producing firms in Tunisia were invited to participate in the study. This number includes 26 Tunisian firms and six Greenfield foreign companies. The survey was administered through face-to-face comprehensive structured interviews based on a questionnaire composed of qualitative/quantitative and close-ended/open-ended questions. The average duration of each interview was three hours, which included individual interviews with several respondents representing various divisions of their companies such as human resources, quality control, chemical engineering and others. Twenty-seven completed surveys have been collected (an 84 per cent response rate). Two of the five non-responding laboratories did not accept the interview because they refused to disclose any information. Two others were in the process of trading cessation. The fifth one was a newly established firm in the market and had not yet started activity.

The survey intended to classify the interviewed firms into two main groups: non-innovation-oriented and innovation-oriented. The latter group was further divided into three sub-groups: weakly and moderately innovative (34 per cent of the sample), catching-up firms (4 per cent) and leader innovative (8.5 per cent). For this purpose, a composite innovation index was constructed in order to measure the firms' innovation inputs, throughputs and outputs[4] based on both quantitative and qualitative indicators. The survey was constructed in a way that would allow for discernment of the success factors behind the intensity of innovation within surveyed firms and to draw conclusions on the efficiency of the Tunisian national innovation system as seen and felt by the respondents, and specifically on the impact of public policies and their efficiency in encouraging interaction between pharmaceutical firms and other actors within the innovation system.

4.2.3.2 Firm-level perspectives on the strengths and weaknesses of the Tunisian context for innovation

According to the surveyed firms, the expansive fiscal policy supporting pharmaceutical producers in Tunisia is less important than the creation of local innovation dynamics (N. Yacoub, 2012). Against the background of competition for structural advantage among firms and countries, the conjunctural policy is rather insignificant (L. Yacoub and N. Yacoub, 2011). At the same time, a small size of the Tunisian pharmaceutical market is seen as a major impediment to investment and development. Despite growing local demand, limited market size still hampers the channelling of financial resources to pharmaceutical R&D, while public financial incentives meant to improve innovation capabilities remain inadequate for financing pharmaceutical research. This conclusion of the survey is in line with the findings of a quantitative study of other Tunisian sectors performed by Koubaa et al. (2010).

Koubaa et al. (2010) also find that highly skilled labour is not a decisive factor for innovation by Tunisian firms. Indeed, human capital is a necessary but not sufficient condition for innovations. This finding confirms that a unified approach that improves local expertise and stimulates local demand is warranted (Arocena and Sutz, 2010). Tunisian pharmaceutical firms seem to be satisfied with the level of human capital available to them. They emphasize the importance of local human capital skills for innovation (N. Yacoub, 2012) and characterize the quality of local human resources as 'good' (77.8 per cent of respondents) or 'excellent' (14.8 per cent). The remaining firms judge it as 'average' because of the lack of practical experience. The surveyed firms state that the Tunisian human resources are appropriate to learning and possess high absorptive capabilities of new technologies. The companies identify academic education, absorptive capabilities, the ability to integrate and adapt to the firm's culture, and the responsive attitude to work as strengths of the Tunisian labour force.

Protection of intellectual property rights is meant to be an incentive to innovation. However, the results of the empirical literature on IPR effects are mixed (Schneider, 2005; N. Yacoub, 2012, 2013). The positive impact is confirmed in the context of countries and sectors that are innovation-makers rather than innovation-takers (N. Yacoub, 2012). In other contexts, the positive impact is not clear and may even be reversed.

Evidence from the Tunisian pharmaceutical industry shows that in the short run, patent protection is an obstacle to innovation because it hinders the 'innovation via imitation' process (N. Yacoub, 2012). In the long run, patent protection generates positive impacts through the facilitation of technology transfer via technology licences, cooperation and collaborative innovation. In order for IPR protection mechanisms to yield benefits, however, the TPIS needs to be strengthened and local innovation capabilities improved to attract foreign R&D investments and partners. Another impediment for the Tunisian pharmaceutical innovation is domestic unavailability of technical resources for research and development, such as equipment, tools and raw materials, up to 80 per cent of which are imported.

4.2.3.3   Firm-level R&D structure and practices

The structure of firm-level R&D is an important indicator and determinant of company's innovation orientation, as it is an important throughput in the innovation process. The structure of firm-level R&D is defined by the frequency of R&D activities, their location (whether they are internalized or externalized) and the intensity of intra-firm knowledge exchange, among other factors.

All surveyed firms perform their R&D activities internally with 70.4 per cent of the respondents housing separate R&D departments, which are mostly engaged in development rather than research. The pharmaceutical firms in Tunisia routinely develop and employ internal information systems based on the use of Internet, Intranet, computers, videoconferencing equipment and so on. Information systems facilitate communication and, thus, knowledge exchange between different departments of the firm, although only 54 per cent of the firms report communication flows within them for scientific and technical purposes, while remaining firms use these technologies for routine administrative and commercial tasks.

Knowledge exchange with external partners offers firms further opportunities to develop knowledge capital and to reduce costs and risks related to R&D activities. KE also means interaction and cooperation with firms, universities and public institutions. Many pharmaceutical firms in Tunisia have recently signed cooperation contracts with medical, engineering and pharmaceutical universities. Within these cooperation agreements, open door days are organized to bring together actors from the public, professional, academic and industrial sectors to discuss the latest achievements in healthcare. For example, the Sanofi-Aventis firm organizes regular competitions to select the best innovative project among students of the faculties of medicine and pharmacy. Despite this, the frequency and scope of public–private interaction in pharmaceuticals falls short of the goals defined by the innovation policy and knowledge exchange within the TPIS remains moderate. The interaction between firms mainly involves industrial licensing and outsourcing some manufacturing tasks, whereas interaction between firms and public entities is limited to routine administrative procedures such as reporting and regulations compliance checks. According to the surveyed firms, long and complicated administrative procedures are a key reason for infrequent communications with public institutions, including limited contact with institutions set up specifically to promote innovation within pharmaceuticals. There is a lack of transparency and dissemination of crucial information related to existing opportunities for the pharmaceutical sector by the ministry of public health and affiliate institutions.

4.3   THE TUNISIAN PHARMACEUTICAL INNOVATION SYSTEM AFTER THE JASMINE REVOLUTION

4.3.1   Change of the Institutional Background after the Revolution

A favourable macroeconomic environment and political stability are important for successful innovation activities by domestic and international companies. Tunisia has traditionally enjoyed a high ranking among countries, presenting a low risk in business dealings, which has contributed to the inflow of pharmaceutical FDI (L. Yacoub and N. Yacoub, 2011). After the revolution, however, the risk of doing business in Tunisia increased, due to political and economic instability and an increased danger of terrorism. International rating agencies such as Standard & Poor and Moody's decreased Tunisia's rating after 2011, as a result. Nevertheless, compared to the other countries in the region, Tunisia is considered a relatively stable country.

Since the revolution, the Tunisian government has undergone restructuring that shows the importance that is placed on key up-to-date concepts such as governance, innovation and sustainable development. The post-revolution ministry of industry is called the Ministry of Industry and Technology; it emphasizes industrial cooperation and innovation. The Ministry has specified a general direction of innovation and technological development and seeks to enforce and improve the accompanying institutions' mission to support business nurseries, technical centres and public research institutions such as the National Institute for Statistics (INS). The post-revolution government seeks to promote cooperation with other governments. For example, in order to facilitate access to new advanced technologies from developed countries, in 2016 the Ministry of Public Health launched a collaborative project between Tunisia and the European Union that supports joint research and the development of mechanisms against sanitary and environmental risks (MPH, 2016).

In addition, new incentives for investment and innovation in high value-added sectors were created, while the existing incentive mechanisms were streamlined. The national programme of research and innovation (NPRI or PNRI in French) was introduced in 2011. As with the PIRD, the goal of this programme is to financially support R&D and innovative firms in industrial sectors (Zayani, 2012) by modernizing firms' production mechanisms, promoting their innovation and enhancing structural competitive capabilities. The programme provides subsidies that cover up to 80 per cent of the research project cost with a limit of 200,000 Tunisian Dinars (90,000 Euros). All industrial firms are eligible for funding if they comply with the following four requirements. First, the project must be original and significantly innovative; second, it must involve the firm and at least one technical centre and one public research structure; third, the firm must fund 20 per cent of the total project cost; finally, the duration of the project must not exceed two years.

The change in the political regime led to the creation of numerous new associations, since before the revolution the associative activities were entirely controlled by the government. As an example, the Laboratory for Social and Solidarity Economy (LabESS) was established in collaboration with the international organization 'Development without Borders' (DWB). LabESS seeks to promote an innovation-driven civil society oriented to social entrepreneurship and sustainable development.

4.3.2   The Human Capital Skills Dilemma

Tunisian pharmaceutical companies indicate that they are satisfied with the preparation of the labour force, as suggested by the survey results. This speaks for a relatively high quality of university education in the country. Indeed, three Tunisian universities were among the top 30 best African universities in 2015, while in 2012 none of them appeared in the top 100. On the world scale, the best Tunisian university was ranked 6719th in 2010 and 2701th in 2015 (CSIC, 2016), which demonstrates a clear improvement over the last five years. The Ministry of Education (ME) continues to implement programmes aimed at further improvement in the quality of university education. In 2016, the ME launched an investment project that will invest 142 million Dinars (65 million Euros) from the World Bank into programmes that facilitate industrial–university cooperation in order to improve the content of academic curricula and to better align it with the requirements of the labour market in the country (Mahjoub, 2016).

On the other hand, the situation in the lower levels of the education system has been deteriorating since the revolution. Each year thousands of students drop out of school; this number reached 100,000 in 2013 (ME, 2016). Poverty, unemployment and the content of academic curricula inadequate to the age capabilities of students are believed to play a major role. This represents a serious problem for the future prospects of Tunisian development and innovation, since high rates of school dropout translate into decreasing human capital, which will be an increasingly important obstacle to technology-led growth and knowledge exchange. In response, the Ministry of Education has attempted to improve the education system content, quality and environment.

4.3.3 Remaining Obstacles to Innovation Catch-Up by the Tunisian Pharmaceutical Companies

Overall, despite recently implemented public policies to build an innovation-driven economy, the IS is still in its infancy. According to the World Economic Forum report of 2009–10 (WEF) the main IS failures in Tunisia are as follows:

- The content and the instruments of existing support programmes often interfere with each other' scope, which reduces their efficiency; such a situation is observed in the case of the upgrade programme, the PIRD and the PNRI;
- The financial aid to SMEs is shared among so many companies that the amount received by each firm is very low compared to the costs of R&D activities;
- Interaction between the actors comprising the National Innovation System is still fragile and not targeted on knowledge exchange;
- The educational system suffers from structural problems;
- The TRIPS agreements prevent Tunisian pharmaceutical firms from engaging in innovation via imitation processes;
- In this context overcoming the weaknesses and consolidating the strengths is necessary to improve the TPIS performance and to generate a genuine innovation-driven catch-up process for the Tunisian pharmaceutical industry.

4.4 CONCLUSIONS

The Jasmine Revolution has brought both threats and opportunities to the innovation perspectives in Tunisia. More time needs to pass in order to fully assess the Revolution's impact. At this stage it is clear that a set of policy measures encouraging technology transfer via cooperation with foreign innovative firms, universities and public and private research institutions is likely to advance TPIS (L. Yacoub, 2014). Whereas other factors, most notably the unstable political environment in the neighbouring countries, may affect the success and the speed of Tunisian IS transformation, local efforts should focus on building structural attractiveness to innovation investors especially in terms of improving R&D capabilities of human capital and stimulating knowledge exchange among all IS actors.

It is crucial to establish an agency that will facilitate technology transfer and will be an intermediary between 'technology producers' and 'technology consumers' (N. Yacoub, 2012). The agency would create a kind of a local 'monopsony technology market' that aims to consolidate the negotiation power of the innovation-seeking Tunisian pharmaceutical firms and increase their opportunities to access new foreign technologies. This implies decentralization of existing institutions (Djeflat, 2012) and a greater involvement of technological parks (M'henni and Arvanitis, 2012).

Beyond the number of innovation support institutions, one of the main challenges is to enforce policies and to introduce mechanisms to control the achievement of the goals. To this end, both policy objectives and the mechanisms of their achievement should be coherent in order to avoid a gap between the intentions of policies and their results. Such a gap may be inherent in Tunisian innovation policy design. It often replicates policies implemented in developed countries that are too ambitious, given the country's resources and the capabilities of domestic firms. This results in a mismatch between the content and objectives of innovation public policy and the innovation strategies and capabilities of local firms. Further streamlining of the Tunisian innovation policy is an imperative action that should lead to a decentralized, cooperative and transparent economic governance structure. Such transformation is in the spirit of the Jasmine Revolution and if it is implemented, the revolution will turn from a potential threat into a genuine opportunity for the take-off of the NSIS in Tunisia.

Other major challenges to the successful development of the Tunisian innovation system include low levels of FDI into research, negligible contributions by the education system toward innovation and inadequate financial support for innovative companies. In a study analysing the country's attractiveness for pharmaceutical FDI, L. Yacoub and N. Yacoub (2011) emphasize the role of the IS in encouraging technology transfer via attracting innovative FDI. Existing pharmaceutical foreign direct investments are mainly market- and/or production-seeking; none of them is mainly innovation-seeking. Tunisia needs to become an attractive destination to research-based FDI. Reforming the country's education system in order to improve and valorise innovation capabilities of domestic human capital may aid in achieving this goal. Human resource skills assessment in Tunisia should be based on qualitative (content, intelligence, practice, etc.) rather than quantitative indicators (tertiary school enrolment, number of university graduates, number of technology students, etc.). Efficient cooperation between industry and universities should promote education approaches that allow students to acquire both academic and practical skills, which are in demand in the labour market. The caps on public subsidies to firms should be relative to the actual R&D

costs. It is necessary to ensure that pharmaceutical firms have the financial resources to perform research and development. One way to do so is by promoting exports, which requires Tunisian pharmaceutical products to conform to European standards in order to access wider foreign markets.

NOTES

1. The Tunisian Investment Incentive Code is available at http://www.tunisieindustrie.nat. tn/fr/download/CFGA/Code.pdf.
2. Unlike acquisition of foreign existing assets (e.g. mergers and acquisitions), a Greenfield investment is intended as a type of foreign direct investments (FDI) where a transnational firm builds up a new asset in a developing country (Calderon et al., 2004).
3. More details of the survey's methodology are given in N. Yacoub, 'A qualitative approach to assess innovation in small infant industries within developing countries. The case of pharmaceuticals in Tunisia', *African Journal of Science, Technology, Innovation and Development*, forthcoming.
4. At a firm level, innovation is a process where a set of inputs interacts via a set of throughputs resulting in a set of outputs (N. Yacoub, 2013). Throughputs are defined by Vermeulen et al. (2003) as a 'black box' of mechanisms, methods and means organized in a way specific to each firm and exploited in the innovation inputs-outputs transformation process. Innovation is an interactive process where outputs are continuously reinstated in the dynamic innovation process as further inputs. At the same time throughputs are continuously revised to answer the evolving innovation process requirements. This dynamic concept of the innovation process at a firm level is illustrated in Figure 4.2.

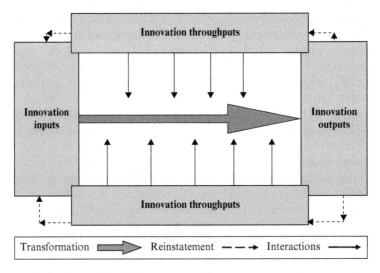

Source: Author's own elaboration.

Figure 4.2   The dynamic innovation process at the firm level

REFERENCES

Agrawal, A., Cockburn, I., Galasso, A., and Oettl, A. (2014). Why are some regions more innovative than others? The role of small firms in the presence of large labs. *Journal of Urban Economics, 81*, 149–165.

Arocena, R., and Sutz, J. (2010). Weak innovation demand in the South: Learning divides and innovation policies. *Science and Public Policy, 37*(8), 571–582.

Aubert, J.-E., Karlsson, M., and Utz, A. (2012). Building knowledge and innovation-driven economies in Arab countries: How to do it. In T. Andersson and A. Djeflat (eds.), *The real issues of the Middle East and the Arab Spring: Addressing research innovation and entrepreneurship* (pp. 359–370). New York, Heidelberg, Dordrecht, London: Springer.

Calderon, C., Loayza, N., and Serven, L. (2004). Greenfield foreign direct investment and mergers and acquisitions: Feedback and macroeconomic effects. *World Bank Policy Research (Working Paper, 3192)*. Washington, DC: World Bank, accessed 8 April 2017 at http://elibrary.worldbank.org/doi/abs/10.1596/1813-9450-3192.

Casadella, V., and Benlahcen-Tlemceni, M. (2006). De lapplicabilité du système national d'innovation dans les pays moins avancés. *Innovations, Cahier d'Economie de l'Innovation, 24*, 59–90.

Consejo Superior de Investigaciones Científicas (CSIC). (2016). Webometrics Ranking of World Universities, accessed 8 April 2017 at http://www.webometrics.info/en/Africa/Tunisia%20.

Djeflat, A. (2012). The relevance of science and technology for Arab Spring and the key role of the knowledge economy. In T. Andersson and A. Djeflat (eds.), *The real issues of the Middle East and the Arab Spring: Addressing research innovation and entrepreneurship* (pp.169–194). New York, Heidelberg, Dordrecht, London: Springer.

Index-mundi. (2016). Tunisie: taux de chômage – Diagrammes historiques de donénes par année. Index-Mundi data portal, accessed 8 April 2017 at http://www.indexmundi.com/g/g.aspx?v=74&c=ts&l=fr.

Koubaa, K., Gabsi, F., and M'henni, H. (2010). Determinants of innovation in emerging country: An empirical study at the Tunisian firm level. *International Journal of Technological Learning, Innovation and Development, 3*(3), 205–225.

Laperche, B., Picard, F., and Yacoub, N. (2013). Origine, fonctionnement et gouvernance de l'innovation multi-partenariale: une lecture néo-institutionnaliste. In S. Boutillier, F. Djellal and D. Uzunidis (eds.), *L'innovation: analyser, anticiper, agir* (pp. 143–174). Bruxelles: Peter Lang, Série Business and Innovation.

Lundvall, B.-Å. (ed.) (1992). *National systems of innovation. Towards a theory of innovation and interactive learning.* London: Pinter.

Mahjoub, Z. (2016, February 26). Tunisie: 142 millions de dinars pour réformer l'enseigenement supérieur. *Réalités*, accessed 8 April 2017 at http://www.realites.com.tn/2016/02/tunisie-142-md-pour-reformer-de-lenseignement-superieur/.

Malerba, F. (2002). Sectoral systems of innovation and production. *Research Policy, 31*(2), 247–264.

March, J. G. (1991). Exploration and exploitation in organizational learning. *Organization Science, 2*, 71–87.

ME. (2016). Statistiques de l'éducation. Ministry of Education of Tunisia, accessed 8 April 2017 at http://www.education.gov.tn/index.php?lan=3.

M'henni, H., and Arvanitis, R. (2012). La résilience des systèmes d'innovation en période de transition: la Tunisie après le 14 Janvier 2011. *Revue Tiers Monde, 4*(212), 57–81.

MPH. (2016). Projet de jumelage entre la Tunisie et l'Union Européenne: l'appui au renforcement de la maîtrise des risques sanitaires et environnementaux, *Ministry of Public Health of Tunisia*, accessed 8 April 2017 at http://www.sante tunisie.rns.tn/fr/index.php/actualites?lang=fr#sthash.qkdoQjRq.dpuf.

Nour, S. S. O. M. (2014). Regional systems of innovation and economic structure in the Arab Region. *Journal of the Knowledge Economy, 5*(3), 481–520.

Schneider, P. H. (2005). International trade, growth and intellectual property rights: A panel data study of developed and developing countries. *Journal of Development Economics, 78*(2), 529–547.

Vermeulen, P. A. M., O'Shaughnessy, K. C., and de Jong, J. P. J. (2003). Innovation in SMEs: An empirical investigation of the input-throughput-output-performance model paper submitted to Research Policy Zoetermeer, June, accessed 19 April 2017 at http://ondernemerschap.panteia.nl/pdf-ez/n200302. pdf.

WEF. (2014–2015). Global competitiveness report, *World Economic Forum*. Davos: WEF, accessed 8 April 2017 at http://reports.weforum.org/global-competitive ness-report-2014-2015/.

Wieczorek, A. J., Hekkert, M. P., Coenen, L., and Harmsen, R. (2015). Broadening the national focus in technological innovation system analysis: The case of offshore wind. *Environmental Innovation and Societal Transitions, 14*, 128–148.

Yacoub, L. (2008). Le programme de mise à niveau de l'industrie: Un moyen efficace de la politique industrielle tunisienne? Laboratoire de Recherche sur l'Industrie et l'Innovation. *Cahiers du Lab* (Document de Travail. RII, 203 Décembre), accessed 8 April 2017 at http://riifr.univ-littoral.fr/wp-content/uploads/2008/12/ doc-203.pdf.

Yacoub, L. (2014). *Les politiques industrielles dans la mondialisation: entre neutralité et volontarisme . . . L'expérience tunisienne*. Sarrebruck: Presses Académiques Francophones.

Yacoub, L., and Yacoub, N. (2011). Quelles politiques d'attractivité? Les déterminants de la localisation des investissements directs étrangers pharmaceutiques en Tunisie. In D. Uzunidis, B. Laperche and S. Boutillier (eds.), *L'Entreprise dans la mondialisation. Contexte et dynamiques d'investissement et de développement* (pp. 405–445). Paris: LeManuscrit.

Yacoub, N. (2012). *The impacts of drugs patentability on pharmaceutical innovation in Tunisia: A theoretical and empirical essay* (Unpublished doctoral dissertation). University of Tunis el Manar, Tunisia and University of Littoral Côte d'Opale, France.

Yacoub, N. (2013). Assessing the pharmaceutical innovation in Tunisia: An empirical survey on the firm's knowledge capital and an analysis of the NSIS. *African Journal of Science, Technology, Innovation and development, 5*(2), 103–118.

Yacoub, N. (2016). A qualitative approach to assess innovation in small infant industries within developing countries: The case of pharmaceuticals in Tunisia. *African Journal of Science, Technology, Innovation and Development*, forthcoming.

Yacoub, N., and Laperche, B. (2010). Stratégies des grandes firmes pharmaceutiques face aux médicaments génériques. Accumulation vs valorisation du capital-savoir. *Innovations, 2*(32), 81–107.

Zayani, Kh. (2012). *Promoting economic development by research and innovation*, accessed 8 April 2017 at http://www.miraproject.eu/workgroups-area/workgroup. wp7/workgroup-documents-library/workshop-on-technology-transfer-and-valo risation-of-research-results-in-the-med-region/presentations-for-the-workshop-on-technology-transfer-and-valorisation-of-research-results-in-the-med-region/ Promoting%20Economic%20Development%20by%20Research%20and%20Inno vation%20-%20SNRI%20-%20Zayani%20Khemaies.pdf.

5. Public policies to orient science, technology, and innovation in healthcare towards inclusive development: evidence from Brazil

Cecilia Tomassini Urti

5.1 INTRODUCTION

In many countries the science, technology, and innovation (STI) policy focus increasingly includes considerations of social dimensions of development (Borrás, 2009; Bortagaray and Gras, 2013; Casas et al., 2013). The ways in which these dimensions are included vary among countries. In some cases, the STI policies integrate social dimensions in a general way, for example, as related to the objectives of social development, equity or social inclusion. In other cases, countries specify the relationship between STI and social dimensions more precisely, for example when the STI policies are used as a mechanism of poverty reduction, strengthening family farmers' production in rural areas, improving services and basic infrastructure, or searching for technologies that give greater autonomy to people with disabilities, among others. The existing literature, however, points to the challenges associated with operationalization of the inclusive development ideas into effective instruments (Bortagaray and Gras, 2013; LALICS, 2014).

The research within the National Innovation System (NIS) perspective studies the ways that production and diffusion of science, technology, and innovation can promote or hinder a development process, which is usually defined by an expansion of economic output without much attention to social development (Arocena and Sutz, 2012; Cozzens, 2009; Papaioannou, 2013; Soares and Cassiolato, 2013). The STI policies and social policies are generally disjointed in these approaches, especially in their effects on economic growth and generation–redistribution of social well-being. The institutions that implement social policies, nevertheless, may potentially play a role as actors of the NIS if they induce innovation processes and the recognition of the need for inclusive development, including through STI policies.

This chapter considers public policies as the key factors in the orientation and direction of the process of social inclusion. To build a preliminary definition of innovation for inclusive development, this chapter considers innovation as an introduction of novelty or improvement in the productive or social sphere resulting in new products, processes or services, and emphasizes the necessary alignment between needs and capabilities in order to address and solve productive and social problems (Arocena and Sutz, 2003). Thus, innovation for inclusive development is defined here at the intersection of capabilities (including STI capabilities) and societal needs, especially as they relate to the most vulnerable populations, in order to address these needs with new knowledge or with the improvement of existing knowledge (Bianco et al., 2010).

The inclusive innovation, or innovation for inclusive development, also has been the focus of attention of several international organizations, which attempt to incorporate this relatively new concept within their frameworks (OECD, 2013; World Bank, 2010). After analyzing a range of documents from several international organizations, Schwachula et al. (2014) point out that the inclusive innovation field is far less influential compared to innovation for economic growth; the latter is attracting more interest because of the promise to meet social challenges of development. The authors observe that the discussion of inclusive innovation within international organizations has not moved beyond its roots in the market, culminating in almost cynical considerations of the poor solely as consumers.

In Brazil, the public policy debate on science, technology, and innovation in health (STI/H) has highlighted the necessity for interaction between healthcare and STI policies (Gadelha, 2006; Guimarães, 2006; Morel et al., 2005). The 2002–14 period in Brazil witnessed a significant growth in public funds allocated to STI and STI/H promotion (MCTI, 2015; Rodrigues and Morel, 2016). In this period the STI/H was noted for its capacity to successfully promote the systemic interactions among a broad range of actors (Szapiro, Vargas and Cassiolato, 2016; Mazzucato and Penna, 2016).

This chapter studies the policy trajectory in promoting STI/H during the period 2002–14 in Brazil and its orientation to social inclusion problems. More specifically, it traces the evolution of the definition of healthcare as an STI policy priority area and the interactions among the healthcare sub-system, the science and technology (S&T) sub-system and the production-innovation sub-system of the Brazilian NIS. The analysis in this chapter is based on fourteen documents of specific policies, laws and programs implemented in STI/H in Brazil and on twenty semi-structured interviews with healthcare policymakers and researchers in the field. This analysis of the level of policy formulation is important for understanding the general framework that shapes the development of an NIS, and the discourse of the stakeholders based on the evolution of ideas and dominant paradigms within the STI on their effects on healthcare and inclusive development.

The chapter is organized in three main sections. Sections 5.1 and 5.2 frame the analysis within the perspective of STI for inclusive development and explore the key perspectives on the relationship between healthcare, inclusive development and STI. Section 5.3 presents the case of STI/H in Brazil. It starts with a brief historical background followed by the description and categorization of the trajectories of STI policies. Finally, the concluding section offers a critical reflection and highlights challenges to future research.

5.2   SCIENCE, TECHNOLOGY, INNOVATION AND INCLUSIVE DEVELOPMENT

The concerns about the relation between STI and social needs in the developing countries have been voiced as early as in the 1970s by the representatives of the so-called Latin American School of Science and Technology Studies. During that time, a disconnect between the S&T activities and the social needs, as well as the absence of endogenous development vision, was highlighted by researchers (Sagasti, 1973; Herrera, 1973; Varsavsky, 1969). For example, Herrera (1973) illustrates such disconnect by low investments in basic and applied research that could promote agricultural productivity, thus, solving the problems of food shortage and malnutrition. A key conclusion of his work is that the deficiencies of the research and development (R&D) systems in Latin America are not as serious as a failure of the R&D activities to serve social needs.

In the last decade, the concerns of a mismatch between R&D activities and social needs have been gaining traction within the NIS approach, in particular in the frameworks that have adopted a broader perspective on the innovation processes and their impacts. An NIS can be viewed narrowly (a restricted set of actors like firms, education and research organizations, financial organization, STI policies, and policies oriented to acquisition, use and diffusion of innovation) or broadly (an expanded set of actors including social organization and demands from social actors together with interconnections between the different sub-systems and their determination by social, cultural, political, and economic contexts) (Cassiolato and Lastres, 2008). The growth of economic inequality and the potential ability of the STI to mitigate this problem within a complex system of actors as broadly defined by the NIS framework offers an opportunity to bring the goals of the STI and social policies together in addressing social needs (Arocena and Sutz, 2012; Cozzens, 2009; Dutrenit and Sutz, 2014; LALICS, 2014; Soares and Cassiolato, 2013).[1]

The idea of inclusive development in addition to the traditional view of growth as an expansion in output includes various measures of social well-being, thus reconciling economic and social goals. In this sense, the inclusive development is more than economic growth; it is related with social justice in the distribution of growth benefits, and with the opportunities to participate in the development process itself. The concept of social inclusion behind this idea is a relational notion where what people are able to do (functioning) or are able to be (capabilities) depends on the context and time (Sen, 1999; Nussbaum, 2011).

Several recent approaches, such as pro-poor innovation (Berdagué, 2005) and grassroots innovation (Gupta, 2010), emphasize the necessity of a more direct link between STI production and social empowering that is normally excluded from the agenda of STI policies. Although these approaches have different theoretical and normative orientations, they usually criticize traditional innovation approaches that do not take into account the social needs of low-income sectors; are based on a belief that new mechanisms for promoting innovation are needed to alleviate poverty; and reject classical models of economic development and investment in STI (Sutz and Tomassini, 2013). Despite the emphasis on capacity-building, empowerment and the pursuit of sustainability of productive entrepreneurship at local or community level, these approaches do not include social policies. In fact, the role of social policies in interaction with STI policies is very marginal in all the innovation literature.

Likewise the NIS studies usually do not directly consider social policies. Yet, the literature distinguishes at least two important ways in which social policies and innovation systems are related. Social policies may be an ex-ante precondition of innovation systems, that is, certain social policies generating welfare and income redistribution are necessary to achieve the equality that would contribute to a successful implementation of an NIS. Within this view, some believe that social equality is one of the key factors behind successful NIS development in the Nordic countries, such as Denmark (Lundvall, 2009). Another approach introduces social policies in the analysis of NIS in an ex-post sense and mostly focuses on the potential consequences that the introduction of new technologies can bring in terms of unemployment, job instability or insecurity, as well as environmental degradation.

Within the field of STI/H, the concerns of inclusive development and the interplay between social and STI policies have been widely discussed. As recognized by the Council on Health Research for Development (COHRED, 2012) healthcare issues cannot be solved by healthcare policies alone, because the development of STI/H must consist of multi-sectoral activities that address economic and social development goals together. The idea of reconciling economic and social objectives in STI promotion has a long history in Brazil and has generated a novel perspective within the healthcare field, The Economic and Industrial Health Complex (CEIS)[2] (Gadelha et al., 2003). The CEIS includes a range of industries such as chemical and biotechnology, mechanical, electronics and materials and services, and intends to link the healthcare production base with the assistance needs of the public healthcare system for ensuring equity in health (Vargas et al., 2012).

5.3   SCIENCE, TECHNOLOGY, INNOVATION IN HEALTHCARE AND INCLUSIVE DEVELOPMENT

Although it is recognized that ensuring population's health is an important step towards strengthening the development path, there is no consensus on the causality in the relation between health, wealth and well-being. From an inclusive development perspective, health is central to guaranteeing the quality of life and economic growth and in this sense health disparities are a threat for social inclusion. As argued by Anand (2004), good health is a prerequisite for people to develop as agents. Nussbaum (2011) includes a broad definition of health in the list of ten central capabilities; for the author, systematic inequalities in health is a denial of equal opportunity. In addition to the contribution to social welfare, high economic returns of investments in public health are noteworthy (Husain, 2010). For example, it is estimated that among countries with high levels of malaria a 10 percent reduction of the disease may be associated with 0.3 percent higher income growth per person per year (Gallup and Sachs, 2001).

Worldwide spending on healthcare R&D has grown in the last decades. In 2009, the global investment in healthcare R&D (public and private) was US$240 billion (Røttingen et al., 2013). The high-income countries account for almost 90 percent of this amount where the business sector is the leading investor, followed by the public sector and other sources such as private non-profit organizations. A huge gap between healthcare R&D in poor countries and healthcare R&D in rich countries, which is even bigger if one factors in a greater need for such R&D in poor countries, given the higher levels of infectious and neglected diseases in such countries (Morel, 2004) and the growing prevalence of non-transmissible diseases in the former. This is the case of Brazil, where old and new health problems coexist. Chronic and degenerative diseases are on the rise, while communicable diseases are still widely spread.

In addition to the need to further develop the STI/H sector, the equity in the access to its products in supporting the health of nations is an important question in developing countries. In this sense, it is imperative to distinguish between advances in health through innovation and advances in equity in health through innovation (Sutz, 2015). With health R&D taking place predominantly in the developed countries, the products often serve the needs of these societies. The developing countries, as a result, lack access to drugs and technologies that are able to address pressing problems in their region, such as limited availability of vaccines to prevent malaria and infectious, respiratory and diarrheic diseases; medications to treat HIV, tuberculosis, cancer and diabetes; and equipment such as software, surveillance systems, diagnostic and medical devices (Morel et al., 2005).

This is an area where private and public interests tend to generate tensions, whereas a power struggle can lead to disjointed orientation towards different economic and social dimensions in the promotion of STI in healthcare. In this process, the government should play a leading role in encouraging interactions and negotiations between the actors, creating mechanisms for establishing priorities and balancing interests in the dissemination of STI results and its orientation towards equity (Gadelha et al., 2003; Morel, 2004; Sutz, 2015).

The relationship between STI and equity in health is strongly related to the capacity of articulation and coordination between the actors of the system (Soares and Cassiolato, 2015). From a broader perspective, the NIS in healthcare includes a wide range of actors and institutions, such as the health system itself, the market, knowledge-generating institutions (educational system, universities and laboratories among others), regulatory, financial, social and economic policies (especially intellectual property rights policies, public procurement policies, industrial and financial policies), civil society organizations and international organizations (Morel et al., 2005).

Two analytical dimensions may help explicate how STI/H policies are oriented towards inclusive development goals: the priority setting and diffusion-use. The priority-setting process indicates which actors and interests are represented in agenda formulation and in resources allocation. The implementation of diffusion-use mechanisms reveals where the policies seek to generate explicit impacts. Then, the selected methodologies and the types of actors involved in these processes are an indicator of the presence or absence of the social inclusion considerations in the STI policy.

5.4 SCIENCE, TECHNOLOGY, AND INNOVATION IN HEALTH IN BRAZIL

5.4.1 A Brief Historical Background

The eighth *Health Conference*, held in 1986, proposed the creation of a public and universal healthcare system in Brazil.[3] Two years later, the Brazilian constitution gave healthcare the status of a primary public good. The constitution had already emphasized the economic and social components of healthcare in the obligation of the state to ensure access to healthcare for all citizens (Bercovici, 2013). Within this context, citizens have a right for adequate healthcare and the provision of such healthcare is an obligation of the government. The Unified Public Healthcare System (SUS),[4] based on the principles of universality, integrality and equity, is the mechanism to fulfill this obligation. The development of the STI/H is among SUS responsibilities, in addition to the typical competences of a state-run healthcare system.[5] Historically, the generalized model to promote the development of STI/H in Brazil was a linear one that assumed a direct causal link between investment in knowledge and technology on the one hand and generation of wealth and well-being on the other. According to Guimarães and Vianna (1994), during the 1990s the institutional promotion of S&T was mainly directed at increasing scientific capacities with little attention given to fostering technological development.

The First STI/H Conference in 1994 was perhaps the first national action to initiate a debate on S&T and healthcare needs in public policy discourse. Following the tradition of healthcare conferences, the First STI/H Conference had the goal of promoting a dialogue between different stakeholders, including the users of the healthcare system, scientists, technicians, politicians, and others. The aims of the Conference were to assess the state of the STI/H, to mobilize participants and to define a new national project to promote S&T in order to deliver solutions for the national healthcare system. In a context where social policy was seen as a subsidiary of economic policy and S&T was conceived only in terms of its capacity to improve competitiveness, the First STI/H Conference recognized the importance of the dual dimension (social and economic) of the relationship between STI and healthcare. The Conference final report highlights that, in an economy oriented to competitiveness, the role of S&T must be at the service of social equity as a condition for achieving competitiveness in a new national project (Morel et al., 1994). The Conference recognized the need for a National Policy on STI/H, necessarily implying a close interaction between the S&T system and the SUS. It was also recognized that the healthcare policy is more complex compared to an STI policy, as the former incorporates all relevant processes such as basic, strategic, induced, applied, and operational research, results diffusion, technology development, scale production in laboratories and industries, quality control, commercialization and services delivery (Morel et al., 1994).

5.4.2 Policy Trajectory to Promote Science, Technology, and Innovation in Healthcare During the Period 2002–14 in Brazil

The 2002–14 period was characterized by the growth in STI public funding in Brazil. According to the MCTI (2015), the expenditures on STI activities went from 1.3 percent of GDP in 2002 to 1.7 percent of GDP in 2013, while expenditures on R&D increased from 1 percent to 1.2 percent during the same period, a growth well above the average rate of other Latin American countries. The importance of the STI/H activities was widely emphasized (Rodrigues and Morel, 2016; Zacca-González et al., 2014) and the sector was recognized as an example of success, in particular when it comes to the capacity to promote systematic interactions among a broad range of actors (Szapiro, Vargas and Cassiolato, 2016; Mazzucato and Penna, 2016). This sub-section details four main periods of the development of STI/H in Brazil. Figure 5.1 summarizes the emergence of major policies and programs for the promotion of STI/H discussed in this chapter.

5.4.2.1 2002–03: Paving the way for the promotion of science, technology, and innovation in healthcare

At the beginning of the century, Brazil started strengthening its governmental support for STI/H via the increased allocation of financial resources and promotion of interaction between public and private actors. A number of specialized funds to support specific sectors, including the Health Fund (CT-Health) and Biotechnology Fund (CT-Bio), were established. The funds were organized through a shared management, with a steering committee formed by ministerial representatives in each field, regulatory agencies (such as the National Health Surveillance Agency and the National Healthcare Foundation), academia, business and industry, in addition to the Ministry of Science, Technology and Innovation (MSTI), the Financier of Studies and Projects (FINEP),[6] and the National Council for Scientific and Technological Development (CNPq 2014).[7] In the case

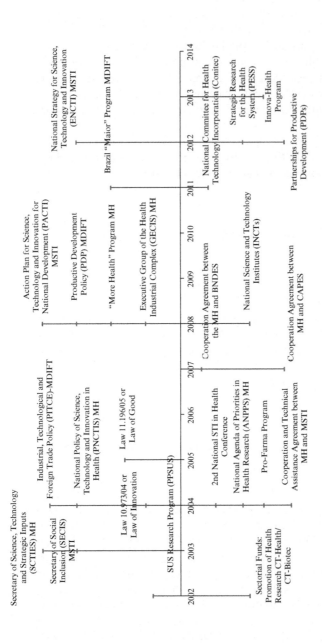

Note: The fourteen official documents analyzed were: 1st National STI in Health Conference; 2nd National STI in Health Conference; National Agenda of Priorities in Health Research (ANPPS); Strategic Research for the Health System (PESS); National Policy of Science, Technology and Innovation in Health (PNCTIS); Law 10.973/04 or Law of Innovation; Industrial, Technological and Foreign Trade Policy (PITCE); Law 11.196/05 or Law of Good; Action Plan for Science, Technology and Innovation for National Development (PACTI); "More Health" Program; Productive Development Policy (PDP); Brazil "Maior" Program; National Strategy for Science, Technology and Innovation (ENCTI); Decree No 837, April 18, 2012 (PPPs Regulation).

Source: Author's elaboration based on the Brazilian official documents.

Figure 5.1 *Emergence of the main policies, laws and instruments for the promotion of Science, Technology, and Innovation in Healthcare in Brazil (2002–14)*

of the *CT-Health*, the Ministry of Healthcare (MH) submits a list of annual priorities of the National Healthcare Policy (NHP) to the steering committee, which suggests priorities in allocating resources to the funds.[8] Additional guidelines to realign the activity of these funds with the STI and the industrial policies were introduced in 2007.[9] Other notable initiatives during this early period include the Research Program for the National Healthcare System (PPSUS) developed by the Department of Science and Technology (DECIT)[10] and the creation of the Secretary of Science, Technology and Strategic Inputs (SCTIE)[11] within the MH, the latter being responsible for the formulation of the first STI/H national policy. Besides which, the social inclusion dimension of the STI policy was translated into the creation of the Secretary for Social Inclusion within the MSTI. This secretary deals with the issues of the diffusion of science and education and of digital inclusion, among others.

5.4.2.2   2004–07: The emergence of the Ministry of Healthcare as a key actor in establishing science, technology, and innovation among healthcare priorities

During this period the first government of President Lula strengthened many social policies, such as cash transfer programs, and launched new ones in the social, industrial, and STI areas. The social mobilization around the public healthcare system increased under the slogan *SUS pra Valer*:[12] universal, humanized, and of quality (Viana and Silva, 2012). Against this backdrop, the Second STI/H National Conference, motivated by the need to reorient the direction of the STI/H production at the national level, was held. The conference recognized a low capacity of the S&T system components to define research priorities in healthcare and proposed that the MH should become the meaningful player in this respect (Guimarães, 2004). More specifically, the need for a national STI/H policy (PNCTIS)[13] and the development of an STI/H priority setting process at the national level was highlighted.

The main goal of the PNCTIS was to contribute to national development by stimulating the production of new knowledge and technologies directed at the needs of the SUS. The operationalization of the PNCTIS ideas led to the creation of the National Agenda of Priorities in Healthcare Research (ANPPS).[14] The prioritization process ensured the participation of stakeholders and institutional actors involved in the consolidation of the national healthcare policy, such as managers, healthcare professionals, service providers, patients, promotion agencies, educational institutions, researchers and others (Guimarães et al., 2006). The agenda has been recognized as the most important political instrument in legitimizing PNCTIS (Pacheco Santos et al., 2011). This agenda, however, consisted of

24 sub-agendas with 823 components, which made it practically impossible to properly prioritize the resources that remained widely dispersed.

Aiming at the operationalizing of the ANPPS and the PNCTIS, the MH, and particularly the DECIT, developed two types of incentive programs for healthcare research. One was oriented to healthcare issues at the national level and the other was aimed at overcoming regional inequalities in this area, focusing research on local health problems, the PPSUS program. Since its establishment, the DECIT has financed nearly 4000 projects, over 40 percent of them in the less economically successful regions of the country, the Midwest, the Northeast and the North. The evolution of funding also shows an increase in the participation of partner institutions, most of them STI agencies such as CNPq and FINEP.[15] The year 2004 also marks the conclusion of an important partnership between the Ministry of Healthcare and the Ministry of Science, Technology and Innovation, which enabled the MH to use the capacities created by the STI agencies and their expertise in project assessment, management, and financing. Later, other cooperation agreements would continue along this path; for example, in 2007 the MH signed an agreement with the Brazilian National Development Bank (BNDES) and in the year 2008 with the Higher Level Personnel Training Coordination (CAPES).[16]

During the 2004–07 period, the innovation concept gains additional traction in the policy discourse, and its general vision, although still weak, generates new challenges in terms of coordination between various actors. In 2004, the Technological and Foreign Trade Policy (PITCE),[17] was the first industrial policy with systemic ideas about innovation; the development of medicines and pharmaceutical products was among its strategic areas and the so-called promising future activities, along with biotechnology, nanotechnology, biomass, and renewable energy. At the same time, the issue of public healthcare system sustainability becomes important, given the sector's strategic role in the economy.[18] Also, during this period two important laws were passed with the goal of supporting the implementation of PICTE, the Law 10.973/04 or the Law of Innovation (2004) and the Law 11.196/05 or the Law of Good (2005). The former aims at supporting STI in the manufacturing sector with the final goal being accelerated industrial development and the technological autonomy of the country. The latter establishes a series of fiscal incentives for companies developing technological innovations in order to reduce the costs and risks of innovation activities for companies.

In 2007, the Lula's second administration presented the Action Plan for Science, Technology and Innovation (PACTI),[19] as a part of the Growth Acceleration Program (PAC).[20] Although the central focus was on economic development, this Plan incorporated the issues of regional equity, popularization of science and the dissemination of knowledge to improve the general living conditions. The relationship between STI and health was promoted primarily through its ability to expand the Brazilian healthcare supplies industry by creating favorable conditions for competitiveness-building, business expansion, and participation in international trade. The policy, however, did not address the ability of science, technology, and innovation to improve public healthcare services or to contribute to better health and quality of life for the general population through the investments in STI/H. On the other hand, PACTI proposed promoting social development via a range of means that included popularization of STI, improving science education, digital inclusion, more intensive research in the areas of food and nutrition security, agriculture and agro-industrial integration, among others.

5.4.2.3   2008–11: Strengthening of interactions between the healthcare sub-systems and the science, technology, innovation, and production sub-systems

In 2008 the Productive Development Policy (PDP)[21] and the More Health Program were launched, both a part of the mentioned Growth Acceleration Program. The PDP was the second industrial policy of the analyzed period. The launch of the PDP occurred when the new main objective of the Brazilian industrial policy was to boost economic growth and to ensure its sustainability. Healthcare appeared in this policy among strategic programs, hand in hand with the Industrial Health Complex (CIS).[22] Also during those years, the MH's More Health Program gained a prominent place in the government discourse. The goal of the program was to increase access to healthcare services, placing healthcare within the Brazilian pattern of development promoted by the PAC. Regarding the promotion of STI, the program recognized the importance of strengthening the CIS, in order to advance the convergence of SUS needs, with the productive structure of the country.

During this period, the main actor to promote STI/H within the MH, the SCTIE, underwent several notable changes in its structure. The SCTIE incorporated the Department of Industrial Complex and Innovation in Healthcare (DECIIS)[23] in 2009.[24] The aim of the DECIIS is to promote the production of prioritized public technologies for the SUS in order to reduce Brazilian healthcare system vulnerability related to the growing trade deficit in the sector, which increased from nearly US$7 billion in 2009 to US$11.5 billion in 2014 mainly due to purchases of medicines and high-tech medical equipment (Massuda, 2015). In response to this situation, SCTIE-DECIIS supported a development of Partnerships for Productive Development (PDPs). Other initiatives during this period included the creation of the Executive Group of the Health Industrial Complex (GECIS). The GECIS has been instrumental in assisting several actions, for example, to define a strategic list of pharmaceutical products for the SUS,[25] introduced market guarantees for domestic companies,[26] and the use of public purchasing power for the development of the CIS,[27] among other things.

The Brazil Maior Plan, launched in 2011 by the first government of President Rousseff, was the third industrial policy implemented in Brazil during the period studied in this chapter. In this policy, innovation was named the engine of competitiveness and economic growth. Within the strategic sectors, the Plan included the medical equipment industry. Also during this period the National Committee for Health Technology Incorporation for the SUS (Conitec) was formed. This Committee has the objective of advising the MH on the issues of incorporation, exclusion or modification of healthcare technologies by the SUS, as well as the creation or adjustment of clinical and therapeutic protocols.

5.4.2.4   2012–14: Reinforcement of the Ministry of Healthcare as inducer of the healthcare priorities within the Science, Technology and Innovation system

In 2012, the MSTI developed the National STI Strategy. This policy strongly emphasized human resources training, as well as the strengthening of institutionalization in order to foster innovation. As a priority area, healthcare was defined by the promotion of pharmaceuticals and a medical industrial complex. The Strategy called for the reduction of Brazil's dependence on foreign suppliers in order to overcome the trade deficit and for increased competitiveness in the international markets, also highlighting the importance of coordination with the national healthcare system.

Within the MH, the Secretary of Science, Technology and Strategic Inputs worked to update research priorities of the Ministry, identifying research lines convergent with the current needs of the healthcare policy. To this end, it held consultations with various departments of the MH, National Health Surveillance Agency, the National Supplemental Health Care Agency, and the FIOCRUZ.[28] The results were published in the 2012 document called Strategic Research for the Health System (PESS).[29] These priorities were framed in the sixteen strategic objectives of the National Healthcare Policy and involved 151 research priority lines.

In 2012, the MH launched the Program for the Development of the Health Industrial Complex (PROCIs)[30] in order to strengthen the manufacturing and innovation infrastructure in the public sector, revitalize the PDPs, and encourage technology transfer in strategic areas for the

SUS. Although the partnership mechanisms between public and private actors were already a part of the MH initiatives, it was in this period when the regulatory mechanisms of PDPs were strengthened.[31] In 2014, the regulation was enhanced by the Decree 2531/2014, which defined PDPs as agreements between public institutions and private entities with the goal of technology development and production, technology transfer, absorption, and training in strategic products, in order to meet the demands of the SUS. The Decree stipulates an annual update of the list of products contained in each group by the MH in coordination with the GECIS. Finally, in 2013 FINEP, BNDES and MH released the program *Innova-Health*. In the broader frame of the *Innova-Enterprise* program, the objective of *Innova-Health* was to reduce technological dependence on the medical and healthcare imports.

5.4.3   Synthesis of the STI Policy Trajectories: Interactions and Priority Setting

The 2002–14 period witnessed a gradual increase in the interaction between actors in the STI and the healthcare sub-systems. In the early 2000s, the mechanisms to promote STI/H activities, such as the creation of the sectorial healthcare funds, and the new institutional framework within the MH, such as the DECIT and the SCTIES, paved the way for the institutionalization of the STI/H promotion. All these changes took place in a context of limited resources allocated to promote STI/H, although over time the financial support increased as the MH gained legitimacy and experience in this new role.

The period 2004–07 brought about the emergence of the Ministry of Healthcare as a key player in the system. A main achievement of the period was the creation of political agreements within the MH itself and with the academic community in the field. The analysis of the policy documents suggests that 2004 marks a turning point in the nature of interactions between the healthcare sub-system and the S&T sub-system. In this year the pharmaceutical industry was recognized by the federal government (through PNCTI) as a key sector of development and, thus, as a target of public support (Gadelha et al., 2012). Also in 2004, the second National Conference on STI in healthcare took place, the first national STI in healthcare policy coordinated by the MH (PNCTIS) was developed, and the first national prioritization of healthcare research (ANPSS) was introduced. Furthermore, during this year, the MH and the MSTI reinforced their partnership.

In the following years, between 2008 and 2011, the promotion of STI/H involved interaction between healthcare, the STI sector, and industry. Two parallel movements were unfolding in the promotion of STI/H. The first movement was a search for explicit mechanisms of coordination derived by the convergence between the industrial and the healthcare policy. The second movement was related to the More Health Program, which was the first social policy to explicitly incorporate production and innovation structures in its agenda. According to Gadelha and Costa (2012), at the time health promotion and improved productivity were viewed as two interrelated dimensions of development. Instead of the more traditional causal pathway from economic goals to social benefits, the new policy approach was based on the social objectives driving economic strategies of development.

The period of 2012–14 was characterized by active implementation of the programs with the goal to strengthen interaction between the sub-systems. During these years, the MH entered the healthcare market in order to try to orient companies' production towards the needs of the SUS through prioritized drugs, medicines and medical equipment using PDPs and the MH's public procurement.

The analyzed STI policies within MSTI and MDIFT stressed the promotion of innovation and technology with the primary goal of accelerated economic growth. However, during the 2002–14 period the social dimension of development was increasingly brought to the forefront. Table 5.1 summarizes the ways in which the issues related to inclusive development and health appeared within the priority areas and objectives of the policies described above.

In general, the MSTI policies seem to recognize some ability of STI to improve the living conditions of marginalized populations. For example, the PACTI (2007) encourages technologies for social development and the ENCTI (2012) recognizes the role STI should play in overcoming poverty and reducing social and regional inequalities. On the other hand, within the MDIFT industrial policy, issues related to social inclusion are mediated by goals such as improving competitiveness or expanding consumer markets. The link with the social component of development comes from strengthening goods and services supply to consumers through increased accessibility, and particularly by promotion of consumer welfare.

The prioritization of health-related issues by the policies implemented during the analyzed period varies, with a changing balance between economic and social objectives. The evolution of the healthcare definition expands beyond the production of medicines, pharmaceutical products, healthcare supplies, and equipment to include the healthcare industrial complex. However, as reported by Gadelha et al. (2012), the industrial policies leave out the production of healthcare services, which are a conduit for the output of the medical manufacturing sector to shape the

Table 5.1   Health and Inclusive Development issues as they appear in the policies

Year	Policy	Ministry	Health issues in the priority areas	STI to inclusive development issues
2004	Industrial, Technological and Foreign Trade Policy (PITCE)	MDIFT	Medicines and pharmaceutical products	Alignment with employment and social inclusion policies as part of the State's strategies
2004	National Policy of Science, Technology and Innovation in Health (PNCTIS)	MH	ANPSS and PESS	STI directed at the needs of the health system and equity
2007	Action Plan for Science, Technology and Innovation for National Development (PACTI)	MSTI	Health supplies	Technologies for social development
2008	More Health Program	MH	Health industrial complex (CIS)	STI in order to converge with the SUS needs
2008	Productive Development Policy (PDP)	MDIFT	Health industrial complex	Social inclusion and reduction of regional disparities through programs promoting competitiveness
2011	Brazil "Maior" Program	MDIFT	Mechanics and electronics systems and health	Expansion of goods and services for consumers through increased accessibility, ensuring quality and safety in health and consumer's welfare
2012	National Strategy for Science, Technology and Innovation (ENCTI)	MSTI	Pharmaceuticals and health industrial complex	Overcome poverty and reduce social and regional inequalities

Source: Author's elaboration based on official documents.

health status of the country's population. On the other hand, the two mechanisms within the MH, ANPSS and PESS, play a central role in setting priorities in healthcare. However, they both struggle to effectively prioritize resources within their extremely broad fields of action. In addition, they lack mechanisms of updating agendas in response to the changes in epidemiological patterns within the country. This adds rigidity to the prioritization process, precisely in an area where flexibility and rapid response capability is required.

5.5   CONCLUSIONS

The incorporation of social dimensions into the STI policies creates a number of implementation challenges, which mostly stem from the poor equipment of policy actors to seamlessly interact and to translate social goals into effective policy instruments. The incorporation of inclusive development goals into the STI agenda implies, above all, abandoning old paradigms that compartmentalize the promotion of STI into separate economic and social components. The incorporation of the social dimensions into STI policies does not suggest a divorce from economic issues, or sole focus on immediate problems of social vulnerabilities but, on the contrary, a harmonious approach where economic development results are channeled to the solution of existing social needs, including those in healthcare.

In Brazil, the MSTI is primarily responsible for the promotion of scientific activities in all areas. The MH traditionally enjoys a secondary role in the promotion of healthcare research. This fact hinders successful communication between STI and healthcare policies, resulting in a gap between the STI production and the healthcare needs of the population (Ministério de Saúde, 2011). In this scheme the STI agencies have a very limited capacity in setting priorities related to healthcare requirements (Guimarães, 2004). The analysis of the recent STI/H evolution shows a transition to a model with a better interaction between the two main drivers of public policies in the area, the MH and MSTI, in which each actor participates within its margin of expertise.

The analyzed trajectory also shows a strengthening of the MH as a key player of the system and especially as a priority inducer of STI capacities towards the healthcare needs of the population. The two attempts to set priorities developed by the MH, the national agenda (ANPSS) and the strategic healthcare research (PESS), made a great effort to define priorities at the national level. However, these agendas had difficulties in effectively prioritizing resources within their wide field of action and were unable to spread through the whole STI sub-system. The prioritization processes of two programs of the MH, PPSUS (with its focus on knowledge generation) and PDPs (with the focus on technological innovation), appear to be successful in building bridges between different sub-systems of the Brazilian economy related to STI, healthcare, and inclusive development.

According to Morel (2002), defining national priorities in healthcare research must be followed by the effective incorporation of the generated knowledge into the national healthcare plan and actions. This dimension remains one of the most neglected during the analyzed period. Most policies do not incorporate explicit incentives to disseminate and use knowledge and technologies to serve the health needs of a specific population. In this case, practical application of PDPs outcomes stimulated by the MH's public procurement and distributed by the SUS may be the most outstanding example of coordination that promoted equity in the access to STI/H. Nevertheless, further research is needed on the actual impacts of the PDPs on the access to medicines of various groups of populations.

Articulating prioritization and diffusion-use strategies seems a key avenue for promotion of STI orientation towards social inclusion. Correctly identifying the areas that lack new knowledge and the areas where knowledge is underutilized could help to rationalize resources and to improve healthcare. In this sense, it is increasingly important to conduct thorough program evaluation. More studies assessing the socio-sanitarian impacts of STI/H promotion are necessary in order to advance our knowledge of the inclusive development strategies. Public policies to improve and sustain the priority-setting processes and the use of STI to the needs of the SUS and to the health problems of the population are needed. However, the analyzed trajectory is in an early stage, while the current economic and political crisis in Brazil raises questions about the long-term sustainability of these initiatives.

NOTES

1. Heightened concerns about these issues within the NIS community can be seen in the unifying topics of a number of meetings and conferences in recent years. For example, the GLOBELICS conference (2011) in Buenos Aires focused on *Innovation, Inequality and Sustainable Development*; the LALICS conference (2013) in Rio de Janeiro was entitled *National Innovation Systems and STI Policy for Inclusive and Sustainable Development* and the GLOBELICS conference (2015) in Habana-Cuba was entitled *Innovation to Reduce Poverty and Inequality for Inclusive and Sustainable Development.*
2. In Portuguese: Complexo Económico Industrial da Saúde.
3. The health conferences are collegiate instances of dialogue between representatives of different social sectors. They are called by the Executive or by the Health Council with

the goal to evaluate health situation and to propose guidelines for the formulation of healthcare policies.
4. In Portuguese: Sistema Único de Saúde.
5. Art. 219 and 218 of the 1988 Brazilian constitution.
6. In Portuguese: Financiadora de Estudos e Projetos.
7. In Portuguese: Conselho Nacional de Desenvolvimento Científico e Tecnológico.
8. Art. 6 of the Decree No 4.143, 2002. Presidency of the Republic, Brazil.
9. A Board of Directors linked to the MSTI was created by Law 11.540.
10. In Portuguese: Departamento de Ciência e Tecnologia.
11. In Portuguese: Secretaria de Ciência,Tecnologia e Insumos Estratégicos.
12. SUS: for real.
13. In Portuguese: Política Nacional de Ciência, Tecnologia e Inovação em Saúde.
14. In Portuguese: Agenda Nacional de Prioridades em Pesquisa de Saúde.
15. Available at http://www.saude.gov.br/pesquisasaude accessed on July 2016.
16. In Portuguese: Coordenação de Aperfeiçoamento de Pessoal de Nível Superior.
17. In Portuguese: Política Industrial, Tecnológica e de Comércio Exterior.
18. An important background of these ideas appears in Gadelha (2003) and Gadelha et al. (2003).
19. In Portuguese: Plano de Ação em Ciência, Tecnologia e Inovação.
20. In Portuguese: Programa de Aceleração do Crescimento.
21. In Portuguese: Política de Desenvolvimento Produtivo.
22. In Portuguese: Complexo Industrial da Saúde.
23. In Portuguese: Departamento do Complexo Industrial e Inovação em Saúde.
24. Presidential Decree 6.860.
25. For example, the Ministerial Ordinance of the MH 978/08, listing prioritized strategic products for the SUS, currently revoked by the Ministerial Ordinance of the MH 3089/2013.
26. For example, the Ministerial Ordinance of the MH 3031/08, an orientation for supplies purchasing in the national pharmo-chemical sector for official pharmaceutical laboratories.
27. Especially Law No 12.349 or the Law of the National Purchasing Power, providing guidelines about Public Administration's tender offers and contracts, as well as the Ministerial Ordinance No 128/08 that established guidelines for medicines and drugs procurement by the SUS through the network of public producers.
28. In Portuguese: Fundação Oswaldo Cruz.
29. In Portuguese: Pesquisa Estrategica para o Sistema de Saúde.
30. In Portuguese: Programa para o Desenvolvimento do Complexo Industrial da Saúde.
31. Decree No 837, April 18, 2012.

REFERENCES

Anand, S. (2004). The concern for equity in health. In S. Anand, F. Peter and A. Sen (eds.), *Public health, ethics, and equity* (pp. 15–21). New York: Oxford University Press.
Arocena, R., and Sutz, J. (eds.) (2003). *Subdesarrollo e innovación. Navegando contra el viento.* Madrid: Cambridge University Press.
Arocena, R., and Sutz, J. (2012). Research and innovation policies for social inclusion: An opportunity for developing countries. *Innovation and Development,* 2(1), 147–158.
Bercovici, G. (2013). Complexo industrial da saúde, desenvolvimento e proteção, *Revista de Direito Sanitário, 14*(2), 9–42.

Berdagué, J. A. (2005). *Pro-poor innovation systems* (Background paper for the International Fund for Agricultural Development), accessed June 1, 2015 at https:// www.ifad.org/documents/10180/a43c92c1-9469-4156-9b64-72dd03cd3260.

Bianco, M., Oliva, S., and Tomassini, C. (2010 July). *Investigación Orientada a la Inclusión Social: complejidades y desafíos para el contrato social de la ciencia en contextos de subdesarrollo.* Paper presented at Conferencia ESOCITE 2010, Buenos Aires, Argentina.

Borrás, S. (2009). *The widening and deepening of innovation policy: What conditions provide for effective governance?* (Paper No. 2009/02). Centre for Innovation, Research and Competence in the Learning Economy, Lund University.

Bortagaray, I., and Gras, N. (2013). Políticas de ciencia, tecnología e innovación para el desarrollo inclusivo: Tendencias cambiantes en América del Sur. In G. Crespi and G. Dutrénit (eds.). *Políticas de Ciencia, Tecnología E Innovación Para El Desarrollo: La Experiencia Latinoamericana* (pp. 263–291). Mexico: Foro Consultivo Científico y Tecnologico, AC and LALICS.

Casas, R., Corona, J. M., and Rivera, R. (2013 November). Políticas de ciencia, tecnología e innovación en América Latina: Entre la competitividad y la inclusión social. Paper presented at the Conferencia LALICS 2013, Rio de Janeiro, Brasil.

Cassiolato, J., and Lastres, H. (2008). *Discussing innovation and development: Converging points between the Latin American school and the Innovation Systems perspective?* (Working Paper Series. No. 08–02). GLOBELICS, accessed June 1, 2016 at http://www.redesist.ie.ufrj.br/ga2012/textos/Cassiolato/Lecture17_GA2008.pdf.

Conselho Nacional de Desenvolvimento Científico e Tecnológico (CNPq). (2014). *Principais resultados dos programas Institutos Nacionais de Ciência e Tecnologia, INCTs,* accessed June 1, 2016 at http://inct.cnpq.br/documents/10180/124986/Apresentacao_Chamada_INCT_2014.pdf/0a4623b3-8191-4c1a-87b4-d8335072 fda2.

Council on Health Research for Development (COHRED). (2012). *Annual Report 2012,* accessed April 5, 2017 at http://www.cohred.org/wp-content/uplo ads/2011/05/COHRED_AR_web-copy-2012.pdf.

Cozzens, S. (2009 October). *Emerging technologies and inequalities: Beyond the technological transition.* Paper presented at the GLOBELICS Conference 2009. Dakar, Senegal.

Dutrenit, G., and Sutz, S. (eds.). (2014). *National innovation systems, social inclusion and development: The Latin American experience.* Cheltenham, UK , Northampton, MA: Edward Elgar Publishing.

Gadelha, C. (2003). The health industrial complex and the need of a dynamic approach on health economics. *Ciência and Saúde Coletiva, 8*(2), 521–535.

Gadelha, C. (2006). Development, health-industrial complex and industrial policy. *Revista de Saúde Pública,* 40(spe), 11–23.

Gadelha, C., and Costa, L. (2012). Health and development in Brazil: Progress and challenges. *Revista de Saúde Pública, 46,* 13–20.

Gadelha, C., Maldonado, J., Vargas, M., Barbosa, P., and Costa, L. (eds.). (2012). *A Dinâmica inovativa do sistema produtivo da saúde.* Rio de Janeiro: FIOCRUZ.

Gadelha, C., Quental, C., and Fialho, B. (2003). Health and innovation: A systemic approach in health industries. *Cadernos de Saúde Pública, 19*(1), 47–59.

Gallup, J. L., and Sachs, J. D. (2001). The economic burden of malaria. *American Society of Tropical Medicine and Hygiene, 64*(1 suppl), 85–96.

Guimarães, R. (2004). Bases para uma política nacional de ciência, tecnologia e inovação em saúde. *Ciência e saúde coletiva, 9*(2), 375–387.

Guimarães, R. (2006). Pesquisa em saúde no Brasil: contexto e desafios. *Revista de Saúde Pública, 40*(Esp.), 3–10.

Guimarães, R., and Vianna, C. M. (1994). Ciência e Tecnologia em Saúde. Tendências Mundiais. Diagnóstico Global e Estado da Arte no Brasil. In *Anais Da I Conferência Nacional de Ciência E Tecnologia Em Saúde – I CNCTS – Ministério Da Saúde*, accessed June 1, 2016 at http://bvsms.saude.gov.br/bvs/publicacoes/anais_conf_nac1.pdf.

Guimarães, R., Santos, L. M. P., Angulo-Tuesta, A., and Serruya, S. J. (2006). Defining and implementing a national policy for science, technology, and innovation in health: Lessons from the Brazilian experience. *Cadernos de Saúde Pública, 22*(99), 1775–1785.

Gupta, A. K. (2010). Innovations for the poor by the poor. *International Journal of Technological Learning, Innovation and Development, 5*(1–2), 28–39.

Herrera, A. (1973). Los determinantes sociales de la política científica en América Latina. Política científica explícita y política científica implícita. *Desarrollo Económico, 13*, 113–134.

Husain, M. J. (2010). Contribution of health to economic development: A survey and overview. *Economics: The Open-Access, Open-Assessment E-Journal, 4*, 1–52.

LALICS. (2014). *LALICS Statements: Contributions from science, technology and innovation to social inclusion*, accessed June 1, 2016 at http://lalics.org/index.php?option=com_content&view=article&id=267&Itemid=239&lang=en.

Lundvall, B.-Å. (2009). *The Danish model and the globalizing learning economy.* (UNU-WIDER Working Paper No.2009/18), accessed June 1, 2016 at https://www.wider.unu.edu/publication/danish-model-and-globalizing-learning-economy.

Massuda, A. (2015). *O papel do Estado. A agenda do Ministério da Saúde na coordenação das ações para inovação, ciência e tecnologia em saúde, Brasilia*, accessed November 1, 2016 at http://www.valor.com.br/sites/default/files/apresentacao_-_adriano_-_o_papel_do_estado_revfinal.pdf.

Mazzucato, M., and Penna, C. (2016). *The Brazilian Innovation System, Brasil: CGEE*, accessed June 1, 2015 at https://www.cgee.org.br/documents/10195/909424/The_Brazilian_Innovation_System-CGEE-MazzucatoandPenna-FullReport.pdf.

Ministério de Ciência, Tecnologia e Inovação (MCTI). (2015). *Indicadores selecionados de ciência, tecnologia e inovação, Brasilia*, accessed June 1, 2015 at http://www.mct.gov.br/upd_blob/0237/237254.pdf.

Ministério de Saúde. (2011). *Pesquisas Estratégicas para o Sistema de Saúde, Brasilia*, accessed June 1, 2015 at http://bvsms.saude.gov.br/bvs/publicacoes/livro_pesquisas_estrategicas_para_o_sus.pdf.

Morel, C. (2004). Health research and the millennium development goals: Global challenges and opportunities, national solutions and policies. *Ciência & Saúde Coletiva, 9*(2), 261–270.

Morel, C. M., Acharya, T., Broun, D., Dangi, A., Elias, C., Ganguly, N. K., and Hotez, P. J. (2005). Health innovation networks to help developing countries address neglected diseases. *Science, 309*(5733), 401–404.

Morel, C. M., Hamilton, D. M., Fleury, S., Viacava, F., Baltar, J. M., and Martins, C. E. (1994). Documento Básico da 1ra CNCTS. In *Anais Da I Conferência Nacional de Ciência E Tecnologia Em Saúde – I CNCTS – Ministério Da Saúde*, accessed June 1, 2015 at http://bvsms.saude.gov.br/bvs/publicacoes/anais_conf_nac1.pdf.

Nussbaum, M. (2011). *Creating capabilities*. Cambridge, MA and London, UK: The Belknap Press of Harvard University Press.

Organisation for Economic Co-operation and Development (OECD). (2013). *Innovation and inclusive development*, accessed June 1, 2015 at https://www.oecd.org/sti/inno/oecd-inclusive-innovation.pdf.

Pacheco Santos, L. M., Moura, E. C., Barradas Barata, R. de C., Serruya, S. J., da Motta, M. L., Silva Elias, F. T., Angulo-Tuesta, A., de Paula, A. P., de Melo, G., Guimarães, R., and Grabois Gadelha, C. A. (2011). Fulfillment of the Brazilian agenda of priorities in health research. *Health Research Policy and Systems*, 9–35.

Papaioannou, T. (2013). *How inclusive can innovation and development be in the 21st century?* (International Workshop on New Models of Innovation for Development, University of Manchester, Manchester, United Kingdom), accessed June 1, 2015 at http://www.cdi.manchester.ac.uk/medialibrary/news_and_events/PapaioannouPreWorkshopPaperUpdate.doc.

Rodrigues, M. L., and Morel, C. (2016). The Brazilian dilemma: Increased scientific production and high publication costs during a global health crisis and major economic downturn. *mBio*, *7*(3), e00907–e00916.

Røttingen, J. A., Regmi, S., Eide, M., Young, A. J., Viergever, R. F., Årdal, C., and Terry, R. F. (2013). Mapping of available health research and development data: What's there, what's missing, and what role is there for a global observatory? *The Lancet*, *382*(9900), 1286–1307.

Sagasti, F. (1973). Underdevelopment, science and technology: The point of view of the underdeveloped countries. *Social Studies of Science*, *3*(1), 47–59.

Schwachula, A., Vila Seoane, M., and Hornidge, A. K. (2014). *Science, technology and innovation in the context of development: An overview of concepts and corresponding policies recommended by international organizations*. (ZEF Working paper series No. 132), accessed June 1, 2015 at https://www.econstor.eu/handle/10419/99990.

Sen, A. (1999). *Development as freedom*. New York: Oxford University Press.

Soares, M. C., and Cassiolato, J. (2013). *Innovation systems and inclusive development: Some evidence based on empirical work*. (International Workshop on New Models of Innovation for Development, University of Manchester, Manchester, United Kingdom), accessed June 1, 2015 at http://www.cdi.manchester.ac.uk/medialibrary/news_and_events/SoaresCassiolatoPreWorkshopPaper.pdf.

Soares, M. C., and Cassiolato, J. (eds.) (2015). *Health innovation systems, equity and development*, accessed June 1, 2015 at http://www.academia.edu/download/46141981/Innovation_Systems_Development_and_Healt20160601-12638-11zpdby.pdf.

Sutz, J. (2015). Is there a role for innovation in health equity? In M. C. Soares and J. Cassiolato (eds.), *Health innovation systems, equity and development* (pp. 87–106). Brazil: e-papers.

Sutz, J., and Tomassini, C. (2013). *Knowledge, innovation, social inclusion and their elusive articulation: When isolated policies are not enough*. (International Workshop on New Models of Innovation for Development, University of Manchester, Manchester, United Kingdom), accessed June 1, 2015 at http://www.cdi.manchester.ac.uk/medialibrary/news_and_events/SutzTomassiniPreWorkshopPaper.pdf.

Vargas, M., Gadelha, C., Silveira, L., and Maldonado, J. (2012). Inovação na indústria química e biotecnológica em saúde: em busca de uma agenda virtuosa. *Rev Saúde Publica*, *46*(spe), 37–40.

Varsavsky, O. (1969). *Ciencia, política y cientificismo*. Buenos Aires: CEPAL.

Viana, A. L., and Silva, H. P. (2012). Desenvolvimento e institucionalidade da Política Social no Brasil. In C. V. Machado, T. Baptista and L. Lima (eds.), *Políticas de saúde no Brasil: continuidades e mudanças* (pp. 31–60). Rio de Janeiro: Fiocruz.

World Bank. (2010). *Innovation policy: A guide for developing countries.* Washington, DC: The World Bank.

Zacca-González, G., Chinchilla-Rodríguez, Z., Vargas-Quesada, B., and Moya-Anegón, F. de (2014). Bibliometric analysis of regional Latin America's scientific output in public health through SCImago Journal and country rank. *BMC Public Health*, *14*(1), 2–11.

6. The role of public policies in promoting innovation and innovation complementarities in developing countries: the case of the Argentinian software industry

Hernán Alejandro Morero

6.1 INTRODUCTION

Successful innovation strategies depend on the creation and integration of new knowledge into the innovation process through diverse internal and external innovative activities (Cassiman and Veugelers, 2002). Firms do not innovate in isolation. There are external influences such as complementary information and knowledge that may become key drivers of a firm's performance. With this background, it becomes increasingly important to understand if internal and external innovation activities are complements or substitutes in the innovation performance of firms for educated policy design.

In this chapter, we highlight the relevance of the study of internal and external innovation complementarities for developing economies and argue that the role of public policies promoting innovation depends on the presence of complementarity (and substitution) between internal and external innovative activities. Our main contribution is to demonstrate the importance of complementarities for development strategies, particularly for the promotion of growth in industrial sectors.

The chapter is organized as follows. Section 6.2 presents a review of the literature on the implications of innovation complementarities for economic development. Section 6.3 illustrates these arguments with a particular case of the Argentinian software sector. This case is exemplary because, during the 1990s, Argentina had policies in place that did not take into account complementarity issues. After 2000, however, a specific industrial policy, designed to promote both internal and external innovation activities in a sector with proven complementarities, shaped the outstanding success of that sector. The experience of the Argentinian software industry suggests that neither substitutability nor complementarities in innovation can be taken for granted; nevertheless, the nature of the innovation process may have powerful effects on the effectiveness of sectoral public policies.

6.2 COMPLEMENTARITIES IN INNOVATION ACTIVITIES: THEORETICAL ARGUMENTS AND EMPIRICAL STUDIES[1]

Several distinct theories predict complementarities in innovation, which translate into various empirical approaches to test these theories and dissimilar predictions generated by the analyses. From a theoretical perspective, there are opposing views around the existence of complementarities between innovative activities. The transaction costs and the property rights theories suggest the prevalence of substitutability relations, whereas the resource-based view (RBV) of the firm approach, the absorptive capacity frameworks and evolutionary theories, point to the presence of complementarities in innovation.

On the one hand, under the tradition of the transaction costs theory (Arrow, 1962; Coase, 1937; Williamson, 1985) and the property rights theory (Grossman and Hart, 1986), the argument revolves around costs of innovative activities; a firm has to decide which of the two governance structures (in-house innovative activities or outsourcing) has the lowest (transaction) costs. In this spirit, the internal development of innovative activities and the external acquisition of knowledge are substitutes.

Alternatively, other theories, such as the RBV approach (Penrose, 1959), mostly present arguments to sustain the hypothesis of complementarity, but they are, to some extent, ambivalent about the merits of each type of knowledge source. The theories stress the heterogeneous and inimitable assets and resources of the firms in order to emphasize the superiority of in-house activities. From a management perspective, as Teece (1986) points out, complementary assets may be crucial for the successful commercialization of an innovation. The key argument is that firms need to expand their access to external sources, and a collaboration with external agents is a way to achieve a better competitive position. At the same time, this approach highlights the benefits of cooperation and knowledge sharing, based on the absorptive capacity concept (partially related to the knowledge spillovers literature). For instance, complementarity could arise because of the need to have internal competences that allow for the effective absorption of external knowledge; internal research and development (R&D) develops the ability of a firm to identify, internalize and use knowledge from the environment (Cohen and Levinthal, 1989), which is known as a firm's absorptive capacity. In a nutshell, the arguments from the resource-based view of the firm approach propose that internal knowledge creation activities usually reduce the inefficiencies of external acquisition and enable the modification and absorption of knowledge from outside the firm. If this is true, one should expect complementarity relations between internal and external sources of knowledge for innovation.

Finally, evolutionary theories and learning economics put forth arguments that emphasize the importance of complementary external and internal knowledge for innovation. C. Freeman (1974) anticipates the absorptive capacity claims, arguing that successful offensive innovation strategies inevitably include R&D efforts, sometimes in basic research, as a way of accessing scientific knowledge from outside the firm. Various innovative strategies of a firm, and their performance, result from the diverse combinations of internal and external sources of knowledge (C. Freeman and Soete, 1997). Related to this, learning economics proposes several distinct types of knowledge such as know-how, know-what, know-why and know-who (Lundvall and Johnson, 1994). It follows that internal and external sources of knowledge may be combined into different learning and innovation modes, for example the Science, Technology and Innovation (STI) mode, focused mainly on codified and technical knowledge management; or the Doing, Using and Interacting (DUI) mode, more focused on the daily learning processes and the knowledge created in informal and formal interactions (Jensen et al., 2007).

Largely, industrial and innovation economics literature studies the degree to which internal and external innovative activities, namely sources of knowledge, are complementary or substitutes for the innovation process, mostly using quantitative analysis. Mohnen and Röller (2005) classify the quantitative strategies to deal with the issue of complementarities into two groups: the correlation method and the direct method; but this chapter suggests that an additional strategy, the association approach, may be a more valid way of testing.

The most common econometric strategy so far has been the so-called correlation approach in which simple correlations between the variables (with or without controls) are analysed. The studies in the correlation approach tradition account for the co-occurrence of external and internal sources of knowledge, but do not test directly their complementarity in relation to innovation results. The second econometric strategy has been to adopt a direct approach, which is concerned with the study of complementarities in direct relation to the performance effects. Unfortunately, this approach usually fails to specify the main determinants of complementarities. Somewhere between these two, there is an intermediate approach in the sense of being stronger than the correlation approach to prove complementarity, but weaker than the direct approach to test it. This intermediate research tradition includes studies that combine diverse statistical techniques, such as multivariate analysis, to establish and explore a complex association between variables that are qualitative in nature, but analysed through quantitative tools. The third separate strand of empirical studies, which has not been properly recognized in the literature and which we propose to term 'association approach', can potentially define complementarity determinants.

As Table 6.1 illustrates and summarizes, the existing empirical literature does not provide conclusive results. Studies that apply the most modern estimation techniques are comparatively scarce. Among these studies, some find complementarity while others point to ambivalent results. The studies in the correlation tradition are less conclusive in general, whereas the results from the association approach tend to be more diffuse and less concerned with testing complementary vs. the substitutable nature of innovations specifically.

6.3   COMPLEMENTARITIES: WHY DEVELOPING ECONOMIES SHOULD CARE?

As can be seen from Table 6.1, empirical studies performed in the context of developing economies do not offer conclusive results on the relationship between internal and external innovative activities. The understanding of the mechanisms that make innovation strategies complements or substitutes in developing countries is arguably of paramount importance for a number of reasons. First, scarce financial resources that developing countries can allocate to innovation policies make a more efficient use of these resources a necessity for successful economic development. In many developing countries, the private sector provides a minor contribution to research and development (R&D) expenditures and efforts, compared to the developed economies. Therefore, the government, through the formulation of public policies, is currently the primary actor boosting development, and an effective allocation of public resources, based on sound knowledge of the mechanisms that firms adopt in their innovative activities, becomes crucially important. Second, the prevalent way of final knowledge utilization (from in-house innovation or acquired outside) in a sector has immediate implications for policy design. If substitutability holds, more 'foreign technology buying' and 'foreign direct investment attraction'-oriented policies are justified, as it is cheaper to buy the wheel instead of inventing it. If complementarity holds, supporting

Table 6.1 Empirical evidence on the relationship between internal and external innovation activities

Empirical strategy	Substitutability	Complementarity	Ambivalent
Correlation approach	Blonigen and Taylor (2000) **Mytelka (1978)** **Basant and Fikkert (1996)** Pisano (1990) Love and Roper (2001)	Arora and Gambardella (1994) **Braga and Willmore (1991)** **Deolalikar and Evenson (1989)** Veugelers (1997) Schmiedeberg (2008)	Audretsch et al. (1996) Veugelers and Cassiman (1999)
Association approach	Doloreux (2015)	**Motta et al. (2007)** **Suarez (2015)**	**Milesi (2006)**
Direct approach		Cassiman and Veugelers (2006) **Hou and Mohnen (2013)** **Morero et al. (2014)**	Love et al. (2014) Lokshin et al. (2008) Schmiedeberg (2008)

Note: Entries in bold indicate studies carried out in the context of emerging economies.

Source: Author's elaboration based on the literature.

local domestic capacities, not only to incorporate foreign technology in a more effective way, but also to develop local technologies that could be combined with foreign and external knowledge, should be a more efficient way to steer technology-led growth.

Many macro policy recommendations coming from international organizations such as the International Monetary Fund or the World Bank are based on macroeconomic theories that implicitly assume a substitutability relation between sources of knowledge, without undertaking an empirical analysis of the micro behaviour involved. In response to empirical micro evidence that supports complementarities, it can be counter-argued that the issue of the internal and external complementarities at a firm level does not imply that macro policies have to support domestic and foreign sources of knowledge complementation. However, that argument fails to recognize the micro–macro interactions (Katz and Astorga, 2014), and the fact that macro policies – such as unrestricted commercial liberalization – have specific micro implications on productivity levels and innovation capacity of heterogeneous firms.

Several studies have shown how macro policies that do not take into account the micro responses of the agents, often presuming an automatic (a somehow 'optimal') response to macro incentives themselves (even in a quite drastic shift of macro reforms), failed to improve productivity levels in the economy (Katz and Bernat, 2012; Milesi, 2002). Firm heterogeneity, socially embedded routinized behaviour, bounded rationality, sectoral differences, political and economic uncertainty, and many other particularities should be taken into account when designing industrial, technological and trade policies aimed at stimulating economic growth. In that sense, complementarities at the firm level matter, not just as a micro issue, but also because of their implications at the macro policymaking concepts. If complementarity holds, macro policies, that presume an automatic ('optimal') response of substituting inefficient internal practices and efforts with external and foreign technology in the environment of an unrestricted competitive pressure will inevitably fail by the micro–macro effect. A full commercial liberalization – often accompanied by an overvalued exchange rate and deregulation reforms – is likely to force defensive substitution strategies and the destruction of firms and employment as an unavoidable micro response. An increase in the underemployment rate is a natural result that erodes quality and optimality of human capital investment allocation in the long run, leading to a slower growth without any impact on the development stage of the country (Bernat, 2006).

The issue of innovation complementarities in developing economies is not a trivial one and one should not take the results observed in developed economies for granted. There are unique traits of the innovative behaviour in firms from developing economies that should be accounted for. Usually, the innovative behaviour of the firms from emerging economies is characterized by a lower importance assigned to R&D effort compared to sales coupled with higher levels of macroeconomic and political uncertainty. In that sense, recommendations based upon research in the context of developed economies have less applicability. That is the reason why there are strong political reasons to consider the question of complementarities in emerging economies. For example, behind policy recommendations of imports liberalization as a base for development strategy, it is implied that developing countries should (almost exclusively) buy technology outside to catch up. Implicitly, this liberalization argument assumes a high degree of substitutability between internal and external sources of knowledge in successful technological development, whether at a micro, a meso or a macro level.

Contrary to this conception, it has been argued that even third world countries have to undertake assimilation efforts of imported technologies in order to effectively adapt, extend or even improve foreign external knowledge (Mytelka, 1978). Public policies are needed in developing countries to encourage firms to consciously get involved in activities that allow 'learning by doing', 'learning by interacting', 'learning by using' and 'learning by failing' processes, as a way to consolidate the in-house capabilities to assimilate foreign knowledge while effectively improving domestic innovation performance. A minimal threshold of internal domestic R&D capabilities and activities is also needed to be involved in a process of technological learning of imported technologies (Katz, 1976). This will affect the actual cost of developing, imitating or buying a specific frontier technology, in the sense that assimilation of foreign high-tech knowledge needs to be complemented with an availability of well-qualified university personnel, to open a window of opportunity so that catching up processes take place effectively (Pérez and Soete, 1988).

The debates on the needs of assimilation efforts in order to implement and develop frontier technologies imply a complementarity view of innovative activities. The existence of complementarity, however, contradicts the substitutability perception, which is embedded into prevailing policy designs based on recommendations to liberalize markets and exports. Proper understanding of how innovation works at a firm level would allow a more educated approach and careful implementation of policy recommendations that may lead to a 'kicking away the ladder' recommendations trap (Chang, 2003, 2013).[2] Contrary to the logic of free-market-oriented policy recommendations, which have mostly failed in the developing countries, recent history has shown that successful policies to develop high-tech sectors in rapidly industrialized Asian economies involved a combination of domestic efforts with external acquisition of technology (Amsden, 2004). It is also recognized that a strategy that merely concentrates on buying foreign equipment, machinery and technology without high domestic learning and training efforts will be futile (Pérez, 2001). On the contrary, such a strategy, combined with unrestricted liberalization and deregulation policies, has destroyed local capacities for the technological catch-up (Katz, 2009).

6.4 AN ILLUSTRATIVE CASE OF APPLICATION IN AN EMERGING ECONOMY: THE SOFTWARE SECTOR OF ARGENTINA

The study of complementarity of innovation activities in developing economies has immediate and crucially important policy implications. The recent (mostly negative) experience of developing countries in their attempts to follow recommendations from international organizations suggests that contextual, historical and political factors matter. This section starts with a contextual presentation of the Argentinian software sectoral policy, which is followed by a rigorous empirical testing of the existence of internal/external innovative complementarities, under the direct approach strategy. The section concludes with a discussion of the recent industrial sectoral policy, highlighting the role of the linkages between innovation complementarities in the sector, policy design and its effects.

6.4.1   The Industrial Policy in the Software Sector of Argentina[3]

In the last decade, the software sector became an important part of Argentinian manufacturing. This change is largely a result of a strong national technology policy implemented in recent years. On the recent growth curve of the sector, two periods can be distinguished. The first one corresponds to the 'convertibility period'[4] from the early 1990s until 2002 (the year when the Argentinian currency, the *peso*, suffered devaluation), and the second cycle of the 'post-convertibility period' running from 2003 to 2015.

In the 1990s the country lacked specific policies and systematic promotion of the software sector, following the Washington Consensus prescriptions. By the end of that decade, software sector sales amounted to 190 million USD and the sector employed about 4500 people, but the sector was stagnant as measured by the number of active firms, market expansion and exports (CESSI, 2012). The devaluation of the Argentinian peso in 2002, combined with a strong public system of higher education, created a favourable environment for the adoption of policies aimed at growth in the software sector.

As an important precondition for software sector success, Argentina has an extended public university system, which is universally accessible, mainly publicly sustained, and enrols more than a million students, that played a fundamental role in the recent development of the sector. The special role of Argentinian universities stems from their deep embeddedness in society and from a common (in Latin America) practice of knowledge generation taking place mostly in public universities and national public research centres, with a very weak contribution from private universities or private firms (Arocena and Sutz, 2005). Argentina has a system of higher education with a wide variety of undergraduate and graduate courses in Computer Sciences. By 2009, there were 41 universities and colleges in the country that granted degrees in Computer Science, with a student population of more than 65,000 degree students and a rate of 2500 graduates per year (SPU, 2009). The overwhelming majority of these students attend national public universities.

The first big step in the development of a comprehensive policy to support the software sector was the enactment of the National Law No. 25.922 (the Software Law) with the goal to promote the software industry in 2004. It instituted an active sectoral policy, and created several policy instruments, such as tax exemptions and reductions selectively applied with greater tax breaks for firms with R&D activities; quality certification process and/or product exports; and import permits and preference access to financing programmes. The law promotes in-house innovative activities (through tax breaks and financing) as well as the external acquisition of knowledge for innovation (through import permits). These policies were the result of a broad consensus of diverse public and private actors with active private sector participation on the part of the Chamber of Software and Computer Services of Argentina (CESSI) and the Chamber of Information and Communications of Argentina (CICOMRA) (Borrastero, 2011).

From 2004, policies that strengthened the Software Law were gradually consolidated, mainly those oriented to financing the SMEs sector. Along with the Law, the Fund for the Promotion of the Software Industry (FONSOFT, by its Spanish acronym) was established, in order to finance various activities of the sector through loans and subsidies from the national budget. FONSOFT is clearly a policy instrument that promotes internal innovative activities and competence-building of firms by giving subsidies to R&D activities. It has two other lines, besides: subsidies to promote entrepreneurship and credits to launch exports and financing technical assistance to develop exportable products and services. Finally, it also has a minor line to support public institutions that provide software training.

Since the creation of the Ministry of Science, Technology and Innovation (MINCYT, by its Spanish acronym), which centralizes and strengthens sectoral policies, between 2007 and 2008, 317 FONSOFT projects were approved, representing a total aid of US$25.2 million.[5] At around the same period, the Argentine Technology Fund (FONTAR), which provides subsidies to upgrade projects of industrial SMEs and public science and technology institutions, began actively supporting innovation projects presented by software SMEs for R&D, technological modernization, patenting costs and so forth. As a result, companies that have accumulated the expertise necessary to engage in complex projects usually have access to credits.

Currently, the Software Law, FONOSOFT and FONTAR are the most specific and relevant national policy instruments for promoting the growth of the sector. The effective coverage of the policy instruments is very high, reaching 50 per cent of the firms. In addition to these instruments, there is a web of sub-national sectoral policies with the goal to promote association and cooperation agreements in support of local and regional clusters and technological poles. The Buenos Aires IT Pole, the Cluster Cordoba Technology and the Rosario Technological Pole (CEPAL, 2011; López and Ramos, 2008), which are consolidated firm spaces, are prime examples of the latter. Other types of initiatives include clusters with incipient growth, led by an important S&T centre (as are the cases of Tandil and Bariloche); weak clusters in regions where software activity has certain importance (as are the cases of Mendoza and Tucuman); and other initiatives less relevant to the objective to create and support an active software presence.

6.4.2   A Direct Approach Application: Complementarity Tests in the Software Sector of Argentina[6]

To apply the method of Cassiman and Veugelers (2006), a technological survey is needed in order to estimate the innovation function. We use a survey from the research project *Capacity of Absorption and Production Systems Connectivity and Local Innovation* by the Carolina Foundation. Thus, the data come from a technological survey conducted in 2011 that covers 257 software and related services producer firms in Argentina, covering the period 2008–10. The sampling is based on the standard practice of preserving the representativeness across firm size distribution, location and participation in public programmes (Barletta et al., 2013).

Testing for complementarities between two variables when the nature of the available data regarding the key variables is discrete implies testing if the objective function is super modular in these arguments. The condition of super modularity between two arguments implies that the function shows complementarity between these arguments, and the condition of sub-modularity shows substitutability (Milgrom and Roberts, 1990; Topkis, 1998). For a detailed explanation of the mathematical and econometric issues regarding the methodology, see Morero et al. (2014) and Morero et al. (2015). For instance, it can be assumed that the innovation function depends on the recurrence to internal and/or external knowledge sources, in addition to traditional structural factors. Table 6.2 gives more details about the construction of the variables. An ordered probit estimation of the innovation function was performed, and the coefficients estimated of the knowledge-sourcing dummies are used to perform the complementarity tests. The dependent variable in the ordered probit model is an ordinal indicator of innovation. Independent variables capture diverse innovative activities by firms, with specific distinction between internal and external activities.

The estimation of the coefficients in the innovation function allows for the specification of a Wald test for inequality restrictions to test for complementarities. The ordered probit specification of the model is:

$$I^{*i}(KS^i_{int}, KS^i_{ext}, Z^i, \delta, \mu) = (1 - KS^i_{int})(1 - KS^i_{ext})\delta_{00} + KS^i_{int}(1 - KS^i_{ext})\delta_{10} +$$
$$KS^i_{ext}(1 - KS^i_{int})\delta_{01} + KS^i_{int}KS^i_{ext}\delta_{11} + \mu Z^i + \omega^i$$

where I^* represents an unobserved index underlying the ordinal responses observed (i.e. it is a latent variable[7]), while KS^i_{int} is the use of internal knowledge sources by firm i, KS^i_{ext} is the use of external knowledge sources by firm i (both binary variables), δ are their estimation coefficients, and Z^i is a set of control variables (*Size, Property* of *Capital, Specialization, Exports, Age, Linkages and Competences*).

The ordered probit estimation is complemented with a probit estimation[8] of the innovation function as a robustness check of the results. Table 6.3 shows the estimates of the different models specified. In all cases, a series of regressions were performed with alternative dependent variables of innovation, and different combinations of control variables were explored. The results presented here correspond to those that have the best fit. To perform a test of complementarity and substitutability, the dummy variables of sources of knowledge for innovation are taken into account (lower panel of Table 6.3). In particular, when the Wald statistic is below 1.642, the corresponding test is accepted, and when the statistic is above 7.094 the test is rejected (Kodde and Palm, 1986). The results indicate that the

Table 6.2   Construction of variables

Innovation	Structural and organizational variables	Knowledge sources
Two **innovation** variables (ordinal and dummy) were considered based on continuous measure of innovation: • *Continuous measure of innovation.* Sum up if the firm introduced new products, new services, improved products, significant improved processes, organizational changes, or developed new commercial channels; and weighting 1 if the innovation was new only for the firm, and 3 if the innovation was new also for the market.	**Size.** Continuous indicator that reflects the number of employees in a firm. **Origin of Capital.** Dummy variable. Adopt 1 if the firm has more than 50% in foreign capital ownership and 0 if the firm has less. **Export Profile.** Continuous variable that measures the percentage of the sales in 2010 coming from exports. **Competences.** Continuous variable. Varies between 1 and 3. It is an average of five ordinal sub-indicators with three modalities each (1 = low, 2 = medium, and 3 = high): R&D structure; Quality standards; Training structure; Quality management indicator; Worker's qualification indicator. **Linkages.** Ordinal variable, taking into account the interactions established by a firm to collective	**Sources.** Taking into account the recurrence to internal sources (internal R&D activities); and the recurrence to external knowledge sources (external R&D, buying of licences or specific software for the firms, or contracting consultancies to innovate), four dummies are calculated according to the combination of recurrence to both sources: • *Not Internal Not External.* Dummy variable. Assumes 1 if the firm has engaged in neither internal nor external innovative activities; 0 otherwise. • *Only Internal.* Dummy variable. Assumes 1 if the firm only engages in internal innovative activities; 0 otherwise. • *Only External.* Dummy variable. Assumes 1 if the firm only engages in external innovative activities; 0 otherwise. • *Internal And External.* Dummy variable. Assumes 1 if the firm engages in both internal and external innovative activities; 0 otherwise. **Specialization.** Three dummies were constructed according to the productive specialization of the firms, taking into account the origin of its sales: • *Specialized in Products.* Adopt 1 if the firm has more than 60% of its sales coming from its own products sales. • *Specialized in Services.* Adopt 1 if the firm has more than 60% of its sales coming from services provision. • *Diversified.* Adopt 1 if the firm has more sales between 40% and 60% coming from services provision and sales between 40% and 60% coming from its own products sales.

- *Ordinal variable.* The indicator establishes three modalities according to the sum from the continuous variable: 1 (low) for a sum between 0 and 5; 2 (medium) for a sum between 6 and 11; and 3 (high) for a sum between 12 and 18.

- *Dummy Variable.* Assumes 0 when the ordinal variable of innovation takes the value low; 1 otherwise.

R&D activities, collective commercial actions, technical or quality assistance. The indicator assumes 3 (high) if the firm interacts with other agents for three or four kinds of interactions, assumes 2 (medium) if the firm interacts for two of the three types, and assumes 1 (low) if the firm interacts only in one kind of these types of linkages, or does not interact with other agents at all.

Categorical Age. Three dummy variables were constructed representing firms founded before 1991, between 1991 and 2001 and after 2001:
- *Age Pre Convertibility.* Assumes 1 if the firm born before 1991.
- *Age Convertibility.* Assumes 1 if the firm born between 1991 and 2001.
- *Age Post Convertibility.* Assumes 1 if the firm born after 2001.

Work Organization. Ordinal variable. Use of agile methodologies in new products, services or processes development. Adopts 1 (low) if the firm never uses agile methodologies, 2 (medium) if the firm uses agile methodologies eventually, and 3 (high) if the firm always uses agile methodologies.

Table 6.3   Estimates of the models specified

	Ordinal probit		Probit	
	Coefficient[a]	Sign[b]	Coefficient[a]	Sign[b]
Knowledge sources dummies				
(intercept)	–	–	−1.594	0.6282**
Not internal not external	–	–	–	–
Only internal	0.4124	(0.5554)	0.2456	(0.5931)
Only external	0.3317	(0.4873)	0.2330	(0.5105)
Internal and external	0.9093	(0.4764)*	0.8233	(0.5022)
Controls				
Size	0.0002	(0.0007)	−0.0009	(0.0008)
Origin of capital	−0.3529	(0.2920)	−0.2040	(0.3514)
Export profile	0.002	(0.0025)	0.0027	(0.0030)
Specialized in services	−0.1568	(0.2118)	−0.3059	(0.2574)
Specialized in products	−0.1622	(0.1982)	−0.2647	(0.2454)
Age	0.0146	(0.0103)	0.0078	(0.0125)
Linkages	0.2525	(0.0972)***	0.3123	(0.1211)***
Competences	0.4044	(0.1949)**	0.4685	(0.2305)**
Log-likelihood	−227.85			
AIC	481.71		–	
Prob > chi2	–		0.0001	
Perc. of correct predictions	0.5247		0.7037	
Complementarity and substitutability tests, Wald statistics				
Supermodularity test	7.79E-20		8.81E-26	
Submodularity test	2.04163		1.918098	

Notes:
([a]) Standard error in parentheses.
([b]) *** Significant at 1%; ** Significant at 5%; * Significant at 10%.

super modularity test is accepted for both models and the sub modularity test is rejected. This indicates that for firms in the Argentinian software sector, internal and external sources of knowledge are complementary for innovation. So, it is more likely to achieve a higher innovation level as measured in this study by relying on complementary innovation strategies, that is, using both internal and external sources of knowledge.

6.4.3   Sectoral Performance, Development Policies and Complementarities

At present, the software sector in Argentina demonstrates high growth rates. In terms of workforce, external sales revenues and total sales, all major indicators grew rapidly between 2003 and 2013. The employment in the sector increased more than threefold between 2003 and 2013, while the total sales and exports increased more than fourfold over the same period (CESSI, 2012).

Regarding the innovation in the Argentinian software sector in the last decade, the data used for this research show an extraordinary performance. First, almost 90 per cent of the innovative software firms from Argentina (about 79 per cent of all software firms in the country) have introduced new products during the period 2008–10. In turn, around 54 per cent of the innovative software firms in Argentina (about 48 per cent of total) introduced new processes. Also, taking into account marketing innovations, the performance in the Argentinian software sectoral system of innovation shows that more than 40 per cent of the innovative firms introduced these kinds of innovations.

The sector shows a remarkable innovation performance by international standards, following comparable survey designs. The Community Innovation Survey indicates that the proportion of innovator firms in the sector (including product innovation) was around 45 per cent in 2008. Another important indicator of innovative performance is the percentage of sales coming from new products. Here, the share of firms whose sales of innovation products exceed 40 per cent represent almost 42 per cent (Uriona et al., 2013).

Evidence from the software and IT services of Argentina allows us to state the existence of complementary relations between internal and external sources of knowledge. These findings tend to support empirically the 'Make & Buy' argument in the related literature (Veugelers and Cassiman, 1999), confirming the idea that successful innovation requires to complement internal sources of knowledge ('making technology') with external sources of knowledge ('buying technology') in a knowledge intensive business services sector, a process that can be of particular relevance in the context of emerging economies.

6.5 CONCLUDING REMARKS

This chapter argues that the issue of innovation complementarities is not a trivial one in emerging economies. It has powerful policy implications for development. The chapter has shown that the industrial policy in the Argentinian software sector has been composed of a set of vertical and horizontal instruments that, as a whole, promote the combination of in-house research activities and the external sourcing of knowledge. The former includes promoting internal R&D activities, sustaining competence-building through the assessment of quality standards, and maintaining a stable and high quality human resource basis formation. Simultaneously, diverse cluster support and import policies facilitated the acquisition of external knowledge via cooperation and interaction among actors. The estimation results suggest that if the government pursued a development strategy for the sector focused solely on FDI attraction and on the purchase of foreign technology, this strategy would not likely be as efficient.

Social science research is complex in terms of theoretical diversity and empirical strategies and often results in contradictive estimation results, which usually form the basis for policy design and implementation. In the case of innovation complementarities, particularly in the context of developing countries, one may see a clear divergence between the fundamentals of common macro policies recommended by the international organizations and the underlying actual economic processes. This chapter shows that the empirical evidence of complementarities in innovative activities by firms, when explicitly incorporated in the economic development of corresponding industrial sectors, may be a powerful tool to ensure policy success. The role of government in developing economies requires not only proper research efforts to understand and leverage specific particularities of the economies, but also an explicit motivation of the empirical research to contribute to the economic growth and well-being of a nation, as happened in the case of the software sector in Argentina.

NOTES

1. See H. Morero (2016) for a more detailed account.
2. Chang (2003) studied the industrial, trade and technological policies followed by the most developed countries when they were still developing economies. Using a historical perspective, he found that a common practice was resorting to interventionist strategies to promote their infant industries and to support the domestic capability of the firms. The author names the pressure received by extant developing countries from those developed economies via international organizations such as the International Monetary Fund, World Bank or World Trade Organization that includes advice to liberalize international trade and investment, privatization, deregulation, conservative macroeconomic policy and a set of 'pro-market' institutions 'kicking away the ladder', used by the developed countries to get to their current economic position (Chang, 2003).
3. This section is based upon Morero et al. (2015) and Uriona et al. (2013).
4. Convertibility is the name of the policy adopted by the Argentine Currency Board, which pegged the currency (peso) to the US dollar between 1991 and 2002.
5. In 2008, an estimated 1000 software firms were active in the country (López and Ramos, 2008), which shows that the coverage of public subsidies – more than 30 per cent of firms – is very high.
6. This section relies partially on Morero et al. (2014).
7. We consider I^* as a latent variable underlying the ordinal variable of innovation used. In

our model, innovation takes 3 levels, so that instead of observing I^* we observe: $I = 1$ if $I^* \leq \tau_1$; $I = 2$ if $\tau_1 \leq I^* \leq \tau_2$ and $I = 3$ if $\tau_2 \leq I^*$. The τ's are unknown 'threshold' parameters that must be estimated along with other parameters of the model.

8. Additional regressions are omitted. A Tobit and an OLS model can be seen in Morero et al. (2014). The Wald test results also hold in those cases.

REFERENCES

Amsden, A. (2004). Import substitution in high-tech industries. *CEPAL Review*, *82*(April), 75–89.

Arocena, R., and Sutz, J. (2005). Latin American universities: From an original revolution to an uncertain transition. *Higher Education*, *50*(4), 573–592.

Arora, A., and Gambardella, A. (1994). Evaluating technological information and utilizing it: Scientific knowledge, technological capability, and external linkages in biotechnology. *Journal of Economic Behavior & Organization*, *24*(1), 91–114.

Arrow, K. (1962). Economic welfare and the allocation of resources for invention. In R. Nelson (ed.), *The rate and the direction of inventive activity* (pp. 609–626). Princeton: Princeton University Press.

Audretsch, D. B., Menkveld, A. J., and Thurik, A. R. (1996). The decision between internal and external R&D. *Journal of Institutional and Theoretical Economics*, *152*(3), 519–530.

Barletta, F., Pereira, M., Robert, V., and Yoguel, G. (2013). Argentina: Dinámica reciente del sector de software y servicios informáticos. *Revista de la CEPAL*, *110*, 137–155.

Basant, R., and Fikkert, B. (1996). The effects of R&D, foreign technology purchase, and domestic and international spillovers on productivity in Indian firms. *Review of Economics and Statistics*, *78*(2), 187–199.

Bernat, G. (2006). Interacciones entre la macroeconomía y la microeconomía en la Argentina de los noventa: efectos sobre el crecimiento, el desarrollo y la distribución del ingreso. *Desarrollo Económico*, *46*(183), 353–384.

Blonigen, B. A., and Taylor, C. T. (2000). R&D intensity and acquisitions in high-technology industries: Evidence from the US electronic and electrical equipment industries. *The Journal of Industrial Economics*, *48*(1), 47–70.

Borrastero, C. (2011). Intervención estatal, transformaciones en los vínculos con el sector privado y crecimiento económico sectorial. El caso del sector de software y servicios informáticos de la ciudad de Córdoba, 2000–2010. *H-Industri@*, *5*(8), 1–35.

Braga, H., and Willmore, L. (1991). Technological imports and technological effort: An analysis of their determinants in Brazilian firms. *The Journal of Industrial Economics*, *39*(4), 421–432.

Cassiman, B., and Veugelers, R. (2002). R&D cooperation and spillovers: Some empirical evidence from Belgium. *The American Economic Review*, *92*(4), 1169–1184.

Cassiman, B., and Veugelers, R. (2006). In search of complementarity in innovation strategy: Internal R&D and external knowledge acquisition. *Management Science*, *52*(1), 68–82.

CEPAL. (2011). *La Inversión Extranjera Directa en América Latina y el Caribe 2010*. Santiago: CEPAL, Naciones Unidas.

CESSI. (2012). *Reporte semestral del Sector de Software y Servicios Informáticos de la República Argentina*. Bs. As, accessed 30 October 2016 at http://www.cessi.org. ar/opssi-reportes-949/index.html.

Chang, H.-J. (2003). Kicking away the ladder: Infant industry promotion in historical perspective. *Oxford Development Studies, 31*(1), 21–32.

Chang, H.-J. (2013). Patada a la escalera: La verdadera historia del libre comercio. *Ensayos de Economía, 22*(42), 27–57.

Coase, R. H. (1937). The nature of the firm. *Economica, 4*(16), 386–405.

Cohen, W., and Levinthal, D. (1989). Innovation and learning: The two faces of R&D. *The Economic Journal, 99*(397), 569–596.

Deolalikar, A. B., and Evenson, R. E. (1989). Technology production and technology purchase in Indian industry: An econometric analysis. *The Review of Economics and Statistics, 71*(4), 687–692.

Doloreux, D. (2015). Use of internal and external sources of knowledge and innovation in the Canadian wine industry. *Canadian Journal of Administrative Sciences/Revue Canadienne des Sciences de l'Administration, 32*(2), 102–112.

Freeman, C. (1974). *The economics of industrial innovation*. Harmondsworth, Middlesex: Penguin Books.

Freeman, C., and Soete, L. (1997). *The economics of industrial innovation* (3rd edn). London: Pinter.

Grossman, S. J., and Hart, O. D. (1986). The costs and benefits of ownership: A theory of vertical and lateral integration. *The Journal of Political Economy, 94*(4), 691–719.

Hou, J., and Mohnen, P. (2013). Complementarity between in-house R&D and technology purchasing: Evidence from Chinese manufacturing firms. *Oxford Development Studies, 41*(3), 343–371.

Jensen, M. B., Johnson, B., Lorenz, E., and Lundvall, B.-Å. (2007). Forms of knowledge and modes of innovation. *Research Policy, 36*(5), 680–693.

Katz, J. (1976). *Importación de tecnología, aprendizaje e industrialización dependiente*. Washington, DC: OAS Programa Regional de Desarrollo Científico y Tecnológico.

Katz, J. (ed.). (2009). *Del Ford Taunus a la soja transgénica*. Buenos Aires: Edhasa.

Katz, J., and Astorga, R. (2014). Interacciones macro-microeconómicas y desarrollo económico: Un estudio comparativo. In G. Dutrénit and J. Sutz (eds.), *Sistemas de Innovación para un desarrollo Inclusivo* (pp. 253–278). México: LALICS / Foro Consultivo Científico y Tecnológico, A.C.

Katz, J., and Bernat, G. (2012). Interacciones entre la macro y la micro en la post convertibilidad: dinámica industrial y restricción externa. *Desarrollo económico, 52*(207), 383–404.

Kodde, D. A., and Palm, F. C. (1986). Wald criteria for jointly testing equality and inequality restrictions. *Econometrica: Journal of the Econometric Society, 54*(5), 1243–1248.

López, A., and Ramos, D. (2008). *La industria de software y servicios informáticos argentina. Tendencias, factores de competitividad y clusters*. Fundación Cenit, accessed 30 October 2016 at http://www.funcex.org.br/material/REDEMER COSUL_BIBLIOGRAFIA/biblioteca/ESTUDOS_ARGENTINA/ARG_182. pdf.

Love, J. H., and Roper, S. (2001). Location and network effects on innovation success: Evidence for UK, German and Irish manufacturing plants. *Research Policy, 30*(4), 643–661.

Love, J. H., Roper, S., and Vahter, P. (2014). Dynamic complementarities in innovation strategies. *Research Policy*, *43*(10), 1774–1784.

Lundvall, B.-Å., and Johnson, B. (1994). The learning economy. *Journal of Industry Studies*, *1*(2), 23–42.

Milesi, D. (2002). Del ajuste macro a la competitividad micro. El caso de las pequeñas y medianas empresas industriales. In R. Bisang, G. Lugones and G. Yoguel (eds.), *Apertura e innovación en la Argentina* (pp. 193–224). Madrid: Editorial Miño y Dávila.

Milesi, D. (2006). *Patrones De Innovación En La Industria Manufacturera Argentina*, Buenos Aires, Argentina: LITTEC, UNGS.

Milgrom, P., and Roberts, J. (1990). The economics of modern manufacturing: Technology, strategy, and organization. *American Economic Review*, *80*(3), 511–528.

Mohnen, P., and Röller, L.-H. (2005). Complementarities in innovation policy. *European Economic Review*, *49*(6), 1431–1450.

Morero, H. (2016). *Innovation complementarities. A state of the art* (Working Paper). University Library of Munich, Germany.

Morero, H. A., Ortiz, P., and Motta, J. (2015 November). *The determinants of innovation complementarities in the software sector. Evidence from Argentina*. Paper presented at the 13th Globelics International Conference, La Habana, Cuba.

Morero, H. A., Ortiz, P., and Wyss, F. (2014). Make or buy to innovate in the software sector. *Pymes, Innovación y Desarrollo*, *2*(3), 79–99.

Motta, J., Morero, H. A., and LLinás, I. (2007). Procesos De Aprendizaje Y De Acumulación De Conocimiento En Las Empresas Autopartistas Argentinas, XII Red PyMes MERCOSUR. Campinas, Brazil.

Mytelka, L. K. (1978). Licensing and technology dependence in the Andean group. *World Development*, *6*(4), 447–459.

Penrose, E. T. (1959). *The theory of the growth of the firm*. New York: Sharpe.

Pérez, C. (2001). Cambio tecnológico y oportunidades de desarrollo como blanco móvil. *Revista de la CEPAL*, *75*, 115–135.

Pérez, C., and Soete, L. (1988). Catching up in technology: Entry barriers and windows of opportunity. In G. Dosi, C. Freeman, R. Nelson, and L. Soete (eds.), *Technical change and economic theory* (pp. 458–479). London: Pinter.

Pisano, G. P. (1990). The R&D boundaries of the firm: An empirical analysis. *Administrative Science Quarterly*, *35*(1), 153–176.

Schmiedeberg, C. (2008). Complementarities of innovation activities: An empirical analysis of the German manufacturing sector. *Research Policy*, *37*(9), 1492–1503.

SPU. (2009). *Anuario de estadísticas universitarias del año 2009*. Ministerio de Educación de la Nación. Buenos Aires, accessed 30 October 2016 at http://repositorio.educacion.gov.ar:8080/dspace/bitstream/handle/123456789/66203/Anuario-2009.pdf.

Suarez, D. (2015). Innovative strategies: When path dependence turns into path creation. Innovation and performance in the Argentinean manufacturing sector. Globelics Working Paper Series No. 2015–04, ISBN: 978-87-92923-09-7, http://www.globelics.org/wp-content/uploads/2015/08/GWP-2015-04.pdf.

Teece, D. J. (1986). Profiting from technological innovation: Implications for integration, collaboration, licensing and public policy. *Research Policy*, *15*(6), 285–305.

Topkis, D. M. (1998). *Supermodularity and complementarity*. Princeton: Princeton University Press.

Uriona, M., Morero, H. A., and Borrastero, C. (2013). 'Catching up' en servicios intensivos en conocimiento: el caso de la producción de software y servicios informáticos de Argentina y Brasil. *Revista Iberoamericana de Ciencia, Tecnología y Sociedad*, 8(24), 117–146.

Veugelers, R. (1997). Internal R&D expenditures and external technology sourcing. *Research Policy*, 26(3), 303–315.

Veugelers, R., and Cassiman, B. (1999). Make and buy in innovation strategies: Evidence from Belgian manufacturing firms. *Research Policy*, 28(1), 63–80.

Williamson, O. (1985). *The economic institutions of capitalism: Firms, markets, relational contracting*. New York: The Free Press.

PART II

Innovation challenges and response strategies
in national and sectoral innovation systems:
a firm-level perspective

7. Health biotechnology in Malaysia: issues and challenges faced by the innovative biotechnology firms

Gulifeiya Abuduxike and Syed Mohamed Aljunid

7.1 INTRODUCTION

Many developing nations have been attempting to develop a robust and competitive biotechnology sector over the last few decades. Biotechnology has been leveraged in several arenas, including healthcare, agriculture, industry, and environment to solve a number of pressing issues as well as to bring economic benefits to the country (Baianu et al., 2004; Daar et al., 2007). Particularly, applications of biotechnology in healthcare and medicine are the most significant as they have enabled prevention and treatment of numerous common as well as some "impossible" diseases and saved millions of people's lives (Boulnois, 2000; Acharya et al., 2004a; Baianu et al., 2004; BIO, 2008). Health biotechnology (HB) is applied mainly in the development of novel drugs, therapeutics and vaccines, genomics, in stem cell research, as well as for the development of numerous molecular diagnostic tests and medical devices to detect, prevent and treat diseases at the molecular level (Acharya et al., 2004a, 2004b).

Biotechnology is increasingly known as one of the sectors that drives global economy development. According to the Organisation for Economic Co-operation and Development (OECD), the economic impact of the biotechnology sector manifests itself in terms of high-return on investments on research and development (R&D), jobs and cost-effective therapeutic treatments and innovative drugs (OECD, 2005; Battelle, 2010; PhRMA, 2012). Biotechnology in Malaysia has been identified as one of the enablers in accelerating the transformation of the country into a knowledge-based economy and an industrialized nation by 2020. During the last decade, there has been remarkable development in the Malaysian biotechnology sector in terms of investments by the private and public sector, the number of biotechnology companies and research centres, patenting intensity, as well as revenues and employment (BiotechCorp, 2014). However, a better understanding of the Malaysian HB sector development and of the challenges it faces is needed in order to ensure its sustainable development and the achievement of its targeted goals by 2020.

7.1.1   Economic Impact of Health Biotechnology Around the World

Biotechnology is playing a vital role in driving the growth of many national economies through science and technology innovation. For instance, according to some estimates, the US biotechnology sector consistently grew by 6.4 per cent in employment during the last decade and provided employment for 96,000 people, despite a decrease in other knowledge-based industries during the same period. From 1993 to 2010, the US invested about US$10.4 billion in basic sciences and gained US$976 billion as a return on investment, simultaneously creating 3.8 million jobs (Battelle/Bio, 2012). Over the years, the US biotech sector revenue is estimated to have grown an average of 10 per cent yearly, and the biopharmaceutical industry is currently one of the major income generators in the US economy, as the export value of biopharmaceutical products reached more than US$267.5 billion from 2005 to 2011 (Carlson, 2016; PhRMA, 2012).

Many developing countries have prioritized the HB sector by setting up national biotechnology policies and investing substantially in programmes that target local health problems. For instance, South Africa kick-started its biotech sector in 2001 with the Department of Science and Technology's National Biotechnology Strategy. The initial investment of US$75 million was planned for allocation through its four major Biotechnology Regional Innovation Centres (BRICs). The BRICs are active platforms from which to support biotechnology R&D, capacity-building, technology transfer and development, and to provide funding with two of them specifically focused on human HB (Cloete et al., 2006). The South African government also has set its ten-year plan for innovation beginning in the year 2008, which targets R&D spending to reach 2 per cent of gross domestic product (GDP) by 2018 (Al-Bader et al., 2009).

Two of the most populous developing countries, China and India, have developed HB sectors with a biopharmaceutical market worth of US$3 billion and US$2 billion in 2007 respectively (Frew et al., 2008). Private biotech firms in both countries have contributed significantly to industry growth by developing affordable and accessible biotech products that have focused on local health problems, such as the indigenously developed hepatitis B vaccine by the Indian innovative HB company Shantha Biotechnics and the only tablet formulation of a cholera vaccine by Shanghai United Cell Biotech, China (Chakma et al., 2011; Frew et al., 2008).

Cuba has invested around US$1 billion to build its HB sector since the 1980s, which brings economic benefits to the country and addresses the local health needs of Cuba. For instance, the Cuban HB sector has developed several innovative vaccines, including the world's first effective vaccine against meningitis B, the Cuban meningococcal BC vaccine (VA-MENGOC-BC®), as a response to its local meningitis B epidemics (Thorsteinsdóttir et al., 2004c; Evenson, 2007). Cuba has more than 300 biotechnology centres. Western Havanna Biocluster employs 12,000 workers and more than 7000 scientists. Cuba exports its HB products to 50 countries with the export value of around US$100 million a year (O'Farrill, 2010).

South Korea is one of the newly industrialized countries that has advanced the HB sector in Asia. The country is also a good example of developing its HB sector by encouraging private sector involvement and investment. The Korean government has invested about US$4.4 billion from 2000–07 in the HB sector with almost half of the R&D budget allocated to basic science (Wong et al., 2004).

7.1.2 The National Health Innovation System and the Role of Biotechnology Firms

Strong and advanced capabilities in Science and Technology (S&T) have become the core engine of economic development, particularly in the sustainable development of biotechnology, as it is a sector characterized by innovative technologies, processes, services and novel products based on innovation. S&T capabilities are the main driver of an effective National Innovation System (NIS) development, with innovation at the core of the technological change (Fischer, 2001; Freeman, 1995; Llerena et al., 2001). The NIS of a country consists of all the public–private entities that contribute to the creation, diffusion, and use of new economically beneficial knowledge, as well as the linkages and interactions between these institutions (Acharya et al., 2004a; Lundvall, 2007).

The NIS theory is applied as a conceptual framework to examine the interactions and linkages between different actors in the system and to assess their roles in the development of new knowledge and technologies using S&T capabilities in a country through knowledge creation and dissemination activities (Lundvall, 1985, 2009). Thus, building an adequate and effective NIS with strong S&T capabilities is essential for the sustainable development of the biotechnology sector (Lundvall, 1985, 2009; Freeman, 1995).

Health-related S&T capabilities determine the efficiency of the health innovation system in a country, which is directly associated with the development of the HB sector. Therefore, in order to have an efficient biotechnology innovation system, building a competent health innovation system is needed, which is mainly determined by knowledge dissemination, interactions and partnerships between diverse actors with varied strengths, to come together and pursue the common goals for health innovation (Juma and Yee-Cheong, 2005; Mahoney and More, 2006).

These innovation actors include HB firms, public universities and research institutions, government and legal/regulatory agencies, education and healthcare systems. Several public sector features in the health innovation system determine the creation of scientific knowledge and its flow between other entities related to biotechnology, such as the traditional educational culture of a country; a basic research foundation; the integration of basic and applied research; funding mechanisms and availability of venture capital; interaction with foreign research institutions and universities; a national biotechnology policy; and the availability of a human capital pool in multidisciplinary, science and technology fields (Bartholomew, 1997).

Researchers have emphasized the role of firms and industries, as they are at the heart of an innovation system, which is driving the transmission of scientific knowledge into specific and tangible health products in the market (Fischer, 2001; Chung, 2002; Lundvall et al., 2002; Niosi, 2003b). Similarly, a biotechnology firm is the key player in the national biotechnology innovation system, which uses its scientific knowledge, expertise, resources and relationships to translate basic research and development into new commercial products and innovative processes to fulfil specific market needs (Abuduxike and Aljunid, 2012; OECD, 1997; Thorsteinsdóttir et al., 2004a, 2004b). As already mentioned, firms are the core entities for driving the growth of the biotechnology sector and there are many factors that impact upon the biotech firms' competitiveness, efficiency and innovativeness. Niosi (2003a) argues that the most vital factor in driving a firm's innovativeness is its capabilities and strong competencies in the biotech sector. At the same time, firms' ability to form alliances also plays an important role in improving their productivity and capabilities. Important types of collaborations include partnerships with research institutions to transfer knowledge; sharing of R&D resources, investments and risks through inter-firm collaboration; and collaboration with foreign companies to exploit foreign knowledge and technology (Niosi, 2003a; Lundvall, 2009).

In this chapter, we attempt to identify the main challenges faced by the Malaysian HB firms in order to evaluate the HB sector in the context of NIS theory. More specifically, we seek to answer the following questions:

● How does the Malaysian HB sector position itself in terms of innovative competitiveness in a global context?

- What are the main challenges and obstacles faced by HB firms in Malaysia?
- What can be done for the sustainable development of this sector from the perspective of HB firms?

7.2 METHODOLOGY

7.2.1 Study Design

This study applies a case study approach, an empirical inquiry that investigates and focuses intensively on a single phenomenon within its real-life context (Yin, 2004). Embedded single case study design is chosen as the most applicable method for this research, which examines more than one unit of analysis. The Malaysian HB sector is the case for this study, and each biotechnology company, public institute and government institution or agency represent multiple subunits of the case study. For the purpose of the study, biotechnology is defined as "the application of science and technology to living organisms, as well as parts, products and models thereof, to alter living or non-living materials for the production of knowledge, goods, and services" (OECD, 2005, p. 9). The focus on health-related biotechnologies suggests that genome-related technologies (such as Bioinformatics) and HB-related contract services (including R&D, clinical development, and manufacturing) are considered as a part of this study, whereas biotechnologies related to agriculture, environment and the industry are excluded.

In a case study, we strive to obtain an in-depth, comprehensive understanding of an issue, event or phenomenon of interest in its natural real-life context (Yin, 2009; Baker and Edwards, 2012). Thus, an attempt was made to cover as many firms related to HB as possible to ensure that our sample is representative of the Malaysian HB sector. A comprehensive sampling frame was developed to include enough cases for the study and volunteer participation was requested from the chosen companies via a formal invitation letter with an information sheet sent out to the participants.

The data was collected through four different sources including the background/historical documents, semi-structured interviews with key informants, a focus group discussion (FGD) with the representatives of the HB companies and a survey. The key informants were selected using a convenient sampling method from high profile management positions or the founders of the corresponded companies. They were chosen based on their expertise and experience in health-related biotechnologies in Malaysia. All interviewed HB companies were requested to fill out a survey after the interview session and in some cases, questionnaires were sent and collected via email. These survey questionnaires were used to obtain some specific supplementary data from companies. Participants in the focus group discussions also were invited from the identified list of key informants who are the main players from the private HB companies in Malaysia.

Subsequently, the following types of analysis were performed separately depending on the data source: (1) systematic content analysis of the data from the secondary research; (2) integrated analysis of the information collected through interviews, FGD and survey based on the common themes such as the main challenges and issues related to R&D capabilities, funding resources, products, niche areas, human capital, collaboration and partnership activities, technology capability and policy and regulations. Respondent validation and triangulation were applied to verify the information obtained from the above sources, which was analysed based on the common themes, using the ATLAS-ti software.

7.3   RESULTS AND DISCUSSION

7.3.1   Science, Technology and Innovation Capabilities of Malaysia

Malaysia started its national S&T policy in the 1980s by setting up various research institutions and agencies to support and strengthen the S&T capacity of the country (MASTIC, 2014).

As a result, all the Science, Technology and Innovation (STI) indicators for Malaysia have shown an increasing trend during the 2000–12 period. This reflects growing financial support and research intensity in S&T areas including biotechnology in Malaysia. For instance, as an important indicator of the research intensity and capacity of a country, the gross expenditure on R&D as a percentage of GDP (GERD/GDP) has increased from 0.5 per cent to 1.13 per cent during the 12-year period until 2012 (MASTIC, 2014). However, Malaysia is lagging behind many developed countries in terms of GERD/GDP, including Finland, Korea, Japan and Sweden, all of which spend more than 3 per cent of their GDP on research and development. In Malaysia, the main sources of funding for R&D activities were from the private sector (56.7 per cent) followed by the government (43.3 per cent). About 66.5 per cent of total Malaysian R&D expenditures were spent on applied research, whereas experimental research and basic research received 16.4 per cent and 17.1 per cent respectively in 2011 (MASTIC, 2014). This is in a stark contrast to the developed countries that have been more committed to basic research.

R&D expenditures on biotechnology and medical and health science accounted for about 11.3 per cent of total R&D expenditure in 2011, which was two to three times less than R&D expenditures on Information and Communication Technology (ICT) and engineering fields (MASTIC, 2014). Moreover, there are huge gaps between these indicators in Malaysia and other developed countries in the region, such as Singapore, South Korea, and Japan. The lack of skilled workforce in S&T areas in Malaysia has been highlighted as one of the obstacles to innovations. This might be the result of consistently fewer students registered in S&T-related subjects compared to other subjects at the undergraduate and postgraduate levels in all types of Malaysian universities (MASTIC, 2014).

According to the Academy of Science Malaysia (ASM), the national S&T Policy II sets the goal of achieving a 60:40 ratio between students in science-related majors and students in the arts fields to ensure the success of the 2020 target. The current ratio, however, is barely 20:80 (ASM, 2013). Since the enactment of the Patent Act in 1983 in Malaysia, the number of patent filings and granted patents has gradually increased. Total patent applications have increased from 5062 in 2003 to 7350 in 2013, where 82.7 per cent of the total number of applications were by foreign applicants. A total of 2691 patents were granted during this time; 88.6 per cent of them were granted to foreign inventors and only 11.4 per cent to local ones, which goes in line with the distribution observed for patent applications (MyIPO, 2013). Similarly, the number of scientific articles in S&T areas has increased from 1048 in 2000 to 5985 in 2009. In terms of the subject fields of the S&T articles, the top research fields include Medicine, Chemistry, Genetics & Molecular Biology, which collectively comprised 24.6 per cent of total article output (MASTIC, 2010).

Malaysia is second after Singapore among the ASEAN countries in terms of the number of S&T publications. However, when comparing the number of patents and publications in Malaysia with selected developed countries, the figures show that Malaysia still lags behind developed countries in terms of R&D output indicators. A number of factors, such as lower R&D expenditures, innovativeness and competitiveness of Malaysian firms, research activities, and the technology transfer capacity of universities and research institutions are likely to contribute to such a state of affairs (OECD, 2016; MASTIC, 2010).

7.3.2 The Health Biotechnology Sector of Malaysia: Facts and Figures

Malaysia is home to a vast range of rich natural resources such as the world's oldest tropical rainforest; it is the 4th mega-diverse nation in

Asia and the 12th in the world with an estimated 15,000 flowering plant species (accounts for 9 per cent of world total) and 185,000 animal species (accounts for 16 per cent of world total) (BiotechCorp, 2008). It is believed that a good infrastructure, political stability, a multiracial and multicultural population coupled with a rich marine ecosystem give Malaysia a competitive advantage in the field of biotechnology (BiotechCorp, 2008).

Since the launching of the National Biotechnology Policy (NBP) in 2005, the Malaysian government has strongly emphasized the development of HB by stating it as the second thrust area in NBP, which focuses on leveraging the country's rich natural diversity and bio generic capacity in the market. The implementation initiatives of NBP were divided into three phases with specific strategies and targets within the timeframe of the Biotechnology Master Plan (BMP) 2005–20 as illustrated in Table 7.1 (BiotechCorp, 2012).

As can be seen in Table 7.2, the biotechnology sector has achieved, and even exceeds, the targets set by the BMP in terms of the amount of investment, number of companies and employment. However, as of the end of 2013, the annual revenue was still far behind the expectation (BiotechCorp, 2014).

The Biotechnology Corporation of Malaysia (BiotechCorp) was established as a one-stop centre for the biotech start-ups and has been acting as a facilitator and advisor to biotechnology companies in Malaysia via a variety of initiatives and programmes including advisory services, seed funding, tax incentives, training, public–private partnerships and business matching. BiotechCorp has defined a BioNexus status, which is the special status awarded to qualified local and international biotechnology companies. By the end of 2013, the number of BioNexus status companies reached 228 with the annual revenue of RM 2.9 billion (BiotechCorp, 2014). The total approved investment for BioNexus status companies reached RM 2.6 billion in 2012 and out of all, 3.7 per cent (RM 97 million) was spent on the R&D expenses by BioNexus status companies (BiotechCorp, 2012).

When comparing the achievements of BioNexus status companies in terms of key indicators in the three subsectors, health care, agriculture and manufacturing, it can be observed that while the level of approved investments for health care biotech companies was lowest among all three sectors (28.3 per cent of total investment for 2005–11), health biotech companies were the group who invested most in R&D activities (54 per cent for 2011). Additionally, the health care subsector had higher revenue (39 per cent for 2011) than other subsectors (BiotechCorp, 2011). These numbers illustrate well the specificity of the HB sector: higher risk in

Table 7.1   Malaysian Biotechnology Master Plan, 2005–20

PHASE 1: Capacity Building (2005–10)
Setting up the building blocks

1   Adoption of policies, plans and strategies
2   Establishment of advisory and implementation Councils
3   Establishment of Malaysian Biotechnology Corporation Sdn Bhd
    (BiotechCorp)
4   Capacity-building in research and development
5   Industrial technology development
6   Develop agricultural, healthcare and industrial biotechnologies
7   Develop legal and intellectual property framework
8   Incentives
9   Bus Business and corporate development through accelerator programs
10 Bioinformatics
11 Skills development
12 Job creation
13 Regional biotechnology hubs
14 Development of BioNexus Malaysia as a brand.

PHASE 2: Science to Business (2011–15)
Unblocking potential for the industry

1   Develop expertise in drug discovery and development based on biodiversity and
    natural resources
2   New products development
3   Technology acquisition
4   Promote Foreign Direct Investment (FDI) participation
5   Intensify spin-off companies
6   Strengthen local and global brands
7   Develop capability in technology licensing
8   Job creation.

PHASE 3: Global Business (2016–20)
Attaining world class status

1   Consolidate strengths and capabilities in technology development
2   Further develop expertise and strength in drug discovery and development
3   Leading edge technology business
4   Maintain leadership in innovation and technology licensing
5   Create greater value through global Malaysian companies
6   Rebranding of Malaysia as a global biotechnology hub.

Source: BiotechCorp Annual Report, 2012. Reprinted with permission.

healthcare R&D projects, long gestation time for return on investments, as well as inadequate knowledge about healthcare biotechnology among investors, explain the relatively low level of investments in the health biotech industry in Malaysia.

Table 7.2   Key indicators for the Biotechnology Industry and achievements, 2013

Key indicators	TARGETS			Phase II Achievements as of 2013
	Phase I (2005–10)	Phase II (2011–15)	Phase III (2016–20)	
Investment by Private Sector and Government	RM6 billion	RM9 billion	RM15 billion	**RM14.8 billion**
Number of BioNexus Companies	25	25	25	**228**
Employment	60 000	80 000	160 000	**83 400**
Annual Revenue	RM20 billion	RM50 billion	RM100 billion	**RM2.9 billion**

Source: BiotechCorp Annual Report, 2014. Reprinted with permission.

We enrich these quantitative indicators by a detailed SWOT analysis of the Malaysian biotech sector, which is based on an extensive study of secondary data from public sources (Table 7.3). The strengths of the Malaysian HB sector are based on Malaysia's stable macro-economic conditions and a strong governmental support. These strengths are met with deficiencies with regard to human capital; specifically skilled knowledge workers for the HB sector are lacking while at the same time hiring foreigners is complicated. Bureaucracy in general poses a weakness for the HB sector. The opportunities for the Malaysian HB sector lie not only in the country's diversity – both in nature and in population – but also in the cost-advantage for both manufacturing and research and development activities. At the same time, such a cost-advantage can also be achieved by neighbouring countries, such as Indonesia and Thailand. However, exploiting the opportunities posed by the Biotechnology Park and the identification of niche markets combined with the creation of a Malaysian biotechnology brand may counteract such threats.

7.3.3   Main Challenges for HB Sector Development: Firms' Perspective

In this section, we present the analysis based on the information obtained from HB companies through semi-structured interviews and FGD as part of the Malaysian health biotechnology sector evaluation. HB companies representing a variety of activities such as molecular diagnostics, medical devices, herbal medicine and natural wellness products, Contract Research Organization (CRO), Contract Manufacturing Organization (CMO) and

Table 7.3   SWOT analysis of Malaysian Biotech Sector

Strengths	Weaknesses
• Strong policy support and political stability • Stable economic growth, vibrant business environment and a well-developed financial system • Recent increase in quality of life and awareness towards preventive medicine • Educated human resource pool with English language proficiency • Government funding support, BioNexus status and tax incentives • IP rights protection • National biotechnology policy • Strong foundation in medical devices and diagnostics manufacturing • Excellent infrastructure and GMP compliant facilities.	• Lack of funding • No clear regulatory pathway for biotech products • No locally produced innovative, novel drug and vaccines in the market yet • Lack of knowledge among investors and stakeholders towards biotechnology • No balanced educational system which corresponds to the biotech industry needs • Lack of local skilled workforce; brain drain • Complicated immigration process for hiring foreign skilled human capital • Bureaucracy, complicated procurement procedure • Lack of support for locally produced biotechnology products • Lack of awareness among medical professionals and general public.
Opportunities	Threats
• Rich biodiversity and natural resources: Over 1000 species of flora are reported to have therapeutic value that can be tapped for medicinal potential • Multiracial population base provides a diverse genetic pool and positions Malaysia as a great hub for clinical trials • Being the 17th largest trading nation with huge potential to export its biotechnology products • Creation of a Malaysian brand by identifying niche markets based on country's strengths in biodiversity and natural resources • Cost competitiveness and free market • Cost effectiveness in conducting research and development • Bio-XCell, the first dedicated Biotechnology Park and ecosystem for biotechnology and industrial biotechnology companies, mainly focus on R&D and manufacturing.	• Competitive regional and global biotechnology environment • Global economic instability • Cost competitive workforce in neighbouring countries, such as Indonesia, Thailand.

Source: Author's own elaboration.

vaccine areas participated in this study. Having a national biotechnology policy with comprehensive agendas and a specific implementing agency such as BiotechCorp is the strength of the Malaysian biotech sector, as many developing countries do not yet have such a comprehensive biotech policy. However, similar to any other policies, NBP Malaysia has some weaknesses, demonstrated during its implementation and enforcement by the government.

The participants indicated numerous challenges and barriers to successful innovations by the HB firms. The major challenges were summarized into five themes based on the information obtained from interviews, FGD and a complementary survey. These challenges are related to (1) Malaysian innovation system for HB development, (2) funding and R&D capabilities, (3) human capital, (4) niche areas and (5) government policy and regulations towards the biotechnology sector (Table 7.4).

7.3.3.1 National Innovation Systems to support the development of the HB sector

The majority of respondents pointed out that an NIS for the development of the biotechnology industry in Malaysia has not yet been established. The institutional and business environment is not conducive to the growth of private HB firms. One of the main barriers that interviewees pointed out is the lack of trust among the various actors within the HB sector and the poor linkages among the various governmental institutions, which impedes a consolidated public policy for the HB innovation system.

We have been hearing from BiotechCorp that there is an ongoing discussion within the Ministry of Health (MOH) about firming up regulations and so on. But it has never happened. We carry around BioNexus status by the government, but other agencies don't recognize it. In Malaysia, there is no link between agencies, they don't talk to each other. [Bioinformatics firm]

There is no clear understanding and close relation between ministries, including, Ministry of Health, Ministry of Science, Technology and Innovation (MOSTI), even like Ministry of International Trade and Industry (MITI). The National Innovation System in Malaysia is still developing; it's not fully developed yet. That's why there is no interaction and integration of resources. [Medical devices firm N1]

I feel that we don't have the biotechnology industry. It's not that we have a good industry and there are no suitable local students. There are no opportunities for the science students. The amount of money the government puts into biotechnology growth is very small. There is no collaboration even at ministerial level; instead of working together, they sometimes compete with each other. [Molecular diagnostics firm N1]

Table 7.4 Summary of the main challenges and barriers faced by HB firms in Malaysia

Main themes	Challenges and barriers
Innovation system of country	• Lack of adequate, conducive innovation system for a sustainable HB sector • Lack of know-how in universities • Lack of linkages/connections between universities, research institutions and health biotech firms • No communication and interconnections between government agencies • A resulting insufficient knowledge dissemination and technology transfer
Funding	• Shortage of funding for HB firms, especially during commercialization stage and for long-term R&D and HB product development • Bureaucracy & lack of transparency in the process of funding allocation • Venture capitalists rarely invest in health biotech startups • Affected by the lack of understanding and practical knowledge of the HB products & technology
Human capital	• Lack of an adequate and necessary local human capital • Insufficient & inadequate knowledge and wrong mental set of new graduates • Lack of training curriculums on practical skills to prepare for industry needs • Mismatching of skill sets of industry and university students • Complicated regulatory process to employ expatriates • Lack of efficient utilization and maintenance of existing research facilities and infrastructure
Niche areas	• Very broad and unclear focus areas in the HB sector • Lack of understanding on HB led to a wrong identification of niche areas • Currently identified areas do not reflect the strengths of Malaysia • Tend to take a short cut and looking for an easy way to get fast result
Government policy and regulations	• Lack of clear regulatory pathway in cutting edge HB areas • Lack of an effective commercialization chain • Difficulty in registering, patenting and commercialization of HB products locally • Some regulations are good, but with poor implementation • Procurement policy by MOH is not favourable to local HB firms and their products • Takes a long time to finalize an act, regulations or guidelines related to HB

Source: Author's own analysis based on the Interviews and FGD.

About commercialization, the universities don't have the funding and also don't have an adequate know-how to get their products progressing through the cycle. [Contract manufacturing organization]

Some HB firms have collaborations with foreign firms in the areas of licensing, training staff and marketing. However, most of the respondents stated that local collaborations are weak or non-existent. Some participants named the lack of trust and confidence in each other's capabilities as the main reasons for sparse local collaborations.

Although there are a lot of resources and encouragement from the government, and there is a strong scientific community in Malaysia, however, there is no scientific communication or collaboration between scientific bodies. Even between universities, there are no successful collaborations. [Molecular diagnostic firm N2]

The Malaysian biotech industry is very young and small with few growing companies. So, when academics look at the industry, they don't think the industry is doing well because only a few front-runners are driving the industry such as Holista, Pure cycle, Bioven, and so on. The understanding of the academics towards these young companies is not sufficient enough to evaluate the HB industry. [Medical device firm N2]

7.3.3.2   Funding issues

Most of the interviewed firms enjoy the BioNexus status and received seed funding to start up business activities; some obtained venture capital (VC) funding for specific projects. However, the availability of VC funds is limited and cannot provide the necessary support to firms in HB. As a result, insufficient funding is mentioned as another major obstacle, along with the relatively low R&D expenditures on HB, a lack of investments and of R&D involvement on the part of governmental research institutions, and insufficient attention to basic research and technology transfer activities among sectors. The study participants raised concerns related to the weaknesses in government policy and enforcement, complicated funding procedures and a lack of transparency in funding evaluation.

Until now we are facing funding challenges. Biotechnology business takes longer time to develop [products] and even banks do not want to provide funding. We don't have the investment to expand the business. This is the problem that most of the companies are facing. I have approached Malaysian Technology Development Corporation (MTDC), but they said they don't have the system to fund this business. [Molecular diagnostics firm N3]

The government is not willing to put money into the vaccine industry because they are very conservative due to the long-time horizon of vaccine development. They prefer short-term investments due to faster turnaround time. Another reason is that investment in the vaccine can be very risky and very few projects can be successful. NineBio can be a good example of a failure in vaccine investment, it failed because of poor planning and misuse of the funds by a few people; in this case, corruption was the root of the problem. [Molecular diagnostics firm N4]

Some companies emphasized that in some instances, stakeholders and staff in regulatory agencies lack scientific knowledge; as a result, they often do not understand new health technologies and products. This lack of understanding significantly affects the process of product registration, funding application, and commercialization of the new local products:

There are lots of challenges in running this company here as the business we are doing is very new in Malaysia. Nobody understands what we are trying to do. We applied to get the MOSTI Techno Fund twice and tried to explain to them what we do, but it's very difficult. Also, we tried to explain to investors what we do, but they don't understand because it's a new industry. I think for us the biggest challenge is the construction because this is an international standard quality facility. [CMO]

I think there is very poor understanding of what biotechnology in Malaysia is, especially amongst the government and industry towards the various stages of product development in biotechnology. And the amount of funding, which we have received, is too small to complete the phase 3 clinical trial for our product and to bring it to the global level. There is no vaccine industry in Malaysia and there is no awareness about vaccines for cancers in particular. [Vaccine and therapeutic firm]

In Malaysia, venture capitalist doesn't really understand the biotechnology industry and what our technology is, because the sector is new. Venture capitalists are not comfortable with investing in biotechnology. When we approach VC investors, we always have difficulty to explain our technology and business. [Medical device firm N3]

7.3.3.3 Human capital issues

There appears to be a mismatch between the human capital needs of the industry and the availability of suitable university graduates. Some firms stated that it is difficult to find employees with the right skill sets that suit particular industry requirements. And in some cases, it is difficult to retain talented or skilled personnel due to a lack of incentives and financial support.

Another biggest challenge for us has been recruitment. Biotechnology, especially bioinformatics, is a new field, only about 10 years old. Not only there are no talents in Malaysia, there is very little talent all over the world. This challenge is not unique to Malaysia. So, it was the biggest challenge for our company. However, we overcame the challenge by going through bioinformatics community and using our own network to look for the right person to work with us. [Genomic/CRO firm]

In comparison to Singapore, the cost of labour is cheaper here in Malaysia, but again they have more expertise in biotechnology. One of the reasons is that Singapore government policy toward hiring expatriates is easier than here, in terms of work permits, the timeline for the application process is much faster than here. [Manufacturing firm]

Some respondents raised the concern over the education system policy and stressed the importance of focused industrial training and strengthened basic research in university curricula, particularly in highly specialized areas such as bioinformatics, genomics, and vaccine and drug development.

Especially in the development of the vaccine field, there is not enough skilled experts or professionals to work in Malaysia. When you look at the vaccine industry, you need to look at two basic things, one is the relevancy of the vaccine in development with the needs of the people, and another one is the manufacturing capabilities. This requires two different kinds of skills and we don't have either one of them. The whole generation of people has lost the knowledge, skills regarding this field and this might be related to our education policies. [Vaccine and therapeutic firm]

In terms of workforce and experience, the differences are so wide. If this company was in the UK and if I was looking for the positions like I am looking for here, I would fill demand three weeks ago. But here I need to do lots of scarifies and recruitment managers could not get what they want. So they need to look at what is the most important technical skill this person needs to have. Probably they are not going to have it all. [CMO]

Some interviewees highlighted that Malaysian institutions possess a good infrastructure in terms of equipment, buildings, and research facilities. However, the common concern was the effective utilization and maintenance of these facilities and equipment. Some respondents mentioned that they are lagging behind many developed countries in terms of technology advancement and availability.

If talk about infrastructure in terms of equipment, buildings, and facilities . . . yes, we have very advanced laboratories with the latest equipment. However, the weakness is a lack of proper use, maintenance of the equipment and there are no skilled people to utilize the specialized equipment. Our problem is that we always invest in equipment and buildings, but not in proper utilization and maintenance. [Molecular diagnostic firm N3]

7.3.3.4 Niche areas

Respondents expressed concerns over the wide and unstructured scope of the biotechnology industry in Malaysia and emphasized the need to identify niche areas, according to the Malaysian strengths and capabilities and to focus on developing these particular sectors.

> In the area of healthcare biotechnology such as diagnostics, medical devices and so on, if you look at innovation by itself, it is very hard to stimulate if you do not provide incentives to the entrepreneurs and researchers. Just think about the research in healthcare, it's very difficult to do if there is no clear focus. Countries like the US, Europe, Cuba, Japan, Korea and others spent a lot of time to create the momentum of the building of healthcare biotechnology. We want to do it in a very short period of time with very broad ambition, I think it is very difficult to do. [Medical device firm N2]

> I think the first thing you have to understand is which part of the biotechnology that you want to focus on. A lot of people misconstrue. If a big pharma comes to Malaysia and sets up a manufacturing plant here, of course, it is not considered as biotechnology. That's real state. You should take it, open it up and then see what sector you want to focus on. Either it is going to be service based, or CRO based or biologic manufacturing or generic manufacturing based. Manufacturing itself is so wide and the problem is, the understanding of that is not clear. [Medical device firm N1]

> I think the lack of focus is the main issue. If the focus were there, we would have the competencies to be built. Then the industry will drive the biotechnology, and the government will have to listen. Now we don't have the competency, only two or three players in each sector, so how are we going to lead the sector? If we have the focus and competency, then we can sit around and tell them we are not being helped here. Now everybody is running in their own direction. This is not the way. [Molecular diagnostics firm N4]

7.3.3.5 Government policy and regulation

Some respondents from the private sector expressed major concerns over the difficulty in accessing the local market due to regulations and restrictions imposed by the MOH procurement policy and other related regulations.

> We faced challenges when we needed to register our products and commercialize the kits. However, there is no single regulatory body that does the registration for the molecular diagnostics and there is no pathway for the registration as well. We have spent a long time and many resources to develop a diagnostic product, but the commercialization was delayed due to no regulatory pathway to register. [Molecular diagnostic firm N1]

There is no local market and support from MOH to buy the products which are manufactured here. There is no support for the BioNexus companies to get into the procurement policies. The entire circular is there. For the myDankit which is the only first molecular diagnostic kit for dengue infection, even though it was recommended to the regulatory agencies, but the Malaysian devices bureau does not accept it. [Molecular diagnostic firm N2]

Of course our product is much cheaper and cost-effective, about 50 per cent. But most of the central procurements are being made only through one or two companies include pharmaniaga. [Orthopedic device firm]

The respondents also stressed that even though regulations exist, implementation may be very poor, so that Malaysian biotech companies often do not have fair access to the local market.

If you look at the 9th and 10th Malaysian plan, everything is there, even the procurement policy. But in terms of the real operation, there is no support. The execution and standard operation of procedures don't exist. [Molecular diagnostic firm N3]

7.3.4 What can Malaysia do to Develop the Sustainable HB Sector?

The study participants were asked about their recommendations and suggestions to improve the current situation and foster HB development. Their responses were summarized based on the main themes identified above (Table 7.5). Almost all respondents agreed that the inadequate innovation system of the country is the basis for most other challenges. With the existing ineffective knowledge dissemination and technology transfer system and a lack of linkages between actors, it is very difficult for new ideas to become tangible innovative products in the local market.

The study participants pointed to a number of areas, where changes are urgently needed for the HB sector to move forward. Foremost, priority should be given to the identification of niche areas, which are targeted to solve the health needs of the local population. For instance, there are some tropical infectious diseases such as Malaria and Dengue Fever, which are endemic in Malaysia and other Southeast Asian countries. Development of health biotech products that help a quick diagnosis, treatment, and prevention (in the form of vaccines) of these diseases could be good examples of the regional niche areas to focus on.

At the same time, the niche areas should reflect the strengths of Malaysia and exploit the advantages in natural resources, rich biodiversity, geographic and racial dynamics in the country and region. The identification process of the niche areas should be transparent, inclusive to all actors in the NIS and well informed of the real situation of the country and health status of the people.

Table 7.5   The main perspective from HB firms to develop the sustainable HB sector in Malaysia

Main aspects	Recommendations and strategies
National Innovation System	• Government should encourage collaborations between private and public sector • There should be the effective knowledge dissemination between universities and firms • Technology transfer offices in the universities should work together with HB firms for the ideas to become tangible HB products in the market • Sectors should be encouraged to share and combine resources to work efficiently on similar research projects
Regulatory aspects	• Clear guidelines, acts and regulations should be set for all HB subsectors, increasing transparency and reduce the bureaucracy in the operation • Existing guidelines should be followed by developing and enacting clear pathways and procedures, especially for locally developed products • A stakeholders approach to decision making should be utilized; all related experts should be included in the decision making process, not only one or two agencies • Regulatory bodies should be knowledgeable and able to act as consultants to HB firms and let them understand the procedure, requirements, etc. • There is a need for an agency that can specifically support and assist HB firms
Niche areas	• Biotech sector should focus on one or two areas of competitive advantages such as biodiversity, natural products • Supported areas should reflect the health needs of the nation, such as infectious diseases as well as non-communicable diseases • Country's assets such as multiracial population and resources should be promoted, protected and effectively utilized in clinical trials • More focus should be given to the basic and fundamental research
Funding	• Fund review procedures and processes should be transparent and devoid of favouritism • Funding mechanisms should be available for the whole production chain of HB • More private sector involvement and investment in the sub sectors is needed • There is a need to attract more Foreign Direct Investments and multinational companies to invest and set up their companies in Malaysia

Table 7.5   (continued)

Main aspects	Recommendations and strategies
	• Collaborations/partnerships between public and private players can be useful in sharing investments, risks and outputs of research, such as IP Intellectual property rights (IPR), revenues etc. Such collaborations may facilitate human capital development
Human capital	• The education system should be modified to suit the industry and niche areas of research and development
	• Universities should make sure new graduates have adequate knowledge capability and practical skills related to biotechnology
	• More specific training and support programs should be provided to improve the qualifications of the labour force
	• Stressing science and technology as the main subjects since primary school education may be a fruitful idea
	• There is a need for additional funding and programs for students to pursue higher degrees, like masters and PhDs according to the needs of the industry

Source: Author's own analysis.

Focusing strategies and resources on promising HB niche areas in Malaysia would facilitate the development of industry hubs that can serve as locomotives for the HB sector and the Malaysian economy. Therefore, once the niche areas are identified, the next step should be the logical allocation of available resources and funding. There are a number of R&D institutions with world-class facilities in various universities in Malaysia, which are working independently on similar projects, without collaboration and resource sharing between them. Such a working culture only results in further weakening the NIS in the country and in a waste of resources.

Thus, R&D resources, existing human capital and funding mechanisms should be mobilized and most importantly coordinated to focus on the identified niche areas. R&D institutions and universities should conduct extensive R&D activities and collaborate with HB firms in the process of technology transfer or the joint development of tangible HB products to be commercialized in the local and global markets.

Throughout the product development (PD) chain, numerous issues are important and should be tackled strategically and wisely. Funding is one of the key mechanisms to drive the PD process smoothly, including R&D, human capital, product development and commercialization. Thus, for the funds to be effective in promoting the areas of high potential, the allocation of available monetary resources should be transparent and devoid of favouritism and corruption.

Currently, the Malaysian government is trying to attract Foreign Direct Investment (FDI) into the biotech sector to foster its development. However, in order to attract FDI, Malaysia should be able to compete with neighbouring countries like Singapore and Taiwan in terms of technology, human capital and advanced R&D capacity. At the same time, other countries such as Thailand, Indonesia and Vietnam also are having competitive advantages in low-cost production and cheaper labour force. All of these factors pose significant challenges to Malaysia in its desire to be the target for FDI in biotechnology.

To overcome these challenges, Malaysia should fully utilize its existing financial resources through its financial institutions and venture capital entities to support the niche areas and create its own unique competitive advantages among these countries. During all the stages of PD, the government should play an active role as a facilitator to support and monitor the HB sector, based on the market demand. Government agencies such as BiotechCorp should continuously support the HB sector by creating unique platforms and opportunities for various NIS actors to collaborate and strengthen the linkages in order to effectively utilize existing resources and capabilities.

HB firms should improve their own capabilities, and strengthen the feasibility and credibility of their business plans in order to secure a sustainable financial support and investment. After the development of an innovative and viable business plan, it is important for a start-up HB company to improve its R&D capacity and competencies based on collaborations and partnership activities with other local and international companies.

Regulations and registration processes pertaining to HB products should be streamlined and simplified. The interviewees suggested that government agencies such as the National Pharmaceutical Control Bureau (NPBC) and the Performance Management and Delivery Unit (PEMANDU) should hire personnel with knowledge and practical experience within the HB field to assist firms. During the policy decision-making process, private firms should be a part of the process, as it directly affects their products, business and daily operations.

It would be helpful to set up a specialized agency with the goal being to support, assist and manage regulatory, collaborative and funding aspects of HB firms. Such a need follows on from the fact that HB is different from other subsectors, as it is directly related to the healthcare system, as well as the economy of the country. The HB sector relies on the expertise of professionals with multidisciplinary knowledge and experience in medicine, chemistry, microbiology, health economics, business and other specialty areas. The proposed specialized agency should be well positioned to assemble a well-qualified staff in one place, which would support, advise and assist the sector to develop its competency in a global arena.

Finally, an inadequate university training in HB-related fields results in a shortage of qualified labour and is another primary obstacle to the success of the Malaysian HB sector. Wider dissemination of information about the role of the HB sector, as well as university training with more emphasis on science-related courses, appear to be promising. Raising new generations of curious, entrepreneurial and innovative graduates is a task of paramount importance to teachers of all levels of education. Universities with biotechnology subjects should introduce more applied curricula that would prepare students for biotech jobs in the future.

7.4   CONCLUSIONS

This chapter evaluated the obstacles and issues faced by HB firms in Malaysia on their journey towards developing a successful, innovative and sustainable HB sector. For countries that aspire to that end, an inadequate innovation system that is unable to support the biotechnology sector is at the root of most challenges. Without improving the Malaysian National Innovation System currently characterized by weak communications, linkages and interactions between sectors related to biotechnology, all challenges identified in this chapter will continuously exist.

Since the NBP launch, the Malaysian government has put considerable effort into the development of the biotechnology sector in the country. However, more specific services and support are needed to strengthen the intellectual property rights and regulatory system, funding mechanisms and public–private collaboration. Focusing more on the fundamental, scientific research and human capital development in S&T will help strengthen the foundation of the HB industry in Malaysia. Meanwhile, the country is well positioned to leverage its natural diversity and multiracial population in order to develop cutting-edge technologies in genomics and bioinformatics and to become a regional hub for clinical trials.

There is considerable room for improvement in human capital development, the funding allocation process and transparency, and identification of niche areas in HB based on local health needs and capabilities. A major change in the education system is warranted in order to improve the qualifications of biotechnology graduates and to change the general attitudes of the younger generation who are expected to think creatively and innovatively.

REFERENCES

Abuduxike, G., and Aljunid, S. M. (2012). Development of health biotechnology in developing countries: Can private-sector players be the prime movers? *Biotechnology Advances, 30*(6), 1589–1601. doi.org/10.1016/j.biotechadv.2012.05.002.

Acharya, T., Daar, A. S., Thorsteinsdóttir, H., Dowdeswell, E., and Singer, P. A. (2004a). Strengthening the role of genomics in global health. *PLoS Medicine, 1*(3), 195–197. doi.org/10.1371/journal.pmed.0010040.

Acharya, T., Kennedy, R., Daar, A. S., and Singer, P. A. (2004b). Biotechnology to improve health in developing countries – A Review. *Mem Inst Oswaldo Cruz, 99*(4), 341–350.

Al-Bader, S., Frew, S. E., Essajee, I., Liu, V. Y., Daar, A. S., and Singer, P. A. (2009). Small but tenacious: South Africa's health biotech sector. *Nature Biotechnology, 27*(5), 427–445. doi.org/10.1038/nbt0509-427.

ASM. (2013). *Enhancing research and development in health sciences.* Kuala Lumpur.

Baianu, I. C., Lozano, P. R., Prisecaru, V. I., and Lin, H. C. (2004). *Applications of novel techniques to health foods, medical and agricultural biotechnology. Cornell University Library*, accessed 26 December 2013 at http://arxiv.org/abs/q-bio/040 6047.

Baker, S., and Edwards, R. (2012). *How many qualitative interviews is enough? Expert voices and early career reflections on sampling and cases in qualitative research*, accessed 15 January 2014 at http://eprints.ncrm.ac.uk/2273.

Bartholomew, S. (1997). National systems of biotechnology innovation: Complex interdependence in the global system. *Journal of International Business Studies, 28*(2), 241–266, accessed 15 January 2014 at http://www.jstor.org/stable/10.2307/155254.

Battelle. (2010). *Driving state economic growth in the 21st century: Advancing the biopharmaceutical sector*, accessed 21 April 2013 at http://www.phrma.org/sites/default/files/pdf/phrmafinal_report_11_15_2010_.pdf.

Battelle/Bio. (2012). *State Bioscience Industry Development 2012*, accessed 17 January 2014 at http://www.bio.org/sites/default/files/v3battelle-bio_2012_indus try_development.pdf.

BIO. (2008). *The guide to biotechnology 2008*, accessed 22 January 2014 at http://www.bio.org/sites/default/files/BiotechGuide2008.pdf.

BiotechCorp. (2008). *Biotechnology industry overview.* Kuala Lumpur.

BiotechCorp. (2011). *Annual report 2011: Accelerating biotechnology commercialisation through global collaboration.* Malaysian Biotechnology Corporation. Kuala Lumpur.

BiotechCorp. (2012). *Annual report 2012: Enriching the nation, securing the future.* Malaysian Biotechnology Corporation. Kuala Lumpur.

BiotechCorp. (2014). *BiotechCorp annual report 2014.* Malaysian Biotechnology Corporation, accessed 22 February 2014 at http://www.biotechcorp.com.my/wp-content/uploads/2011/11/publications/Annual_Report_2011.pdf.

Boulnois, G. J. (2000). Drug discovery in the new millennium: The pivotal role of biotechnology. *Trends in Biotechnology, 18*(1), 31–33, accessed 21 March 2012 at http://www.ncbi.nlm.nih.gov/pubmed/20127553.

Carlson, R. (2016). Estimating the biotech sector's contribution to the US economy. *Nature Biotechnology, 34*(3), 247–255.

Chakma, J., Masum, H., Perampaladas, K., Heys, J., and Singer, P. A. (2011). Indian vaccine innovation: The case of Shantha Biotechnics. *Globalization and Health*, 7(1), 9. doi.org/10.1186/1744-8603-7-9.

Chung, S. (2002). Building a national innovation system through regional innovation systems. *Technovation*, 22(8), 485–491. doi.org/10.1016/S0166-4972(01)00035-9.

Cloete, T. E., Nel, L. H., and Theron, J. (2006). Biotechnology in South Africa. *Trends in Biotechnology*, 24(12), 557–562. doi.org/10.1016/j.tibtech.2006.10.009.

Daar, A. S., Berndtson, K., Persad, D. L., and Singer, P. A. (2007). How can developing countries harness biotechnology to improve health? *BMC Public Health*, 7, 346. doi.org/10.1186/1471-2458-7-346.

Evenson, D. (2007). Cuba's biotechnology revolution. *MEDICC Review*, 9(1), 8–10, accessed 12 January 2016 at http://www.medicc.org/mediccreview/articles/mr_57.pdf.

Fischer, M. M. (2001). Innovation, knowledge creation and systems of innovation. *The Annals of Regional Science*, 35(2), 199–216. doi.org/10.1007/s001680000034

Freeman, C. (1995). The "national system of innovation" in historical perspective. *Cambridge Journal of Economics*, 19(March 1993), 5–24, accessed 6 January 2014 at http://cje.oxfordjournals.org/content/19/1/5.short.

Frew, S. E., Kettler, H. E., and Singer, P. A. (2008). The Indian and Chinese health biotechnology industries: Potential champions of global health? *Health Affairs (Project Hope)*, 27(4), 1029–1041. doi.org/10.1377/hlthaff.27.4.1029.

Juma, C., and Yee-Cheong, L. (2005). Reinventing global health: The role of science, technology, and innovation. *Lancet*, 365(9464), 1105–1107. doi.org/10.1016/S0140-6736(05)71147-8.

Llerena, P., Matt, M., Avadikyan, A., Bach, L., Cohendet, P., Dupouët, O., and Edler, J. (2001). *Innovation policy in the knowledge-based economy* (P. Llerena and M. Matt, eds.). Berlin Heidelberg New York: Springer, accessed 6 January 2014 at http://books.google.com/books?hl=en&lr=&id=PlGv1O5HCzUC&oi=fnd&pg=PR7&dq=Innovation+Policy+in+a+Knowledge-Based+Economy&ots=H7Y7f_Rs-F&sig=6lHbnFuTDpWVyZg4Su003jdcx3c.

Lundvall, B.-Å. (1985). *Product innovation and user-producer interaction*. Aalborg, accessed 6 January 2014 at http://vbn.aau.dk/files/7556474/user-producer.pdf.

Lundvall, B.-Å. (2007). *Innovation system research and policy: Where it came from and where it might go*. CAS seminar, Oslo. Oslo, accessed 26 September 2013 at http://vbn.aau.dk/fbspretrieve/13354006/Postscript_Vinnova_version.doc.

Lundvall, B.-Å. (2009). Innovation as an interactive process: From user-producer interaction to the national system of innovation. *African Journal of Science, Technology, Innovation and Development*, 1(283), 10–34, accessed 7 January 2014 at http://www.ajstid.com/abstractlundvall.pdf.

Lundvall, B.-Å. et al. (2002). National systems of production, innovation and competence building. *Research Policy*, 31(2), 213–231. doi.org/10.1016/S0048-7333(01)00137-8.

Mahoney, R. T., and More, C. M. (2006). A global health innovation system (GHIS). *Innovation Strategy Today*, 2(1), 1–12, accessed 16 October 2013 at www.biodevelopments.org/innovation/index.htm.

MASTIC. (2010). *Malaysian science and technology indicators 2011*. Chapter 11: Bibliometrics.

MASTIC. (2014). *Malaysian Science, Technology and Innovation (STI) indicators Report 2013*. Kuala Lumpur, accessed 20 November 2015 at http://www.mastic.gov.my/documents/10156/d914d686-7d35-4b8b-bc9e-f3fcb5e93f79.

MyIPO. (2013). *Statistical booklet 2013*. Kuala Lumpur.

Niosi, J. (2003a). Alliances are not enough explaining rapid growth in biotechnology firms. *Research Policy*, *32*(5), 737–750, accessed 6 January 2014 at http://www.sciencedirect.com/science/article/pii/S0048733302000835.

Niosi, J. (2003b). Regional systems of innovation as evolving complex systems. In *Proceedings of the DRUID Summer Conference* (p. 2). Montréal Canada, accessed 29 April 2014 at http://www.druid.dk/conferences/summer2003/Abstracts/NIOSI.pdf.

O'Farrill, A. C. (2010). *The Cuban biotechnology: Innovation and universal health care*. University of Bremen. Pisa, Italy.

OECD. (1997). *National Innovation Systems*. Paris, accessed 29 April 2014 at www.oecd.org.gov.

OECD. (2005). *A framework for biotechnology statistics. Organisation for Economic Co-operation and Development*.

OECD. (2016). *Main science and technology indicators: No. patents applications in biotechnology sector applications filed under PCT. OECD STAT*, accessed 26 February 2016 at https://data.oecd.org/gdp/gross-domestic-product-gdp.htm.

PhRMA. (2012). *Growth platform for economies around the world*.

Thorsteinsdóttir, H., Quach, U., Daar, A. S., and Singer, P. A. (2004a). Conclusions: Promoting biotechnology innovation in developing countries. *Nature Biotechnology*, *22 Suppl*, DC48-52. doi.org/10.1038/nbt1204supp-DC48.

Thorsteinsdóttir, H., Quach, U., Martin, D. K., Daar, A. S., and Singer, P. A. (2004b). Introduction: Promoting global health through biotechnology. *Nature Biotechnology*, *22*(December), DC3-7. doi.org/10.1038/nbt1204supp-DC3.

Thorsteinsdóttir, H., Sáenz, T. W., Quach, U., Daar, A. S., and Singer, P. A. (2004c). Cuba – Innovation through synergy. *Nature Biotechnology*, *22 Suppl*, DC19-24. doi.org/10.1038/nbt1204supp-DC19.

Wong, J., Quach, U., Thorsteinsdóttir, H., Singer, P. A., and Daar, A. S. (2004). South Korean biotechnology – A rising industrial and scientific powerhouse. *Nature Biotechnology*, *22 Suppl*(December), DC42-7. doi.org/10.1038/nbt1204supp-DC42.

Yin, R. K. (2004). *Complementary methods for research in education* (3rd edn, p. 26). Washington, DC: American Educational Research Association.

Yin, R. K. (2009). Designing case studies: Identifying your case(s) and establishing the logic of your case study. In *Case study research: Design and methods* (4th edn, pp. 25–66). SAGE Publications, Inc.

8. Collaborating to innovate: the case of the Nigerian mining industry

Oluseye Oladayo Jegede

8.1 INTRODUCTION

Numerous studies investigated National Innovation Systems (NISs) in both developed and developing countries (Alo, 1995; Adeoti, 2002; Adeoti and Adeoti, 2005; Adeyeye et al., 2013; Adeyeye et al., 2016; Ajao et al., 2015; Jegede et al., 2012; Jegede et al., 2013; NACETEM, 2011; Lundvall et al., 2009; Oyelaran-Oyeyinka et al., 1996; Oyelaran-Oyeyinka, 1997, 2001, 2002, 2003a, 2003b, 2005, 2006; Radwan and Pellegrini, 2010). Most of these studies have narrowly focused on the national level, neglecting the sub-sectoral differences. Indeed, no detailed sub-sectoral study can be identified in the literature on the impact of collaboration on innovation in the mining industry in Nigeria. Thus, this chapter studies the incidence and impact of collaboration in the mining sector in Nigeria with the goal of developing a framework that improves innovation in the industry and contributes to the development of the mining sector in Nigeria.

The specific objectives of the study are (1) to determine the prevalence of innovations and the incidence of collaborations in the mining industry in Nigeria; (2) to identify the collaboration partners and location of collaborating partners in the Sectoral Mining Innovation System in Nigeria; and (3) to examine the impact of collaboration on innovation in the mining industry in Nigeria.

8.2 INNOVATION SYSTEM RESEARCH IN THE CONTEXT OF DEVELOPING COUNTRIES

Existing research on the application of the innovation system (IS) approach in the context of developing countries, and in Africa in particular, shows that certain modifications of the concept originally developed within the developed world are necessary for its applicability

(Iizuka, 2013; Sutz and Tomasini, 2013; Cozzens and Sutz, 2014). Within the existing debate, Ajao and colleagues (2014) identified four research gaps which exist in the IS literature when it comes to Africa and other developing countries. First, innovation cannot be narrowly viewed through the lens of technologically new or significantly improved products or processes alone. Other dimensions, such as non-technological innovations, for example organizational and market innovations, are also important (Eurostat/OECD, 2005). Surveys carried out in Africa show a high prevalence of non-technological innovations (AU–NEPAD, 2010).

Second, Ajao et al. (2014) observe that the majority of research on African countries and their NISs show weak interactions among key actors/stakeholders. This may be because interactions and collaborations have often been defined by formal or legal binding agreements, such as memoranda of understanding, joint ventures, licensing, franchise and others. Ajao and Jegede (2014), on the other hand, report that *informal* interactions among actors within the NIS in African countries are prevalent.

Third, the measures of innovation activity exclude the informal sector. Innovation surveys in accordance with the first, the second and the third edition of the Oslo Manual leave out the informal sector and micro enterprises. In developing countries and specifically in Africa, this is likely to lead to substantial distortions in the measurement of innovation because the informal sector may represent as much as 75 per cent of a country's economic activity (ILO, 2002). Substantial evidence exists on the higher levels of innovativeness and increased productivity within these informal organizations (Müller, 2010; Daniels, 2010; Bhaduri and Sheikh, 2012).

Finally, the overly aggregated view of the four elements identified in the Nigerian innovation system by Tiffin (1997) – education and research, industrial production, finance, and public policy and regulation – may hinder the proper identification and operationalization of all of the active actors that are important for the promotion of innovation and knowledge generation and diffusion. Each of these four elements contains actors that perform specific activities towards the actualization of Nigeria's NIS. The principle is that every economic actor must fit within a clearly defined element, otherwise the systems approach is considered inappropriate in the innovation measurement. For instance, within the government element, there are many actors with different functions and only some of them have the ability to promote the NIS.

8.3   COLLABORATIONS WITHIN THE NATIONAL INNOVATION SYSTEM IN NIGERIA

The continuous search for knowledge within the NIS leads to interactions between the various actors (Ilori, 2006). According to Cervantes (1999), interactions within the NIS may be of the following types:

- University–industry interactions;
- Government–industry interactions;
- Research institute–industry interactions; and
- Any combination of the above.

Oyebisi et al. (1996) carried out an assessment of the linkages between universities and enterprises in Nigerian engineering and the agro-allied sectors. They found that linkages between firms as well as between firms and research and development (R&D) institutes are mostly on an ad-hoc basis. These interactions tend to be weak with the capacity to become strong. Oyewale (2006) studied Nigeria's research system and the culture of patenting within pharmaceuticals, food science and technology, and metallurgy and materials science in Nigerian universities. The study showed that only about 10 per cent of the respondents had ever applied for a patent. The study recommended that technology brokerage organisations, like the intellectual property and technology transfer offices, science parks and others, are established to facilitate interaction between academia, government and industry. Isola et al. (2010) examined R&D capabilities and productivity in science and technology in selected Nigerian universities and research institutes. The study showed intermediate to high levels of interaction among researchers in the universities and research institutes but weak linkages with government and industry. NACETEM (2011), in a nationwide survey of firms in the manufacturing sector in Nigeria, found out that the firms collaborated more with customers, suppliers of equipment and raw materials, and competitors than they did with universities/higher institutions. The study also showed that collaborations with government had a very low prevalence. Siyanbola et al. (2012) found that R&D institutes in the Federal Ministry of Science and Technology in Nigeria have successfully produced over 100 commercially viable R&D products in the areas of agriculture, industry, engineering and health. The study observed, however, that these products were yet to be commercialized due to the weak relationships between government and academia. The study suggested a solution to the problem of low commercialization through active collaboration and networking support from other governmental actors and firms. Based on results that involved indigenous oil and gas services firms in Nigeria, Jegede et al. (2013) concluded that for improved participation of indigenous firms in business and economic activities in the oil and gas sector in Nigeria, there is a need for greater collaboration and knowledge-sharing among indigenous firms and other actors in the IS, most notably, multinational companies.

8.4 METHODOLOGY

8.4.1 Sampling

The sample for this study includes 150 purposively selected mining, exploration, quarrying, processing and dredging and construction companies in the South West of Nigeria. Primary and secondary data sources were used for the study covering the period 2011–13. Primary data sources include completed questionnaires, structured interviews and field observations. Secondary data came from published sources, companies' annual reports, information from the National Bureau of Statistics and others. A structured questionnaire was administered in each firm, eliciting information on the profiles and activities of the companies and the types of innovations present. The questionnaire also obtained information on the prevalence of product, process and organizational innovations in the mining companies, the incidence of collaboration for innovation activities, the type of collaboration and location of collaborating partners, amongst others. It was drafted using the Community Innovation Survey (CIS) 4, which is based on the Oslo Manual (EuroStat/OECD, 2005) that is widely used for innovation surveys around the globe. The study used information obtained from the questionnaire to determine the impact of collaboration on the innovation performance in the mining companies in Nigeria. Scheduled interviews were used to ascertain and supplement the information from the questionnaire. Secondary data were collected from relevant government agencies, journals, books, monographs, the Internet and companies' annual reports. Both descriptive and inferential statistical techniques were employed for data analysis.

8.4.2 Study Variables and their Measurement

Some of the variables measured in this study could not be directly captured, in such cases proxies and surrogate variables were used. The main dependent variable is innovation prevalence, which was measured by the incidence of product, process and organizational innovations. Product innovation was measured via two proxy dummy variables, indicating whether companies introduced a new or significantly improved product or a new or significantly improved service. Process innovation was measured via three proxy variables indicating whether companies introduced: (i) new or significantly improved methods of mining or prospecting for natural resources; (ii) new or significantly improved logistics, delivery or distribution methods for inputs, goods or services; and (iii) new or significantly improved supporting activities for companies' processes, such as maintenance systems or operations for purchasing, accounting or computing. The prevalence of process innovation was measured on a two-item code, yes or no. Organizational innovation was measured by three variables indicating if companies implemented within the reference period: (i) new business practices for organizing procedures (i.e. supply chain management, business re-engineering, knowledge management, lean production and quality management); (ii) new methods of organizing work responsibilities and decision-making (i.e. first use of a new system of employee responsibilities, team work, decentralization, integrating/de-integrating different departments or activities, education/ training systems); and (iii) new methods of organizing external relations with other firms or public institutions (i.e. first use of alliances, partner-ships, outsourcing or sub-contracting). The prevalence of organizational innovation was also measured on a two-point item code, yes or no.

Linkage between the mining companies with other actors for innovation was measured by the incidence of collaborations among sampled companies. This was done by asking if the companies collaborated with any other actor for their innovation activities. The presence of linkages was measured using a binary variable, yes or no. The types of coop-eration partners and their locations were grouped into the following categories: (i) other enterprises within the enterprise group; (ii) suppliers of equipment, materials, components, or software; (iii) clients or customers; (iv) competitors in the sector; (v) consultants, commercial labs, or private R&D institutes; (vi) universities; and (vii) public research institutes or other higher education institutions.

Government or public research institutes were subdivided into six categories: Nigeria, other African countries, Europe, United States, Asian and other countries. Additionally, the types of cooperative partners that the mining enterprises found to be most important for their innovation activities was indicated with an open-ended question. The frequency was used to determine the most important cooperative partners (Eurostat/OECD, 2005).

8.4.3 Model Specification and Statistical Analysis

The impact of collaboration with other actors on innovation performance was analysed using binary regression with innovation prevalence as the dependent variable and the incidence of collaboration as the key independent variable, reflected in the following equation:

$$log\ (odds)_i = log\ (y_i/1\text{-}y_i) = a + bX_i + e_i \qquad (8.1)$$

where subscript i indicates firms; Y is innovation prevalence (product, process or organizational); a is an intercept (constant variable), b is the slope (constant variable), e is an error term and X is the incidence of collaboration. The empirical model estimated originally included two control variables (employee size and turnover), which were statistically insignificant and were not included in the final analysis.

8.5   RESULTS AND DISCUSSION

8.5.1   Nigerian Mining and Prevalent Types of Innovation

The most prevalent activity in the mining industry in Nigeria is quarrying (27.4 per cent), closely followed by construction (20.8 per cent), exploration (19.8 per cent) and small-scale mining (16.0 per cent).[1] Activities such as rock/mineral processing and dredging ranked lowest in the industry with a prevalence of 8.5 per cent and 7.5 per cent respectively. The mining sector in Southwestern Nigeria is unique in its own way and conceals an array of characteristics that considerably differ among industries. For example, the quarrying industry is well organized, and so is the construction industry. The small-scale mining industry, on the other hand, is largely unorganized and is dominated by artisan independent miners. Due to their business model – mainly consulting – exploration companies may not necessarily be a registered mining company, when compared to other companies in the sector.

Table 8.1 shows the frequency of the different innovation types identified in this study. On the whole, 77.4 per cent of the firms were innovative during the reference period, with organizational innovation ranking first (68.9 per cent) followed by process innovation (64.2 per cent) and product innovation (34.9 per cent). These values are lower than what was recorded in an innovation survey conducted in Nigerian manufacturing sectors (NACETEM, 2011), which showed that about 82 per cent of the sample had implemented at least one innovation type within the reference period (2005–07). Process and organizational innovations were more prevalent, implemented by 63.3 per cent and 62.8 per cent of the firms, respectively, while about 53.4 per cent of the firms implemented product innovation (NACETEM, 2011).

Table 8.1	*Prevalence of innovations in the mining industry in Southwestern Nigeria*

Type and nature of innovation	Prevalence (%)
(i) New or significantly improved raw materials (rock, sand, minerals)	14.2
(ii) New or significantly improved exploration technology/ techniques	27.4
Product innovation [at least one of (i) or (ii)]	**34.9**
(iii) New or significantly improved method of mining from ore or gange	33.0
(iv) New or significantly improved mining logistic and delivery methods	46.2
(v) New or significantly improved support activities for inputs and processing	34.0
Process innovation [at least one of (iii), (iv) or (v)]	**64.2**
(vi) Introduction of new business practices for organizing procedures	35.8
(vii) New methods of organizing work responsibilities and decision-making	34.9
(viii) New methods of organizing external relations with other firms	50.9
Organizational innovation [at least one of (vi), (vii) or (viii)]	**68.9**
Overall innovation [at least one of (i) to (viii) above]	**77.4**

Source:	Author's own elaboration based on the survey.

More specifically, Table 8.1 shows that product innovation was expressed as an introduction of new or significantly improved mineral/raw materials like Granite, Bauxite, Galena, Zinc Blende, amongst others (14.2 per cent) and as an introduction of new or significantly improved exploration techniques/services like magnetic surveys, electromagnetic surveys, radiometric surveys and others (27.4 per cent). Process innovation was expressed as the introduction of new or significantly improved methods of mining such as pitting and trenching, auger drilling, diamond drilling and rotary percussion drilling (33 per cent). Other innovative practices included significantly improved logistics, delivery or distribution methods for inputs such as just-in-time and total quality management (46.2 per cent). Some companies used new or significantly improved supporting activities for the company's production processes like computer-aided mining or technology/work stations upgrade (34 per cent). Organizational innovation comprised the introduction of new business practices for organizing procedures (35.8 per cent) such as supply chain management, business re-engineering, lean production and quality management, new methods of organizing work responsibilities and decision-making (34.9 per cent). Other types of organizational innovation included the first use of teamwork, decentralization, integrating/de-integrating different departments or activities, new methods of organizing external relations with other firms or public institutions (50.9 per cent), such as first use of alliances, partnerships, outsourcing or sub-contracting.

8.5.2 Linkage of Actors in the Nigerian Mining Sector

As far as internal sources of innovation are concerned, the R&D activities, the human and financial resources of firms, their innovative practices and the R&D intensity of their industries all bring a certain stock of information and knowledge into a firm's internal learning process. Firms tend to complement their in-house capacity for knowledge creation through the acquisition of knowledge from external sources – external learning. This is widely referred to in the literature as 'collaboration' or 'linkages' or 'cooperation' or 'networking' with other actors within the IS. This study thus considered collaboration as well as the advantages that firms might derive from these when located close (geographically or in cyber space) to the actors involved in their networks.

Several previous studies (Romijn and Albaladejo, 2002; Lundvall et al., 2009; Lundvall, 2010) have highlighted the importance of a number of stakeholders within an IS that firms may network or collaborate with. The literature shows that, among others, customers, suppliers, trade associations, higher education and research institutions are important sources of information for the firms' innovation activities. The findings of the conducted survey are in line with the existing empirical evidence. About 83 per cent of the firms collaborated with other actors. The surveyed companies collaborated mostly with competitors (64.2 per cent), suppliers (64.2 per cent) and customers (63.2 per cent). Some 37.7 per cent of the companies collaborated with other firms within their group. Collaboration with consultants and private R&D institutions had a prevalence of 27.4 per cent, whereas the incidence of collaboration with universities and public R&D institutions was 17.9 per cent and 3.8 per cent respectively. Since competitors, suppliers and customers are the most established cooperating partners and the main sources of knowledge for innovative activities, it can be concluded that these are the key actors that shape the market (Table 8.2).

At the same time, it is interesting to note that for Nigerian mining

Table 8.2 Type and location of collaborating partners

	Total (% of all firms)	Origin of the collaborators					
		Nigeria (%)	Other Africa (%)	Asia (%)	Europe (%)	United States (%)	Other countries (%)
Enterprises within group	**37.7**	17.0	0	9.4	7.5	0	3.8
Suppliers	**64.2**	25.5	0.9	22.6	12.3	0.9	1.9
Customers	**63.2**	61.3	0	0.9	0.9	0	0
Competitors	**64.2**	63.2	0	0.9	0	0	0
Consultants, private R&D	**20.7**	7.5	0	8.5	0	2.8	1.9
Universities	**23.5**	17.9	0	0	2.8	1.9	0.9
Government, public R&D	**3.8**	3.8	0	0	0	0	0

Source: Author's own elaboration based on the survey.

companies it seems that Nigerian partners are the first choice, especially when relying on competitors or customers. Hardly any collaboration exists with partners coming from other African nations, demonstrating that there is a huge untapped potential for regional collaboration. The potential, however, for international collaboration is even higher. With the exception of suppliers – where Nigerian mining companies rely to some extent on Asian and European collaborators – very few of the mining companies are international in terms of their collaboration pattern for their innovation processes. This reflects a situation where the mining innovation system is dominated by what is often called 'local buzz', an interactive learning process at the local or national level (Bathelt et al., 2004; Isaksen, 2003; Storper and Venables, 2004). This is unfortunate as the inflow of extra-national information and knowledge is crucial, especially in the context of a developing country (Pietrobelli and Rabellotti, 2011). At the same time, the reliance on quite a high amount of international suppliers may point towards another problem of the Nigerian mining sector: a strong reliance on technology from outside the country seems to indicate a lack of skilled and technological advanced local suppliers.

The companies were asked to name their most valuable cooperating partner. About 20 per cent of companies pointed to enterprises within their own group. Another 20 per cent stated that it was their suppliers of inputs and equipment, another 18.9 per cent said consultants, commercial laboratories and private R&D institutes, 17.8 per cent of companies indicated competitors, while 5.6 per cent specified universities/higher institutions. Government was the least valuable cooperation partner (1.1 per cent). In that, the results of this survey differ from the surveys conducted within other sectors, for example, in the service sector in Nigeria customers are often found to be the most important cooperation partner for innovation (Jegede et al., 2012).

8.5.3 Impact of Collaboration on Innovation

Table 8.3 shows that collaboration has no significant impact on product innovation at the 1, 5 or 10 per cent levels of significance but it significantly affects process innovation, indicating that if the companies collaborate with other actors, they are likely to implement process innovation by a log (odds) of 3.18 ($p < 0.01$). Furthermore, Table 8.3 shows that collaboration has a significant impact on organizational innovation, indicating that if the companies collaborate with other actors, they are more likely to implement organizational innovation by a log (odds) of 2.97 ($p < 0.05$).

Table 8.3   Impact of collaboration on various types of innovation

Variable	Product	Process	Organizational
Linkage with other actors	20.88	3.18***	2.97***
	(9474.57)	(0.79)	(0.69)
Constant	−21.20	−2.08***	−1.61**
	(9474.57)	(0.75)	(0.63)
McFalden R-squared	0.208	0.194	0.198
LR-statistic	12.812	26.811	26.084
Prob (LR-statistic)	0.998	0.000	0.000
Mean dependent var	0.249	0.642	0.689
Av. loglikelihood	0.216	−0.526	−0.497

Notes: *** = significant at the 0.01 level; ** = significant at the 0.05 level.

8.6   CONCLUSION

The results of this study show that the majority of formal mining companies in Nigeria are innovative and collaborate with other actors within the mining IS. Collaboration activities appear to be associated with innovation within mining firms, at least for the case of process innovation. During the study period, companies collaborated more with market-related actors than institution-related actors. It is particularly important to facilitate interactions between knowledge institutions and mining companies using appropriate policies, which may help in building up a lacking social capital that facilitates these interactions. For the mining companies, to expand their knowledge capital for innovation and enhanced productivity it is useful to make concerted efforts to cooperate with knowledge institutions, market agents and with government as well as other key actors of the IS including foreign R&D laboratories.

One should keep in mind a number of limitations of this study and its conclusions. The study used data from 150 mining companies, which represent approximately 10 per cent of the total population of mining companies registered with the Mining Cadastre Office in Nigeria as of December 2010. All companies surveyed were located in the southwestern part of Nigeria leaving behind five other zones potentially limiting the generalizability of the findings to all mining firms in the country. In addition, the study has established an association between collaboration and certain types of innovative activities but further research is needed to explore the causation (mechanism) in this relationship.

NOTE

1. The quarrying companies blast rocks and sell them on the market to individuals or contractors to be used for building houses, offices, bridges and other construction work while the construction companies are companies that also blast rocks but use them as raw materials in their own business activities. The exploration companies exist mostly as small business units, as a consulting arm of small and medium enterprises, or as consulting units of an academic institution. The processing companies blast rocks and process them for aesthetic purposes (tiles for floors and walls) and those that mine gems and cut them into gemstones for jewellery making. The activities of dredging companies include sucking and pumping sand from streams and rivers. Sands collected from rivers are usually friable and are used as basic raw materials in the glass industry.

REFERENCES

Adeoti, J., and Adeoti, A. (2005). Biotechnology R&D partnership for industrial innovation in Nigeria. *Technovation*, *25*(4), 349–365.

Adeoti, J. O. (2002). Building technological capability in the less developed countries: The role of a national system of innovation. *Science and Public Policy*, *29*(2), 95–104.

Adeyeye, A. D., Jegede, O. O., and Akinwale, O. Y. (2013). The impact of technology innovation and R&D on firm's performance: An analysis of Nigeria's service sector. *International Journal of Technology Learning, Innovation and Development*, *6*(4), 374–395.

Adeyeye, A. D., Jegede, O. O., Oluwadare, A. J., and Aremu, F. S. (2016). Micro-level determinants of innovation: Analysis of the Nigerian manufacturing sector. *Innovation and Development*, *6*(1), 1–14.

African Union–New Partnership for Africa's Development (AU–NEPAD). (2010). *African Innovation Outlook 2010*. Pretoria: AU–NEPAD.

Ajao, B. F., and Jegede, O. O. (2014). *Formal interactions versus informal interactions in the national innovation system: Concept and issues* (Gordon Research Seminar). Waterville Valley, United States.

Ajao, B. F., Oluwadare, A. J., Jegede, O. O., and Egbetokun, A. A (2014 October). *Towards the future of innovation systems research: An agenda.* Paper presented at the 12th Globelics Conference, Addis Ababa. Ethiopia.

Ajao, B. F., Oyebisi, T., Aderemi, H., and Jegede, O. (2015). Status and impact of strategic technology alliances among telecommunications firms in Nigeria. *International Journal of Business Performance Management*, *16*(2/3), 339–351.

Alo, B. (1995). University-based applied research and innovation in Nigeria. In M. O. Ogbu, O. O. Banji and M. H. Mlawa (eds.), *Technology policy and practice in Africa* (pp. 238–248). Ottawa: IDRC.

Bathelt, H., Malmberg, A., and Maskell, P. (2004). Clusters and knowledge: Local buzz, global pipelines and the process of knowledge creation. *Progress in Human Geography*, *28*(1), 31–56.

Bhaduri, S., and Sheikh, F. A. (2012). *Measuring informal innovations: Study of grassroots innovation of Kashmir* (9th Globelics Academy), 12 September 2016 at www.globelicsacademy.net/2013_pdf/.../Sheikh%20full%20paper.pdf.

Cervantes, M. (1999). Public/Private Partnership in Science and Technology:

An overview (STI Review No. 23, Public/Private Partnerships in Science and Technology). Paris: OECD.

Cozzens, S., and Sutz, J. (2014). Innovation in informal settings: Reflections and proposals for a research agenda. *Innovation and Development, 4*(1), 5–31.

Daniels, S. (2010). *Making Do: Innovation in Kenya's informal economy: An investigation of indigenous innovation in Africa,* 4 June 2016 at https://books.google.com/books?id=W_ghblkxXY4C&pg=PA117&lpg=PA117&dq=Making+Do:+Innovation+in+Kenya%E2%80%99s+Informal+Economy.+Analogue+Digital&source=bl&ots=Zc4Vgv0GbX&sig=fP1I9qd8LSOZNSjYa5OsLy-h1i4&hl=en&sa=X&ved=0ahUKEwiO-_Ty8YzQAhWERCYKHSidAUkQ6AEIKzAC#v=onepage&q=Making%20Do%3A%20Innovation%20in%20Kenya%E2%80%99s%20Informal%20Economy.%20Analogue%20Digital&f=false.

Eurostat/OECD. (2005). *Proposed guidelines for collecting and interpreting technological innovation data: Oslo Manual* (3rd edn). Paris: OECD.

Iizuka, M. (2013). *Innovation systems framework: Still useful in the new global context?* (UNI-MERIT Working Paper No. 2013-005), 12 September 2016 at http://www.merit.unu.edu/publications/wppdf/2013/wp2013-005.pdf.

Ilori, M. O. (2006). From science to technology and innovation management. *Inaugural Lecture Series, 191,* 9–10.

International Labour Organisation (ILO). (2002). *Women and men in the informal economy: A statistical picture.* Geneva: ILO.

Isaksen, A. (2003 June). *Learning, globalization, and the electronics cluster in horten: Discussing the local buzz—global pipeline argument.* Paper presented at The DRUID Summer Conference on Creating, Sharing and Transferring Knowledge: The Role of Geography, Institutions and Organizations, 12 September 2016 at http://www.druid.dk/conferences/summer2003/papers/ISAKSEN.pdf.

Isola, O. O., Ogundari, I. O., and Siyanbola, W. O. (2010 July). *The Nigerian National Innovation System: A critical look at research & development (R&D) and innovation capabilities in selected universities.* Paper presented at the PICMET 2010 Technology Management for Global Economic Growth Conference, 12 September 2016 at http://ieeexplore.ieee.org/xpls/abs_all.jsp?arnumber=5603446.

Jegede, O. O., Ilori, M. O., Sonibare, J. A., Oluwale, B. A., and Siyanbola, W. O. (2012). Factors influencing innovation and competitiveness in the service sector in Nigeria: A sub-sectoral approach. *Journal of Management, 2*(3), 69–79.

Jegede, O. O., Ilori, M. O., Sonibare, J. A., Oluwale, B. A., and Siyanbola, W. O. (2013). Knowledge sharing and innovation as it effects the local content in the oil and gas industry in Nigeria. *African Journal of Science, Technology, Innovation and Development, 5*(1), 31–38.

Lundvall, B.-Å. (2010). *National systems of innovation: Toward a theory of innovation and interactive learning.* London: Anthem Press.

Lundvall, B.-Å., Joseph, K. J., Chaminade, C., and Vang, J. (eds.). (2009). *Handbook of innovation systems and developing countries: Building domestic capabilities in a global setting.* Cheltenham, UK and Northampton, MA: Edward Elgar Publishing.

Müller, J. (2010 March). *Befit for change: Social construction of endogenous technology in the South.* Paper presented at the FAU Conference Workshop 4 on Community Entrepreneurs and Local Economic Development, Grenaa, Denmark, 4 June 2016 at http://vbn.aau.dk/ws/files/32179758/BEFIT%20FOR%20CHANGE.doc.

NACETEM. (2011). *Assessment of innovation capability in the manufacturing sector in Nigeria* (Monograph Series, No 4). Ile-Ife: NACETEM.

Oyebisi, T. O., Ilori, M. O., and Nassar, M. L. (1996). Industry–academic relations: An assessment of the linkages between a university and some enterprises in Nigeria. *Technovation*, *16*(4), 203–215.

Oyelaran-Oyeyinka, B. (1997). Technological learning in African industry: A study of engineering firms in Nigeria. *Science and Public Policy*, *24*(5), 309–318.

Oyelaran-Oyeyinka, B. (2001). *Networks and linkages in African manufacturing cluster: A Nigerian Case Study* (INTECH Discussion Paper No. 2001-5), 12 September 2016 at http://www.intech.unu.edu/publications/discussion-papers/2001-5.pdf.

Oyelaran-Oyeyinka, B. (2002). *Manufacturing response in a National System of Innovation: Evidence from the brewing firms in Nigeria* (INTECH Discussion Paper No. 2002-3), 12 September 2016 at http://www.intech.unu.edu/publications/discussion-papers/2002-3.pdf.

Oyelaran-Oyeyinka, B. (2003a). Innovation and learning by firms in Nigeria: The role of size, skills and ownership. *International Journal of Business and Society*, *4*(1), 1–22.

Oyelaran-Oyeyinka, B. (2003b). Knowledge networks and technological capabilities in African clusters. *Science, Technology and Society*, *8*(1), 1–24.

Oyelaran-Oyeyinka, B. (2005). Inter-firm collaboration and competitive pressures: SME footwear clusters in Nigeria. *International Journal of Technology and Globalisation*, *1*(3–4), 343–360.

Oyelaran-Oyeyinka, B. (2006). Systems of innovation and underdevelopment: An institutional perspective. *Science, Technology and Society*, *11*(2), 236–269.

Oyelaran-Oyeyinka, B., Laditan, G. O. A., and Esubiyi, A. O. (1996). Industrial innovation in Sub-Saharan Africa: The manufacturing sector in Nigeria. *Research Policy*, *25*(7), 1081–1096.

Oyewale, A. A. (2006). *Nigeria's research system and the culture of patenting. Intellectual property rights for business and society*. Paper presented at the Dynamics of Institutions and Markets in Europe International Conference, 16 June 2016 at http://www.dime-eu.org/files/active/0/Oyewale.pdf.

Pietrobelli, C., and Rabellotti, R. (2011). The global dimension of innovation systems: Linking innovation systems and global value chains. In B.-Å. Lundvall, K. Joseph, C. Chaminade and J. Vang (eds.), *Handbook of innovation systems and developing countries: Building domestic capabilities in a global setting* (pp. 214–240). Cheltenham, UK and Northampton, MA: Edward Elgar Publishing.

Radwan, I., and Pellegrini, G. (2010). *Knowledge, productivity, and innovation in Nigeria: Creating a new economy*. Washington, DC: The World Bank.

Romijn, H., and Albaladejo, M. (2002). Determinants of innovation capability in small electronics and software firms in southeast England. *Research Policy*, *31*, 1053–1067.

Siyanbola, W. O., Olamade, O. O., Yusuff, S. A., and Abubakar, K. (2012). Strategic approach to R&D commercialization in Nigeria. *International Journal of Innovation, Management and Technology*, *3*(4), 382–386.

Storper, M., and Venables, A. (2004). Buzz: Face-to-face contact and the urban economy. *Journal of Economic Geography*, *4*(4), 351–370.

Sutz, J., and Tomasini, C. (2013). *Knowledge, innovation, social inclusion and their elusive articulation: When isolated policies are not enough.* (International workshop on new models of innovation for development), 12 September 2016 at http://www.cdi.manchester.ac.uk/medialibrary/news_and_events/SutzTomassini PreWorkshopPaper.pdf.

Tiffin, S. (1997 May). *Building science and technology innovation systems in Africa.* Paper presented at the 1st Regional Workshop on The Restructuring of National Science and Technology Systems in Africa, Lagos, Nigeria.

9. Collaboration among Hungarian SMEs in innovation

László Csonka

9.1 INTRODUCTION

Companies today rely more than ever on external knowledge sources in research, development and innovation (RDI). Current economic trends, such as the growing knowledge-intensity of products and the ever-increasing speed of development, force firms to establish partnerships in order to cope with those challenges. Global expansion at the company level is not only driven by a wider exploitation of knowledge generated in the home country, but also by the relocation of certain research and development (R&D) and innovation functions in order to tap into sources of new knowledge and technology globally (Edler et al., 2002; Edler, 2008; Inzelt, 2010; Taggart, 1998).

This has resulted in an increase of inter-company and public–private collaboration in research and development (Roijakkers and Hagedoorn, 2006; Ozman, 2009; Perkman and Walsh, 2007). This increase of formal and informal collaboration has gone hand in hand with a change in the typical innovation model. In contrast to the earlier conception of innovation as a linear model, innovation is now understood as an interactive process which relies heavily on the flow of knowledge among different actors in the RDI process (Chesbrough, 2003; Inzelt, 2010).

The spread of RDI collaboration is commonly exemplified by the practice of large multinational companies (MNCs), which not only transform their own RDI processes but those of their partners and of the environment in which they operate (Cantwell and Bellak, 1997; Narula and Zanfei, 2005; Iammarino and McCann, 2013). The globalisation process and the spread of MNCs have triggered a series of adjustments in the economies of developing countries. Both smaller and larger economic actors in these countries have found new opportunities by joining international networks. In order to exploit these new opportunities, the R&D and innovation practices of many small- and medium-sized enterprises (SMEs) have changed with new forms of interaction and collaboration emerging

(Bougrain and Haudeville, 2002; Gomes-Casseres, 1997). Due to their ability to innovate by exploiting knowledge created outside the company, SMEs tend to display higher R&D productivity compared to larger companies (Audretsch and Vivarelli, 1996).

In contrast to the active research on MNCs' practices and impacts, our knowledge on the RDI collaboration patterns by SMEs, and on RDI collaborations in transition economies in particular, is rather limited. Current research (Rothwell, 1991; Narula, 2002; Lee, 2007) predominantly focuses on SMEs' practices outside of this context. The understanding of the ways successful SMEs in transition and post-transition countries join international collaboration networks and what kinds of partnerships they tend to establish in their R&D and innovation processes is crucial for the catching-up process. The literature suggests that learning by interacting with the most advanced partners internationally is key to successful technological development (Freeman and Hagedoorn, 1994; Radosevic, 1999; Inzelt, 2000; Csonka, 2010).

SMEs depend upon external information and knowledge due to their limited internal (human and other) resources. In the case of SMEs active in a global environment, external relationships are becoming both more extensive and geographically more dispersed. The development of information and communications technology (ICT) has made the creation and maintenance of such distant relationships much easier, and, as a result, has made networking more accessible for SMEs. In an open and, at the same time, relatively small economy such as Hungary, it is crucial for local enterprises to be connected with international partners. However, we lack a clear view about the collaborations of Hungarian SMEs in the R&D and innovation process. This chapter explores the way Hungarian SMEs (with R&D and innovation activity) collaborate with external partners. As such, it contributes to a better understanding of the main motivations, supporting and limiting factors of collaboration and networking, and how best to support more Hungarian SMEs joining global R&D networks.

The rest of the chapter is structured the following way. The next section offers a short review of the literature on RDI collaboration and networking in order to better understand the main challenges and opportunities for SMEs. The third section briefly introduces the data sources and research methodology on which the empirical research is based, whilst the fourth section analyses the RDI networking activity of Hungarian SMEs and its international aspects. It shows that there is only a small – but active and committed – core of enterprises that have already realised the potential benefits of collaboration. The chapter ends by concluding that enhancing RDI collaborations should be promoted with the broader innovation system of the country in mind.

9.2   CURRENT LITERATURE ON SMES' RDI COLLABORATION

Since the 1980s economists increasingly have emphasised the relevance of an interactive, systemic view of innovation in contrast to the traditional linear models (Nelson and Winter, 1982; Kline and Rosenberg, 1986) driven by the growing complexity and knowledge intensity of RDI and by cross-fertilisation of previously distinct fields of technology (Narula, 2001). Knowledge has become the main source of competitiveness with more actors engaged in knowledge generation, distribution and utilisation. There is a growing territory – mainly outside the core competences of companies – where inter-company (or even inter-sectoral) collaboration and networks become more important.

Collaboration is a loose concept, which encompasses a vast array of different activities. The term may denote formal or informal partnerships; it could be analysed at various levels (from individual to national); and it could involve many different activities. Sometimes it is used as an umbrella term for interactions ranging from the simplest types of contribution to innovation, to collaborations where partners work closely together to achieve a common goal (Katz and Martin, 1997 cited in Inzelt, 2004). These partners could be individuals, organisations or countries.

This chapter focuses on inter-company collaborations. Previously, most inter-company collaborations had some form of equity base, such as joint ventures. However, in the last three decades the prevalence of non-equity-based agreements, such as strategic alliances and networks, has constantly grown (Hagedoorn, 2002). Non-equity based forms are also better suited to bring together partners from various sectors and represent a more flexible way of cooperation. Building R&D collaborations is a complicated process crucially dependent on trust and openness among other factors. Finding appropriate external partners is time consuming; in the search process companies benefit from permanence when they find the best options (Csonka, 2009). The preference for stability of the established R&D links facilitates the development of a set of linkages into networks, which can spread across borders driven by the globalisation of the economy.

Networking has become a very popular topic overarching disciplinary boundaries. Studies such as Dunning (1995) on 'alliance capitalism', Castells' (1996) view of the network enterprise (and network society) or Ohmae (1990) and Freeman and Soete (1997) on the disappearance of companies' boundaries, all point towards the fundamental change in the economy, which is transformed by increasing reliance on external relations. This line of thinking has led to the emergence of the 'open innovation' era (Chesbrough, 2003), which means that companies should make a far greater use of external ideas and technologies for their own innovation process, whilst letting their unused ideas be used by other companies. This requires each company to open up its business model and allow more external ideas and technologies to flow in from the outside and more internal knowledge flow out (Chesbrough, 2006 cited in OECD, 2008). This should be seen as the most flexible way of collaboration, enabling the globalisation of innovation, user-supplier integration or outsourcing of R&D (OECD, 2008).

In the literature, networks take many different forms, from a buyer's network to R&D networks (see for example Fischer, 2006 or Richter, 2000), and an enterprise can be a part of many different networks at the same time (von Tunzelmann, 2004). One particular line of literature discusses the issue of knowledge management in innovation networks (de Man, 2008; Cappellin and Wink, 2009). It is especially important for actors in less developed economies to fully benefit from these partnerships and good knowledge management is vital for success. Geographically, the regional (intra- or inter-national) approach is becoming more compelling in the literature in addition to the research on global networks (Cooke, 2001; Boschma and Frenken, 2010). These latter studies are born out of the realisation that the internationalisation of R&D and innovation activities – and thus of collaboration – is developing into a decisive trend, transforming the economic landscape. The trend dates back to the early 1990s when scholars (Howells, 1990; Archibugi and Michie, 1997) started to analyse its implications and tried to identify the motivation behind, and the degree of, internationalisation (e.g. Kuemmerle, 1999; von Zedtwitz and Gassmann, 2002; Sachwald, 2008).

There is some evidence that SMEs investing in R&D and innovation activities are more productive if they can utilise external knowledge sources (Audretsch and Vivarelli, 1996). It appears that only a small share of Hungarian SMEs internationalise their RDI activities and/or networking, whereas a large part of these companies focus on serving a small local market. R&D and innovation efforts as well as internationalisation in this field are also influenced by the industry in which the SMEs operate. Empirical literature suggests that SMEs in high-tech industries are more actively internationalising their RDI activities (Archibugi and Iammarino, 2002; Narula, 2004; Antalóczy and Halász, 2011). There is also evidence that SMEs in the transition economies of Central and Eastern Europe are more internationalised than SMEs from large West European economies. This result, however, is also influenced by managerial capabilities as well as by the geographical location of companies (Glas et al., 1999).

The Hungarian research in this field is much less detailed. Innovation networking is usually studied from a regional point of view (e.g. Csizmadia and Grósz, 2009) and most of the literature focuses on innovation within clusters (e.g. Buzás and Lengyel, 2002). More literature can be found on university–industry collaboration (e.g. Inzelt, 2004) – which usually emphasises the importance of knowledge utilisation and knowledge spillovers and elaborates the challenges associated with these processes (e.g. Varga, 2007). Inzelt (2003) and Inzelt and Szerb (2003) found evidence of a positive relationship between collaboration and R&D activities among SMEs in Hungary. Recently, the NETINNOV project dealt with related issues (Csizmadia and Grósz, 2011) concluding that the collaboration practices of Hungarian companies are underdeveloped and weak.

9.3 RESEARCH METHODOLOGY AND SAMPLE

As mentioned above, there are relatively few empirical data available on the RDI and networking activity of SMEs in general – and of those in Hungary in particular. In order to fill this gap in the literature, a project was undertaken based on an online survey, interviews and secondary analysis carried out during the period 2010–11. In the absence of a uniform register of Hungarian RDI-active SMEs, a variety of sources were used to compile a research sample. The target group of SMEs was divided into three sub-groups: RDI-active companies, companies involved in RDI-supported governmental programmes and random companies in high-tech industries. The data on the companies came from several sources that include the Hungarian Central Statistical Office R&D survey, a list of winners in government R&D programmes, membership lists of various associations representing specific high-tech industries such as biotechnology and medical instruments, other entrepreneurial datasets available online, and 'snowballing'. Based on these sources, the researchers compiled a list of e-mail addresses for 1110 SMEs (a non-representative sample) from four industries: (a) biotechnology, (b) medical instruments, (c) information technology and (d) engineering services. The survey produced 246 valid responses – a response rate of 22 per cent.

The online survey included seven groups of questions: (1) general characteristics of the SME, (2) innovation activity of the SME, (3) participation in networks, (4) competitiveness, (5) position in the international field, (6) motivations and (7) basic data. This chapter focuses on the SMEs' participation in networks and brings in other parts of the survey only if they have additional explanatory power for the main research focus.

The online survey produced 246 responses from the four selected industries but more than a quarter of these responses could not be attributed to one of the target industries. Overall, engineering services firms had the highest response rate of about 65 per cent with the lowest response rate of about 12 per cent from the medical instruments companies. The response rate for the remaining two sectors was around 20 per cent. As a result, engineering services firms comprised 35 per cent of the sample, followed by IT companies (26 per cent), non-classified firms (20 per cent), medical instruments (14 per cent) and biotechnology (5 per cent – reflecting the small size of this industry in Hungary).

The statistical and sectoral lists show that, although the research primarily focused on RDI-active companies, 22.7 per cent of the sample was not involved in innovation activities at all, whilst 77.3 per cent reported that they were innovative.[1] This mixture – atypical of traditional statistical surveys – offered some opportunity to understand the main differences between the two groups and those factors which are most crucial for becoming an innovative, internationally active SME. Sixty per cent of the respondents were from Budapest, Hungary's capital, and 40 per cent were located in the provinces. This distribution shows a slightly better balance than the actual distribution of RDI activity in Hungary, which is heavily centred in Budapest. Most of the surveyed SMEs (44 per cent) were established between 1991 and 2000, whereas the 'old' enterprises (pre-1991) and younger ones (2001–05) were almost equally represented (22.8 and 23.7 per cent respectively) among the respondents. The newly established companies were the smallest group (9 per cent) in the sample, and the great majority are owned by Hungarian nationals or enterprises, whilst 20 per cent of all the SMEs are co-owned by a Hungarian and international company group.

9.4   RESULTS AND DISCUSSION

This section presents the main findings from the online survey with the focus on the networking activity of Hungarian SMEs, preceded by a short review of the general economic environment in Hungary (based on available statistics) and a comparison of the national trends to those discovered among surveyed companies.

9.4.1   Innovativeness and Networking in the Hungarian Economy

The R&D and innovation performance of the Hungarian economy is not placed among the best or lags behind (many) countries in the European Union. According to the Innovation Scoreboard of the European Commission (EC, 2016), Hungary is only among the moderate innovators, ranking 20th among the 28 member countries. The gross domestic expenditure on R&D (GERD) was around 1.4 per cent of GDP in 2013–15. The level of GERD to GDP fluctuated between 0.92 and 0.99 for almost a decade (2001–08) and started to grow only after 2009. Since that time, modest growth has been mainly fuelled from foreign sources (amounting to 15 per cent of the total, for example from EU Structural Funds) and by the growth of expenditures by businesses (although the latter's share grew only from 46 to 48 per cent from 2009–14). The business sector is still a much weaker source of R&D funding than in leading innovative countries. A glance at the various elements of the EU's Summary Innovation Index shows that businesses' R&D expenditures in Hungary are only 76 per cent of the EU average, whilst non-R&D innovation expenditures are slightly above (102 per cent).[2]

Despite positive dynamics of the R&D and innovation activities in Hungary, the country lags behind the EU average in RDI collaboration and entrepreneurship performance as measured by the EU Innovation Index.[3] Hungarian SMEs innovating in-house amount only to 38 per cent of the EU average, whilst innovative SMEs collaborating with others reach 54 per cent of the EU-28 average. This suggests that there is a huge gap in the innovativeness of Hungarian SMEs compared to their European counterparts. Looking at the innovation activities of enterprises by size, Hungary falls behind both the European innovation leaders and other countries of a similar size. It is notable that, whilst 55 per cent of enterprises with over 250 employees are innovative (this proportion is comparable to that of the Netherlands or Norway), only 15 per cent of the smallest enterprises (with 10–49 employees) are involved in such activities. This is much less than in other countries that show outstanding innovation performance. The difference is not explained by sectoral differences; it rather seems that Hungarian small enterprises – even in the most knowledge-intensive sectors – are less innovative (Inzelt, 2011).

In an innovation ecosystem characterised by a low general level of activity and a weak performance of the small business sector, advanced networking is not to be expected. According to the Hungarian Central Statistical Office (HCSO) based on Community Innovation Survey (CIS) 2012 results (Eurostat, 2012), a total of 43 per cent of innovative enterprises are involved in some kind of innovation collaboration (Table 9.1).

Table 9.1 shows that – similar to the innovativeness of the enterprises – there are great differences in collaboration efforts by size of enterprise. The most innovative group (250+ employees) proves to be the most active in collaboration (67 per cent) followed by medium-sized (54 per cent) and by the least innovative group of small enterprises (37 per cent). There are very few enterprises among the smallest firms, which are capable of

Table 9.1   Innovation collaboration among innovative enterprises by type
of partner (in %, 2008–10)

Collaborative partner	Involved innovative enterprises	Innovative enterprises by size categories (no. of employees)		
		10–49	50–249	More than 250
Suppliers	**27.9%**	**23.3%**	**31.8%**	**39.9%**
Higher education	**21.4%**	11.1%	**29.1%**	**49.6%**
Experts, private research organisations	**21.3%**	13.2%	**28.3%**	**40.7%**
Customers	20.6%	**17.1%**	23.4%	29.4%
Competitors	17.0%	**15.1%**	18.6%	21.9%
Other member of company group	13.7%	5.0%	20.3%	36.8%
Public research organisations	10.2%	6.3%	12.3%	22.4%
Any form of collaboration	43.2%	32.1%	54.2%	66.8%

Note: Bold numbers indicate the three top collaboration partners (by firm size).

Source: HCSO (2012).

innovating in-house, and even fewer capable of collaborating compared to the medium-sized enterprises. The table also reveals that suppliers, Higher Education and private research organisations are the most important partners in innovation collaboration, but there are remarkable differences in the rankings of partners by size of the enterprise. The largest companies tend to turn to knowledge-generating organisations in the public or private spheres, whilst the smaller enterprises search for partners in their familiar business environment. That is why suppliers are the most important collaborative partners for medium-sized enterprises – ahead of higher education and private research organisations – whereas small enterprises are looking for partners among their suppliers, customers or even among their competitors instead of the knowledge-generating organisations.

9.4.2   Participation in Networks

Among the firms surveyed, only 4 per cent of the responding firms had more than 50 employees (none more than 130). This suggests that the majority of survey respondents represent the group of enterprises, which, based on the official national statistics presented in the previous section,

Table 9.2   Participation in various types of networks

Network membership	No. of SMEs	% of the respondents
Any kind of network	51	20.7
National network	40	16.3
● professional associations	27	11.0
● chambers	11	4.5
International network	24	9.8
● professional associations	9	3.7
● chambers	3	1.2
National networks	40	16.3
● R&D	18	7.3
● Innovation	11	4.5
● Sales	7	2.8
● Purchase	7	2.8
● Production	1	0.4
International networks	24	9.8
● R&D	12	4.9
● Innovation	6	2.4
● Sales	12	4.9
● Purchase	3	1.2

Note: Multiple answers were possible.

Source: INNOTARS research programme (2008) supported by the National Innovation Office. Survey was conducted among small and medium enterprises in Hungary to understand factors that influence innovation in these companies.

appears to be the least innovative and rarely engaged in collaboration. It is therefore not surprising that only one-fifth of the respondents reported participation in any kind of network (Table 9.2). Although the number is in line with other sources of data (see HCSO, 2012), based on the selection of the sample (RDI active, internationalised companies), one might expect a higher-than-average level of activity among the respondents. Instead, the sample – although not representative – seems to align with the general practice of innovative companies in Hungary. The fact that the surveyed firms are more internationalised[4] than the average Hungarian SMEs does not seem to significantly influence their innovation practices. If we accept that innovative enterprises are generally more open towards and active in collaboration, this small number of actually collaborating SMEs in the sample is not particularly promising for the whole Hungarian economy.

It is clear from Table 9.2 that, among the various networks, national collaborations – and, within these, those with professional associations – are more common than any international collaboration. Only 10 per cent of the respondents were involved in international networks – which is a very low number and suggests that knowledge flows or knowledge acquisition from abroad is not common among Hungarian SMEs. Inactive participation in international knowledge networks may prevent Hungarian firms from keeping up with competition in producing internationally competitive products. One similarity between national and international networks is the preference given to professional associations as opposed to chambers. The picture among non-innovative firms is even less positive. These types of firms have reported participation exclusively in national networks and their share remains below 27 per cent.

Looking at the networks by their main function, we found some differences between national and international networking. Among national collaboration, R&D networks are the most common, followed by innovation networks, whilst in the international arena R&D and sales networks are the types most frequently used (Table 9.2). It seems from the lower panel of Table 9.2 that SMEs have established more diverse forms of collaboration in their home country than abroad. Whilst, in the national networks, R&D and innovation both seem to be an important objective of collaboration, there are many more R&D networks than networks aimed at innovation activities at the international level. This can be explained by the complexity of the innovation process and by the difficulties of finding an appropriate partner. Further, various EU R&D programmes may have facilitated the establishment of R&D collaboration, contributing to the frequency of this type of partnership at an international level. Another interpretation of these data may be that Hungarian SMEs are more open to collaboration at the beginning of the innovation process and they tend to rely on their own resources or on old trustworthy partners when arriving at the pre-competitive and competitive final stages of the process. It is a continuous process to develop new external business relations and mature existing ones into a higher level of collaboration. Collaboration in R&D – and even more in innovation – needs some common (past) experience, a good understanding of the other partner's operation and, above all, trust (Csonka, 2010). All this requires resources, commitment, and time. As a result, SMEs may be limited in starting such collaboration due to resource constraints. Geographical proximity also plays an important role in developing such relations as it is much easier to develop and maintain complex partnerships through face-to-face contact than with the help of current IT tools. Therefore, we may expect that the current sales/purchase partnerships will develop over time into R&D partnerships and more diversified innovation networks. The relatively long duration of the average national and to a lesser extent international network participation among the surveyed firms lends indirect support to these expectations.

Whilst network membership of a duration of less than two years is rather rare in national networks (14 per cent), it is relatively more common at the international level (27 per cent). According to these numbers, national networks are a few years more mature than their international counterparts. This may support the previous statement about the maturing of R&D and innovation collaboration and about a process where Hungarian companies first establish national contacts before venturing into the international arena.

The analysis of survey data suggests that national memberships in professional associations and chambers are the most mature types of collaboration, with 40–70 per cent of respondents being members of such networks for more than five years. They are followed by R&D networks, where more than 80 per cent of members have collaborated for 3–5 years. On the other hand, innovation networks show the largest variation in the length of participation. There are only new partnerships in R&D and innovation networks. Interestingly, among international networks, R&D networks on average are even more mature than their national counterparts, since two-thirds of their members have been partners for more than five years. (This could be related to the impact of the EU RTD Framework Programmes.) The same is true for international sales networks. On the other hand, the membership in international innovation networks, professional associations and chambers are all younger (most commonly 1–2 years old) than in the case of national ones.

Establishing external linkages in various networks is only one part of the process. The success of these partnerships is even more dependent on the type and intensity of collaboration realised within these networks. The survey contained a question about the intensity of interaction in the various networks. In the case of national networks, 'daily interaction' was the most common answer followed by interacting 'a couple of times a year' and, to a lesser extent, 'weekly/monthly' interaction. In the frame of international networks, 'daily interaction' and 'irregular' were the typical answers and other types were not very common. This information underpins the view that national contacts are easier to maintain (on a more intense level). It is a positive result that the number of companies mentioning that they have only a passive membership of their networks was minimal both at national and international levels, but even this passive collaboration may serve as an important channel of information-gathering for the companies.

The survey explored the most important networking partners of SMEs, and produced a trend similar to that recorded in the HCSO data described above but with some notable differences. The most important partners, generally, are customers, suppliers and – in our case – Higher Education Institutions (HEIs). These are not only the most important types of partner but they are partners with intensive relationships. Additionally, other members of the same company group are mentioned as partners for the most intensive collaboration. At the same time, competitors are rarely mentioned as a networking partner and most often they interact with each other monthly or even less often. Foreign partners based in Hungary also appear in national networks – but in very few cases compared to their active role in international networks. At the international level – understandably – they are the most common partner, followed by customers and HEIs. Networking activity can be very intense with foreign partners ('daily') but equally irregular also. Many SMEs mentioned a more intense relationship with the customers than with HEIs. Table 9.3 shows the collaboration intensity by the various types of partner in this chapter.

The tables show that, although only a small proportion of Hungarian SMEs collaborate in the innovation process with external partners, those who do so have established durable and intense collaboration with a variety of partners. Their collaboration activity is more focused on Hungary than abroad, but the two seem to be closely linked.

9.4.3   Motivations for Networking

The formation of networks, as well as the composition of partners, depends at least in part on the motivation, expectations and aims of the participants. Local or national relationships often develop organically. Moving out to the international field is much more crucial in the life of an SME and such distant relationships require more resources. It also requires more commitment and is associated with greater risk, but the potential gains are also higher than in the case of local or arm's-length relationships. The choice of a specific network to participate in requires strategic thinking and long-term planning from the SMEs, which is hardly typical of Hungarian SMEs (Csonka, 2010).

According to the survey results, the most important motivation for engaging in international networks is the development of existing business relationships; carrying it to the next level and gaining potential market advantage may be the reason behind such motivation. It is followed by technology-related motivations (access and acceleration) and the fact that enterprises take these technology-related motivations as being more impor-tant than finance is quite remarkable. However, the average values hide the fact that finance is regarded as very important by the second largest group of respondents. This situation is likely to be counterbalanced by the view of those companies which are already successful in the market and whose main barrier to international networking is not funding but rather a lack of appropriate partners (Inzelt, 2011). The acquisition of special

Table 9.3 *Networking intensity by type of partner*

Participation intensity	Type of innovation partner							
	Suppliers**	Customers	Universities	Foreign partners	Company group members	Colleges	Competitors	Public research organization
National networks								
Active*								
● Daily	26	24	24	6	13	11	3	
● Weekly	16	13	13	3			3	
● Few times a year	27	13	10	3		4	4	1
● Irregular	3		3	3			3	
Passive	6	6	6	6		3	3	3
International networks								
Active	3							
● Daily	12	9	6	12			3	6
● Weekly		6	6		6			
● Few times a year		3	3	3		3	3	
● Irregular	6	12	12	12			9	
Passive	6	3	3	3		3	3	3

Notes:
* Not all respondents detailed active collaboration.
** Contains parts-suppliers, high-tech suppliers, technology suppliers from SMEs to MNCs.

Source: INNOTARS_08 project.

knowledge or technology also emerged as an important motivation for international networking. This suggests that many enterprises have realised that a successful international expansion is unthinkable without an up-to-date product or technology. Cost-based competition is not so beneficial in the long run, especially in those high-tech industries that were the target of this analysis. Instead, a competitive advantage needs to be generated and this can be obtained via collaboration. The speeding up of the RDI process proves to have modest importance for the respondents. This may be explained by the SMEs' targeted markets, which are niche markets where they are not forced into a speed competition. Interestingly, neither external push factors (acquiring state support) nor internal push factors (deficiency in human resources) play an important role in networking. Most respondents label these factors as not important for SMEs.

Summing up, it seems that international RDI networking is mostly driven by potential advantages (pull factors) such as the development of contacts, new knowledge or technology. In cases of financial or technological motivation, opinions among the respondents are divided but, clearly, push factors are not considered relevant – which poses challenges for any policy striving to improve the international networking of SMEs.

9.5   CONCLUSIONS

The international literature on the importance of RDI networking has grown quickly over the last 20 years, but, until recently, most of the studies paid little attention to the SME networking practices. At the same time, these enterprises are traditionally more reliant on external sources of knowledge compared to multinational corporations. The available evidence suggests a connection between RDI activities and networking, internationalisation and the level of technology involved, although this chapter based on a survey among Hungarian SMEs in four high-technology industries provided only partial confirmation of those theories.

Considering the empirical evidence available from international studies, the knowledge of RDI networking (and networking of Hungarian SMEs in general) is limited. Based on what we know, international trends and European public policy seem to gradually change the prevalence of collaborations. Based on the national statistics, the number of innovation companies in Hungary who are highly active in networking is very small, and they are typically larger companies. The smaller the enterprise, the smaller is the chance that it will be innovative and active in collaboration. The respondents to the survey analysed in this chapter were predominantly medium and small. Although the vast majority are innovative, less than one-third are involved in any kind of networking. This is in line with – or even below – the national average. The low level of activity might be the consequence of the lack of funding and the low level of innovativeness and R&D. Additionally, in many cases the enterprises themselves do not regard their set of contacts as a network (even if it would qualify as one).

The few examples of networking in the sample suggests that SMEs are active in participating not only in 'traditional' (sales, production) networks but also in R&D and innovation networks both at national and (to a lesser extent) international levels. However, a large part of these networks rather serve as information gatherers and not innovation developers. The data reveals the ubiquity of information sharing networks (based on professional associations and chambers). Compared to this type of collaboration, others, such as intra-company group collaboration and university–industry networks, are less common. The data also shows that only a few substantial RDI networks (measured by maturity and intensity of collaboration) exist in the collaboration 'portfolio' of the respondents.

Some of the respondents are committed to establishing durable relationships and actively collaborate with their partners. This could not be possible without strategic thinking and planning ahead which is not characteristic of Hungarian enterprises, but it can ensure the best return on the resources invested in networking. RDI-network forming, developing and tasking is, of course, time-consuming, and the responses reveal that the whole process may take five years or more before the necessary level of trust is generated among the partners. The SMEs' responses also suggest that it is generally a process started with national partners and that international expansion only follows after a few years' delay. Once networks are established, either nationally or internationally, the enterprises attempt to maintain them as long as possible. This is mirrored by the fact that the length of participation in the various networks tends to be medium to long term (over three years) with both national and international networks.

Analysing the SMEs' motivation for participating in networks, it is clear that developing already existing relations further is the primary reason. Generally, the potential benefits of networks are the most important factors (such as new knowledge or more rapid RDI processes) in entering into new partnerships. A much more divisive motivation is that of the additional funding available through networks – which appears to be irrelevant for the surveyed companies. This is an important lesson for policymakers, stressing that top-down initiatives might not be effective in countering market forces. A different situation is created by the EU RTD Framework programmes which seem to influence the collaborative activity of Hungarian SMEs. However its attraction is not primarily additional funding but access to international cutting-edge knowledge.

In Hungary, the unstable economic and RDI environment hinders the prospects for long-term planning by economic actors. This is critical if launching such a time-consuming and risky process as RDI networking is under consideration. In addition to this, in a weakly supportive environment it should be no surprise that the networking activity of Hungarian SMEs is lagging behind the European average. RDI and networking could stimulate each other in a positive environment. Therefore, in Hungary the RDI system – and first of all the linkages within the business sector and between business and research organisations – needs to be further developed. Such a reinforced system could generate much more effective RDI networking than any other direct government measure with the same target.

NOTES

1. Only in the medical instruments and engineering services sectors did the proportion of non-innovative companies exceed 10 per cent of the respondents.
2. (www.ksh.hu, http://ec.europa.eu/growth/industry/innovation/facts-figures/scoreboards/index_en.htm).
3. The EU Innovation Index is a composite of multiple components each consisting of various indicators. One of the components is labelled 'Linkages & Entrepreneurship'. It shows the largest gap between the European average and Hungarian performance.
4. A 2011 survey (Baranyi et al., 2012) estimated that around 30 per cent of SMEs are active on international markets, whilst in this research sample their share is almost 80 per cent.

REFERENCES

Antalóczy, K., and Halász, G. (2011). Magyar biotechnológiai kis- és középvállalkozások jellemzői és nemzetköziesedésük. *Külgazdaság, LV(9–10)*, 78–100.

Archibugi, D., and Iammarino, S. (2002). The globalization of technological innovation: Definition and evidence. *Review of International Political Economy, 9*(1), 98–122.

Archibugi, D., and Michie, J. (eds.) (1997). *Technology, globalisation and economic performance*. Cambridge: Cambridge University Press.

Audretsch, D., and Vivarelli, M. (1996). Firm size and R&D spillovers: Evidence from Italy. *Small Business Economics, 8*, 249–258.

Baranyi, M., Endrődi-Kovács, V., Miklós, G., Nagy, Gy. S., and Palánkai, T. (2012). *Internationalisation (transnationalisation) of the enterprise sector.* (BCE Working paper), Budapest, accessed 8 September 2014 at http://unipub.lib.uni-corvinus.hu/586/.

Boschma, R., and Frenken, K. (2010). The spatial evolution of innovation networks. A proximity perspective. In R. Boschma (ed.), *The handbook of evolutionary economic geography* (pp. 120–135). Cheltenham, UK and Northampton, MA: Edward Elgar Publishing.

Bougrain, F., and Haudeville, B. (2002). Innovation, collaboration, and SMEs internal research capacities. *Research Policy, 31*(5), 735–747.

Buzás, N., and Lengyel, I. (eds.) (2002). *Ipari parkok fejlődési lehetőségei: regionális gazdaságfejlesztés, innovációs folyamatok és klaszterek.* Szeged: Jate Press.

Cantwell, J., and Bellak, C. (1997). Small latecomer countries in a globalising environment: Constraints and opportunities for catching-up. *Development and International Cooperation, 13*(24–25), 139–179.

Cappellin, R., and Wink, R. (2009). *International knowledge and innovation networks: Knowledge creation and innovation in medium technology clusters.* Cheltenham, UK and Northampton, MA: Edward Elgar Publishing.

Castells, M. (1996). *The rise of the network society.* Oxford: Blackwell.

Chesbrough, H. (2003). *Open innovation.* Boston: Harvard Business School Press.

Chesbrough, H. W. (2006). The era of open innovation. *Managing Innovation and Change, 127*(3), 34–41.

Cooke, P. (2001). Regional innovation systems, clusters and the knowledge economy. *Industrial and Corporate Change, 10*(4), 945–974.

Csizmadia, Z., and Grósz, A. (2009). *Vállalati innovációs kérdőíves felmérés a Dél-dunántúli régióban. Research report, MTA-RKK,* Pécs-Győr, accessed 10 September 2014 at http://www.ddriu.hu/userfiles/File/DDRIU_Zarotanulmany. pdf.

Csizmadia, Z., and Grósz, A. (2011). *Innováció és együttműködés – A kapcsolatok innovációra gyakorolt hatása.* MTA-RKK, Pécs-Győr, accessed 10 September 2014 at http://docplayer.hu/762505-Innovacio-es-egyuttmukodes-a-kapcsolath alozatok-innovaciora-gyakorolt-hatasa.html.

Csonka, L. (2009). Regional university knowledge centres: In search for regional benefits. *Social Research, 20*(3), 59–74.

Csonka, L. (2010). Hálózatok az autóiparban: tanulás a kutatás-fejlesztés és innováció érdekében. *Külgazdaság, LIII*(7–8), 89–109.

De Man, A. P. (2008). *Knowledge management and innovation in networks.* Cheltenham, UK and Northampton, MA: Edward Elgar Publishing.

Dunning, J. H. (1995). Reappraising the eclectic paradigm in an age of alliance capitalism. *Journal of International Business Studies, 26*, 461–491.

Edler, J., Meyer-Krahmer, F., and Reger, G. (2002). Changes in the strategic management of technology: Results of a global benchmarking study. *R&D Management, 32*(2), 149–164.

Edler, J. (2008). The role of international collaboration in the framework programme. Brussels: European Commission.

European Commission (EC). (2016). *European innovation scoreboard, 2016,* accessed 24 May 2016 at http://ec.europa.eu/growth/industry/innovation/facts-figures/scoreboards_hu.

Eurostat. (2012). Community innovation survey 2012. European Commission, accessed 24 May 2016 at http://ec.europa.eu/eurostat/web/microdata/commu nity-innovation-survey.

Fischer, M. M. (2006). The new economy and networking. In M. M. Fischer (ed.), *Innovation, networks, and knowledge spillovers* (pp. 95–115). Heidelberg: Springer.

Freeman, C., and Hagedoorn, J. (1994). Catching up or falling behind: Patterns in international interfirm technology partnering. *World Development, 22*(5), 771–780.

Freeman, C., and Soete, L. (1997). *The economics of industrial innovation.* London: Pinter Publishers.

Glas, M., Hisrich, R. D., Vahcic, A., and Antoncic, B. (1999). The internationalisation of SMEs in transition economies: Evidence from Slovenia. *Global Focus, 11*(4) 107–124.

Gomes-Casseres, B. (1997). Alliance strategies of small firms. *Small Business Economics*, *9*(1), 33–44.
Hagedoorn, J. (2002). Inter-firm R&D partnerships: An overview of major trends and patterns since 1960. *Research Policy*, *31*, 477–492.
HCSO. (2012). *Innováció*. Budapest: KSH.
Howells, J. (1990). The internationalisation of R&D and the development of global research networks. *Regional Studies*, *24*, 495–512.
Iammarino, S., and McCann, P. (2013). *Multinationals and economic geography: Location, technology and innovation*. Cheltenham, UK and Northampton, MA: Edward Elgar Publishing.
Inzelt, A. (2000). Foreign direct investment in R&D: Skin-deep and soul-deep cooperation. *Science and Public Policy*, *27*(4), 241–251.
Inzelt, A. (2003). A kicsik K+F és innovációs tevékenysége. *Külgazdaság*, *47*(11), 24–42.
Inzelt, A. (2004). The evolution of university–industry–government relationships during transition. *Research Policy*, *33*, 975–995.
Inzelt, A. (2010). Collaborations in the open innovation era. In N. Ekekwe (ed.), *Nanotechnology and microelectronics, global diffusion, economics and policy* (pp. 61–86). Hershey, PA: IGI Global.
Inzelt, A. (2011). Innováció és nemzetköziesedés a kicsik világában. Egy e-felvétel eredményei. *Külgazdaság*, *LV*(9–10), 122–154.
Inzelt, A., and Szerb, L. (2003). Az innovációs aktivitás vizsgálata ökonometriai módszerek alkalmazásával. *Közgazdasági Szemle*, *L*, 1002–1021.
Kline, S. J., and Rosenberg, N. (1986). An overview of innovation. In R. Landau and R. Rosenberg (eds.), *The positive sum strategy*. Washington, DC: National Academy Press.
Kuemmerle, W. (1999). The drivers of foreign direct investment into research and development: An empirical investigation. *Journal of International Business Studies*, *30*(1), 1–24.
Lee, C. (2007). Strategic alliances influence on small and medium firm performance. *Journal of Business Research*, *60*, 731–741.
Narula, R. (2004). R&D collaboration by SMEs: New opportunities and limitations in the face of globalisation. *Technovation*, *24*(2), 153–161.
Narula, R. (2002). R&D collaboration by SMEs: Some analytical issues and evidence. In F. Contractor and A. Lorange (eds.), *Cooperative strategies and alliances*. Oxford: Pergamon Press.
Narula, R. (2001). *Multinational firms, regional integration and globalising markets: Implications for developing countries*. MERIT (Infonomics Research Memorandum Series 036), accessed 11 May 2016 at http://econpapers.repec.org/paper/unmumamer/2001035.htm.
Narula, R., and Zanfei, A. (2005). Globalization of innovation: The role of multinational enterprises. In J. Fagerberg and D. Mowery (eds.), *The Oxford handbook of innovation* (pp. 318–45). Oxford and New York: Oxford University Press.
Nelson, R., and Winter, S. (1982). *An evolutionary theory of economic change*. Cambridge: Harvard University Press.
OECD. (2008). *Open innovation in global networks*. Paris: OECD.
Ohmae, K. (1990). *The borderless world*. New York: Harper.
Ozman, M. (2009). Inter-firm networks and innovation: A survey of literature. *Economics of Innovation and New Technology*, *18*(1), 39–67.

Perkmann, M., and Walsh, K. (2007). University–industry relationships and open innovation: Towards a research agenda. *International Journal of Management Reviews*, *9*(4), 259–280.

Radosevic, S. (1999). *Restructuring and reintegration of S&T systems in economies in transition, Final Report* (TSER project, SPRU). Brighton, accessed 12 May 2016 at http://cordis.europa.eu/docs/publications/7088/70885211-6_en.pdf.

Richter, F. J. (2000). *Strategic networks – The art of Japanese interfirm cooperation.* New York: International Business Press.

Roijakkers, N., and Hagedoorn, J. (2006). Inter-firm R&D partnering in pharmaceutical biotechnology since 1975: Trends, patterns, and networks. *Research Policy*, *35*(3), 431–446.

Rothwell, R. (1991). External networking and innovation in small and medium-sized manufacturing firms in Europe. *Technovation*, *11*(2), 93–112.

Sachwald, F. (2008). Location choices within global innovation networks: The case of Europe. *Journal of Technology Transfer*, *33*, 364–378.

Taggart, J. H. (1998). Strategy shifts in MNC subsidiaries. *Strategic Management Journal*, *19*(7), 663–681.

Varga, A. (2007). Localized knowledge inputs and innovation: The role of spatially mediated knowledge spillovers in the new EU member countries from Central Europe: The case of Hungary. *Acta Oeconomica*, *57*(1), 1–20.

von Tunzelmann, N. (2004). Network alignment in the catching-up economies of Europe. In F. McGowan, S. Radosevic and N. von Tunzelmann (eds.), *The emerging industrial structure of the wider Europe* (pp. 23–37). London: Routledge.

von Zedtwitz, M., and Gassmann, O. (2002). Market versus technology drive in R&D internationalization: Four different patterns of managing research and development. *Research Policy*, *31*(4), 569–588.

10. The developmental university in emerging innovation systems: the case of the Universidad Mayor de San Simón, Bolivia

Carlos Gonzalo Acevedo Peña, Walter Mauricio Hernán Céspedes Quiroga and José Eduardo Zambrana Montán

10.1 INTRODUCTION

There is a strong need to generate a normative, financial and institutional environment that facilitates interactive dynamics of collaboration between research universities, the government and the industrial sector in many developing countries including Bolivia. Given a certain autonomy that universities often enjoy, they are well positioned to promote internal transformations and to adopt a proactive role in initiating and developing collaborations with other actors, thus enhancing the positive impact on society of university research activities.

This chapter shares the experience and lessons learned from implementing several initiatives launched by a public university in order to make its internal and external innovation environment more dynamic. The university in focus is Universidad Mayor de San Simón (UMSS), the second largest public university in Bolivia located in the Cochabamba region. This university aims to enhance the impact of its research activities on regional and national development. To this end, it has adopted a systemic perspective and proactive institutional attitudes to promote innovation by developing transdisciplinary platforms of interaction in a context of major social, cultural and political transformations in Bolivia.

The chapter presents a case study based on eight years of participatory action research by the authors who performed academic and policymaking roles during the study period. The primary data from the university technology transfer unit (UTT) and from public sources constitute the basis of the analysis. The lessons learned at UMSS can be useful to build fruitful long-term relations, not necessarily focussed on state-centred or market-centred initiatives, but aiming at inclusive development aspirations.

10.2 THEORETICAL FRAMEWORK

10.2.1 National Innovation Systems (NISs)

The concept of the National Innovation System (NIS) has been widely used by policymakers and studied by academics in the last decades. Lundvall et al. (2009) defined the national system of innovation as an 'open, evolving and complex system that encompasses relationships within and between organizations, institutions and socio-economic structures, which determine the rate and direction of innovation and competence-building emanating from processes of science-based and experience-based learning' (p. 6).

In the case of developing countries, especially in Latin America, the concept of the NIS has been used as the basis for economic development policies, but it is still unclear how operative this concept is in specific contexts. Edquist and Hommen (1999) argue that the systemic approach to the innovation process explicitly recognizes the potentially complex interdependencies and possibilities for multiple kinds of interactions among its various elements. In this light, many empirical studies recognize that university–industry–government interactions are key elements in the systemic process of innovation. The Triple Helix model of university–industry–government relations (Etzkowitz, 2008) shows the interaction of the three elements in a system and tries to capture the dynamics of both communication and organization as an overlay of exchange relations that feed back to the institutional arrangements (Leydesdorff and Meyer, 2003). In this model, industry operates within the Triple Helix context as the locus of production; government as the source of contractual relations that guarantee stable interactions and exchange; and the university as a source of new knowledge and technology, the generative principle of knowledge-based economies (Etzkowitz, 2003). In the Bolivian context, however, it was pointed out that the Triple Helix Model should be supplemented by the fourth element, meaningful societal participation.

According to Lundvall (2010) the NIS concept is based on two main assumptions: (i) the most fundamental resource in modern society is knowledge and, accordingly, the most important process is learning; and (ii) learning is predominantly interactive and, therefore, a socially embedded process, which cannot be understood without taking into consideration its institutional and cultural context. Looking at developing countries, Sutz (2012) argued that this condition can be partially explained as an 'innovation as learning' systemic failure, due to the relative weakness of innovation processes in developing countries and the lack of opportunities to learn through such processes. This failure is systemic because it is built-in to the productive specialization of most developing countries where the learning content of productive activities is weak. In such circumstances, universities play a key role in learning and innovation but the specific position and functions of universities and their mechanisms of interactions within the NISs of developing countries are not clearly defined, mostly as a result of NIS context dependency.

10.2.2   Universities in National Innovation Systems

A sizable proportion of the research capabilities of the Latin American countries is concentrated in universities. Recently, the institutional relevance of universities as facilitators of social and economic development in society, via their research activities, has been increasingly emphasized. Vaccarezza (2011) argues that current Latin American research suffers from a double periphery status: it occupies a relatively marginal position within the international scientific community and is not fully able to integrate into the 'context of application' marked by innovation and production flows of international capital. This situation becomes even more critical in the Bolivian case, where, according to the Vice-Ministry of Science and Technology (VCyT, 2011), about 90 per cent of the country's research capabilities are mainly located at public universities. As a result, the last two decades saw intensified efforts to embed universities into the NIS with the goal of their active participation in the socio-economic development of their regions.

For centuries, the main two missions of the universities were teaching and research. Nowadays, it is believed that universities should have more than these two missions. Brundenius et al. (2009) propose the 'third mission' of universities to further the relationships of universities and the society to which they belong. Similarly, the concept of 'Mode 2 science-production' contends that knowledge is produced based on a fluid dialogue between the academy and other actors. Unlike Mode 1, in which knowledge is mostly generated by academic actors within a specific community, in Mode 2, knowledge is produced in a context of application involving a much broader range of perspectives. Mode 2 is transdisciplinary and not only draws on disciplinary contributions but also on new frameworks beyond them; it is characterized by a heterogeneity of skills, by a preference for flatter hierarchies and transient organizational structures. It is more socially accountable and reflexive than Mode 1.

In Bolivia, most policymakers still regard universities, especially public ones, as potential 'knowledge generators' to facilitate socio-economic development by transferring research results, technology and innovation. Bramwell and Wolfe (2008) maintain that this mechanistic view of the way basic scientific research translates into commercial products demonstrates a misconception of the commercialization process and the role of universities herein. The flow of knowledge drives innovation, but knowledge transfer from universities to industry is a complex process that involves many different actors. Brundenius et al. (2009) argue that linking universities closer to users is fundamental for enhancing their role in relation to economic development. Especially in countries where a significant proportion of the research effort is located at universities, it is important to find ways to enhance the interaction between universities and industry as well as with other users in society.

This non-isolated or self-sufficient understanding of universities' role represents a basic foundation of new emerging concepts. Etzkowitz (2008) – looking at some experiences in California (USA) – proposed the concept of the 'entrepreneurial university'. He argues that the 'capitalization of knowledge' is the heart of a new mission for the university, linking universities to knowledge users more tightly and establishing the university as an economic actor in its own right. This model is impractical in the Bolivian context, since the values of the public university are strongly linked to social concerns and social common sense is not perceptive to such institutional behaviour. Additionally, Bolivia does not have well-developed institutional or public normative structures with respect to intellectual property and technology transfer procedures.

In developing countries, the concept of a developmental university seems to be more appropriate to the existing context, for example in Bolivia. Brundenius et al. (2009) define a developmental university as an open entity that interacts with different groups in society, including industries, but it does not have profit-making as one of its missions. Its major goal is to contribute to social and economic development while at the same time safeguarding a certain degree of autonomy. Within the Latin American context, Arocena et al. (2015) went further, arguing that such universities are committed specifically to social inclusion through knowledge and, more generally, to the democratization of knowledge, along three main avenues: democratization of access to higher education, democratization of research agendas and democratization of knowledge diffusion. Additionally, they point out that developmental universities are those involved in the production of learning and innovation processes, which foster inclusive development.

It follows from the discussion above that universities have the power to determine the way in which different university bodies interact and contribute widely to society. Universities can be the test laboratories for adapting and creating new demand-driven mechanisms to support NIS strategies and to help overcome developmental challenges. Under this umbrella, university bodies, like technology transfer offices, can play a crucial role in leading institutional transformations and linking university research dynamics with socio-productive demands. Wahab et al. (2012) refer to Maskus (2004) and contend that the technology transfer concept involves not only the transfer of technological information or knowledge but also shaping the technology recipient's capability to learn and absorb technology into practical market applications. More recently, a number of scholars have argued that the main role of technology transfer units at universities is to build the legitimacy of university actions into society (Codner et al., 2013; O'Kane et al., 2014), defined as a 'generalized perception or assumption that the actions of an entity are desirable, proper, or appropriate within some socially constructed system of norms, values, beliefs, and definitions' (Suchman, 1995, p. 574).

10.3   THE CASE OF THE UNIVERSIDAD MAYOR DE SAN SIMÓN

10.3.1   The Context of the Study

Bolivia's state reforms, started in 2006, recognized the need to develop innovation policies to foster an NIS. The NIS was first presented as a tool of the National Development Plan (2006–11) aimed at strengthening the national research capabilities and linkages with the productive sectors. In 2013, the VCyT presented a 2014–25 National Plan of Science, Technology and Innovation (ST&I), developed after a wide participatory process, which included representatives from several social movements. The plan divided institutions within the system based on bilateral and trilateral relations between three main interacting sectors: (i) the government, (ii) the knowledge-generating sector and (iii) the recipient sector of ST&I. In addition to the traditional institutions in the former two groups – universities and industries – the plan explicitly included indigenous groups and social grass-roots organizations to play a role as both knowledge generators and recipients of ST&I. A more diversified approach adopted by the plan aimed to be more socially inclusive by recognizing academic and non-academic 'native and indigenous' knowledge as a source for demand-oriented innovation (Acevedo et al., 2015).

The VCyT report (2011) estimates that more than a half of the Bolivian research capabilities are located in public universities, while only 4 per cent of research activities in the country focused on experimental development. This reflects low orientation towards the generation of the own knowledge and low knowledge absorptive capability of the national industries. Currently, the interactions between Bolivian universities and the industry are scarce. This appears to be the case for many countries of the global south where market demand for knowledge is extremely low, resulting in the underutilization of the (weak) knowledge that is available and a further weakening of knowledge capabilities in developing countries (Arocena and Sutz, 2014).

The Universidad Mayor de San Simón (UMSS) was created in 1832. It is a public university, declared as an autonomous one in 1931. It is also a part of the Bolivian University System (SUB) and currently is the second largest university in the country, enrolling approximately 65,000 students as of 2014. The University offers about 82 undergraduate courses within 11 faculties and one technical school. Graduate programmes, mostly specialization and master programmes, are primarily oriented at training professionals for the local and national markets. Students in these programmes are usually people already holding a job, wishing to improve their skills in order to enhance their performance at work, and increase their chances when competing in the labour market. Unlike undergraduate education, which is fully funded by the government, graduate training requires students to pay full tuition. Only research-based graduate programmes implemented with the support of international cooperation offer scholarships or other forms of financial aid. Research is one of the three core functions of UMSS, together with education (training of professionals), and community outreach. The Directorate for Scientific and Technological Research (DICyT) is the university body in charge of managing and organizing the research system at UMSS. The research capabilities at UMSS are formed by 42 research units and 219 researchers (Rectorado-Vicerrectorado, 2012).

10.3.2 Research Activities Background

The development of research capacities at UMSS has historically been dependent on international cooperation – most notably with Sweden – and, more recently, on funds coming from the Direct Hydrocarbon Taxes (IDH) collected and distributed by the central government. This support has allowed the creation of scientific competences, physical infrastructure and the acquisition of modern scientific equipment. However, the absence of institutional strategies and priorities to support research resulted in a scattered landscape of research at UMSS. The research community had to face often opposing demands to align research activities with 'real life' and the needs of the region and to establish and build its presence in the international research community.

The accumulation of research resources along the different faculties had a direct relationship with the prioritized fields of international research cooperation. More than 50 per cent of research resources and activities at UMSS have been, and are still, centred in the Faculties of Science and Technology and Agronomy. All financial resources allocated to research centres follow a procedure developed by DICyT for the prompt and transparent selection of research proposals following international standards. Other Bolivian universities replicated the procedures developed and implemented at UMSS. Recent efforts at UMSS also included defining a new, more inclusive and contextualized research agenda that promotes local economic development.

10.3.3   The University Technology Transfer Unit and its Activities

The Technology Transfer Unit at UMSS was created in 2004 within the Faculty of Science and Technology (FCyT). UTT started its operation with the creation of a database of the available research resources at FCyT (equipment, laboratories, services, human resources) that could be used to offer research services to industries. The first years of operations revealed that there was no demand for research services from the industry, while demands of a greater university contribution to solving social problems were mounting. Therefore, the original supply-based UTT business concept proved to be impractical in the Bolivian context for a number of reasons. Large firms were mostly self-sufficient and did not see value in university collaboration. Medium-sized companies showed more interest in collaborating with university research centres, but lacked the funding to invest in research activities and expressed concerns about intellectual property issues. Small and micro firms were interested in getting support from the university. Nevertheless, collaboration was hindered by firms' inability to formulate clear requirements, a lack of funding, a low level of training, short-term vision focused mostly on marketing, and a low level of collaboration with other institutions due to widespread mistrust.

In response to these challenges, in 2006, UTT adopted a new approach for interaction processes. The Innovation Systems (IS) approach was adopted as a basis for the UTT research initiatives in an attempt to increase the impact of UMSS research activities in local socio-economic development. Using funds (mainly for mobilization and training activities) from an external supporter, UTT created an innovation programme at UMSS, which partnered with the Scandinavian Institute of Competitiveness and Development (SICD) at the Blekinge Institute of Technology

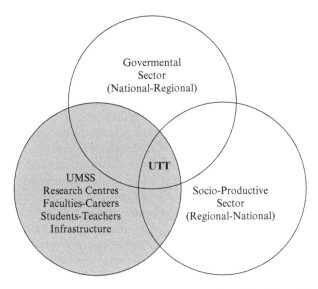

Source: Authors' own elaboration based on the Triple Helix model of innovation (Etzkowitz, 2008).

Figure 10.1   Innovation structure adopted by Technology Transfer Unit (UTT) at Universidad Mayor de San Simón (UMSS)

(www.sicd.se). This partnership helped to shape the vision of the university's participation in socio-economic development and to operationalize innovation processes as co-evolutionary interactions among non-isolated institutions in dynamic relations.

In terms of Trojer (2014), innovation consists of co-evolving processes, where relevance and context of application and implication constitute essential elements. These processes at UMSS were structured in terms of the Triple Helix (university–industry–government) model of innovation, because it was also easier to build a common understanding framework in non-academic contexts (Figure 10.1). However, the question of how these co-evolving processes are carried out was better answered by the concept of Mode 2 knowledge production. Furthermore, Trojer (2014) highlights that co-evolution is not only a hand in hand process between actors within and outside universities. It is an integrating process between Mode 2 researchers and predominantly Mode 1 researchers and partners in society.

The innovation programme promoted by UTT aimed 'to develop at UMSS institutional competences and capabilities for studying, promoting and actively participating in systems and processes of innovation at the local, regional and national levels' (UTT, 2006, p. 9). This objective defined the activities performed by UTT inside and outside the university. On the one hand, it built up an innovation culture and capabilities at UMSS, sensitizing research activities towards socio-productive demands, inspired by the Mode 2 knowledge production paradigm. On the other hand, it linked research resources with the demand from the industry by promoting cluster development and by generating an innovation system environment based on the Triple Helix model of innovation.

According to UTT (2015), the main actions promoted by UTT are oriented towards developing an efficient system of innovation management at UMSS; making the academic community (professors and researchers) more dynamic, participating in activities related to innovation systems (regional and national); developing information systems and standard procedures for contracts with external actors, taking into account intellectual property aspects; studying innovation systems and cluster development; promoting cluster development in the Cochabamba region, supporting innovation system dynamics; and generating capabilities to influence innovation policies at the regional and national levels.

10.3.4   Systemic Interaction Approach: Cluster Development

Cluster development was adopted by UTT as a permanent platform of interaction, from where specific demands (from governments and socio-productive actors) can be articulated. The goal was to coordinate multidisciplinary research activities and to find synergies with other institutions to meet those demands. After an empirical context diagnosis, UTT chose to start cluster activities within the diverse food sector in Cochabamba. The decision was based on the presence of significant research capabilities related to this sector at UMSS, the long food industry specialization of the region and the special attention the government pays to the food industry in its economic development plans.

Starting in 2007, UTT put considerable effort into attracting the main institutions in the region, such as regional government, SMEs, business associations, financial agencies and other supporting agencies, to be a part of the clustering processes. A series of meetings was held with various stakeholders and potential participants where UTT informed about research capabilities of UMSS and highlighted the significance of interaction within innovation processes with the goal to gather a critical mass of institutions and people committed to participating in cluster initiatives.

The 'Food Cluster Cochabamba' by UTT was launched in 2008. It was open to any SME and government body (regional and local) with activities linked to the food sector. From the university side, several research centres and laboratories of services located in the Faculty of Science and Technology were involved, including the Food and Natural Products Centre (CAPN), Agro-Industrial Technology Centre (CTA), Biotechnology Centre (CBT) and others.

Inspired by the Food Cluster initiative, and responding to the explicit request from the leather industry, the 'Leather Cluster Cochabamba' was created in late 2008 with the aim to support linkages between research centres such as the Water and Environmental Sanitation Centre (CASA), Agro-industrial Technology Centre (CTA), Industry Development Research Centre (CIDI) and Manufacturing, and Technology Development Program (PDTF). Both sectors (Food and Leather) enjoy a long industrial tradition in the Cochabamba region and have been prioritized in development programmes for the region.

The Innovation Program at UTT organized bi-annual planning workshops for each cluster. These workshops were dialogue-based forums to generate a shared long-term vision and to openly design short-term common agendas for collaboration. Annual agendas were built based on strengths expressed from the productive sectors and by making common demands visible, as well as presenting research results and the services available in research centres. Besides, in order to facilitate the generation of ideas for collaboration, both clusters organized annual guided tours to university research centres, showcasing the equipment and its main functions. Meetings of researchers, industry representatives and government officials to discuss technical issues related to new proposals for cluster initiatives were also organized. Activities prioritized by each cluster were discussed in detail by an advisory board, composed of volunteer and committed cluster members who showed particular interest in implementing specific cluster initiatives. A 'cluster facilitator' provided by UTT supported each cluster. This person was in charge of organizing the allocation of resources, projects management and networking, while fostering trust-building and dynamic dialogue arenas. Interactions within clusters dynamics were open and mostly informal.

According to UTT (2015), by 2014, the Food and Leather Cluster initiatives had gathered about 120 productive units and firms, 15 government bodies, 21 research units at UMSS and 9 sectorial institutions. Approximately 800 people from the main three sectors – academy, government and industry – have been involved directly in diverse Food and Leather Cluster initiatives. Additionally, UTT has mobilized more than 500 students to support different cluster initiatives linking them to their academic activities (research projects, short studies, surveys, industrial practices, training courses and local productive fairs).

In the first years of our cluster development experience, the participation of productive units and firms was promoted by their association leaders. However, cluster arenas were focused on giving voice directly to the firms. Representatives from business associations had their own agendas and claims, competing for sectorial leadership. This context, at the beginning, made processes of demand identification and trust-building more difficult. However, business associations proved good partners – mobilizing entrepreneurs, supporting defined activities and involving cluster members in their own supporting programmes. In the case of the Food Cluster Cochabamba, the more dynamic entrepreneurs and producers in cluster initiatives have been those only weakly or not linked at all to business associations.

Looking at government bodies, an unstable political context and continuous turnover of public officials at the regional level have complicated the structuring of long-term supporting programmes. However, cluster development was included in the Annual Working Plan (POA) of the regional Secretariat of Productive Development. On the other hand, a more stable central government allowed for the establishment of more dynamic relationships, in particular with the VCyT, which linked some international supporting training programmes, such as CYTED[1] and Sur-Sur, to the cluster initiatives and used the UTT infrastructure and cluster networks as regional references for the implementation of sectorial supporting programmes.

The dynamics of clusters has enhanced the visibility of UTT within the university and society. Thus in 2010, the vice-chancellor of UMSS formally acknowledged the UTT as a university unit in the Faculty of S&T, with a cross-facultative scope of operation. This recognition allowed UTT to involve research centres from other faculties, including Agronomy, Economy, Biochemistry and Sociology among others, into innovation programmes. Research centres at UMSS demonstrated great interest in participating in cluster initiatives and within innovation systems. Despite this fact, active participation of research centres in cluster initiatives was limited by the low S&T demands and the lack of financial resources for fostering university collaboration with productive units. However, UTT was able to meet most of the low-technology demand (in terms of knowledge generation, laboratory tests and pilot practices) by facilitating the access of students and researchers to research centres and productive infrastructures.

Most of the initiatives in both clusters conformed to the five main guidelines described by Sölvell et al. (2003): research and networking; policy action; innovation and technology; commercial cooperation; and education and training. Whereas it is difficult to measure the specific effects that the two cluster initiatives had on firms, with the university, the reorientation of a share of resources towards cluster causes was obvious, as well as the development of new dialogue channels, which facilitated collaborations and influenced the research agenda at UMSS.

10.3.5   Mode 2 and Innovation Culture: UMSS Research Community

A multidisciplinary team of researchers across university faculties, named the UMSS Innovation Team, was officially created in 2012 based on the initial group of scholars linked to cluster development. It now includes about 35 researchers representing diverse disciplines and about 20 university research units. The team's goal is to promote a more dynamic research community at UMSS, fostering both innovation culture and Mode 2 practices institutionally. The team holds annual meetings to discuss collaboration initiatives aimed at the development of national and regional innovation systems from within the university. Many of the team participants are members of national and international research networks within their disciplines.

Another UTT initiative, the Technology-Based Enterprise Incubator (EMBATE), was started in 2010 with the goal to promote innovation and entrepreneurship culture among students. Using resources of the research centres located in the Faculty of S&T, the incubator supports selected technology-based business ideas from students and organizes competitions involving business ideas, which should teach students how to generate proposals based on entrepreneurial ideas. In its early stages, EMBATE was linked to the Bolivian start-up network led by the VCyT. In 2012, the VCyT organized local training activities (transferring entrepreneurship and start-up models developed by the 'Instituto Politécnico Nacional de Mexico' Start-Up Unit to 12 Bolivian universities including UMSS) using the UTT infrastructure. EMBATE was recognized by the national government as a useful node for national and international universities linked to its network. More recently, in 2015, the national significance of EMBATE was confirmed by a proposal for Latin-American start-ups supported by CYTED.

Over the years, UMSS gradually achieved considerable improvements in the size and the quality of the research community, enhanced a number of research facilities, strengthened the management of research and the overall execution of research activities, and created a positive research environment and culture by the adoption of appropriate routines and practices. According to Arocena et al. (2015), developmental universities are characterized as universities that provide effective incentives to include in their research agendas, problems whose solutions can lead to the democratization of knowledge. UMSS is still far from those ambitions, but its efforts are going in that direction, thus we propose an ex-post categorization of UMSS experiences as a 'developmental university' approach. The developmental university approach has a place in emerging innovation systems in Bolivia, playing a key role for the democratization of knowledge and inclusive development ambitions.

10.4   CONCLUSIONS AND REMARKS

In this chapter we categorize (ex-post) the empirical practices and reforms adopted by UMSS as a 'developmental university' approach. Through the experience described above UMSS developed its own institutional competences and mechanisms to influence national and regional socio-economic development. The presented case study suggests that building an innovation system, at least in the beginning, is more about building social relationships than technical and scientific components.

The experience gained by the technology transfer unit at UMSS has demonstrated that offering research services to the industry in a context of a non-dynamic productive system in Bolivia does not work. Thus, the systemic approaches of interaction, adopted since 2007 by UTT, fostered more dynamic interaction between the university, the government and the socio-productive actors. These initiatives shaped a dual role for UTT, promoting innovation system dynamics inside and outside the university and permeating the institutional borders. UTT proved in practice that the concept framework given by Mode 2 science production and the Triple Helix model of innovation makes the communication of the idea of innovation systems easier for both academic and non-academic agents and generates open environments of interaction and trust-building. The UMSS experience demonstrates how universities can play an active role in building and shaping emerging innovation system dynamics in developing countries such as Bolivia.

In 2013, the VCyT proposed a demand-based innovation model within the framework of an emerging Bolivian Innovation System. This model recognizes the key role of universities within an interactive innovation process that is shaped by local demand and the need to enhance local knowledge production processes by making them transdisciplinary, participatory, and socially inclusive. In this general context, public universities are challenged to develop more open collaboration dynamics with socio-productive actors.

The cluster development initiative at UMSS created communication channels that allowed the building of common agendas of collaboration and made the socio-productive demands visible to academic and government actors. Although the technology gap between research centres, and the absorptive capability in the productive sector, limited the dynamics of the collaboration programmes implemented, the programmes helped firms to survive, improving their current productive processes in accordance with sectorial regulations. Open dialogue arenas gave important input towards building more democratic research agendas at universities. The success of cluster development in Bolivia will depend on the capacity to build closer and long-term relationships based on the principles of complementarity with industrial sectors.

The intermediary role of UTT in managing innovation processes has been recognized by government bodies thanks to its ability to leverage existing networks and to identify researchers capable of attending to social needs, to understand productive sector dynamics, and to be able to share knowledge with policymakers at national and regional levels while working on ST&I research and policy proposals. UTT also played a role as a manager of funds, giving an institutional umbrella to cluster initiatives, which are mostly based on trust and informal relationships. UTT promoted co-evolutionary processes of interaction within innovation where institutional barriers were penetrated and common arenas of dialogue were shaped. Its actions further legitimized university activities in society, providing the opportunity to make them more participative and democratic. However, the UTT experience suggests that greater resources are needed in order to improve the absorptive capacity of the productive sectors, allowing an effective use of the university research efforts to address socio-productive demands. Institutional and national intellectual property regulations are also needed to foster the democratization of knowledge and to privilege the endogenous knowledge production aimed at promoting inclusive development ambitions.

NOTE

1. CYTED is a platform that promotes and supports multilateral cooperation in science and technology (www.cyted.org).

REFERENCES

Acevedo, C., Céspedes, M., and Zambrana, E. (2015). National policies of innovation: Building an inclusive system of innovation. *Journal of Entrepreneurship and Innovation Management*, 4(1), 63–82.

Arocena, R., and Sutz, J. (2014). Innovation and democratisation of knowledge as a contribution to inclusive development. In G. Dutrénit and J. Sutz (eds.), *National innovation systems, social inclusion and development: The Latin American experience* (pp. 15 33). Cheltenham, UK and Northampton, MA: Edward Elgar Publishing.

Arocena, R., Göransson, B., and Sutz, J. (2015). Knowledge policies and universities in developing countries: Inclusive development and the 'developmental university'. *Technology in Society*, *41*(0), 10–20.

Bramwell, A., and Wolfe, D. A. (2008). Universities and regional economic development: The entrepreneurial University of Waterloo, *Research Policy*, *37*(8), 1175–1187.

Brundenius, C., Lundvall, B.-Å., and Sutz, J. (2009). The role of universities in innovation systems in developing countries: Developmental university systems – empirical, analytical and normative perspectives. In B.-Å. Lundvall, K. J. Joseph, C. Chaminade and J. Vang (eds.), *Handbook of innovation systems and developing countries: Building domestic capabilities in a global setting* (pp. 311–333). Cheltenham, UK and Northampton, MA: Edward Elgar Publishing.

Codner, D., Baudry, G., and Becerra, P. (2013). Las oficinas de transferencia de conocimiento como instrumento de las universidades para su interacción con el entorno, *Universidades*, *58*, 24–32.

DICyT. (2012). *Concept note: Research cooperation between SIDA and UMSS 2013–2022*. Cochabamba, Bolivia: UMSS.

Edquist, C., and Hommen, L. (1999). Systems of innovation: Theory and policy for the demand side, *Technology in Society*, *21*(1), 63–79.

Etzkowitz, H. (2003). Innovation in innovation: The Triple Helix of university–industry–government relations, *Social Science Information*, *42*(3), 293–337.

Etzkowitz, H. (2008). *The Triple Helix: University–industry–government innovation in action*, New York and London: Routledge.

Leydesdorff, L., and Meyer, M. (2003). Triple Helix of university–industry–government relations. *Scientometrics*, *58*(2), 191–203.

Lundvall, B.-Å. (ed.). (2010). *National systems of innovation: Toward a theory of innovation and interactive learning*. London and New York: Anthem Press.

Lundvall, B.-Å., Vang, J., Joseph, K. J., and Chaminade, C. (2009). Innovation system research and developing countries. In B.-Å. Lundvall, K. J. Joseph, C. Chaminade and J. Vang (eds.), *Handbook of innovation systems and developing countries. Building domestic capabilities in a global setting* (pp. 1–30). Cheltenham, UK and Northampton, MA: Edward Elgar Publishing.

Maskus, K. E. (2004). *Encouraging international technology transfer*, Geneva, Switzerland: International Centre for Trade and Sustainable Development (ICTSD) and United Nations Conference on Trade and Development (UNCTAD).

O'Kane, C., Mangematin, V., Geoghegan, W., and Fitzgerald, C. (2014). University technology transfer offices: The search for identity to build legitimacy. *Research Policy*, *44*(2), 421–437.

Rectorado-Vicerrectorado. (2012). *Universidad en Cifras 2012*. Cochabamba, Bolivia: UMSS.

Sölvell, Ö., Lindqvist, G., and Ketels, C. (2003). *The Cluster Initiative Greenbook*. Stockholm, Sweden: Ivory Tower AB.

Suchman, M. C. (1995). Managing legitimacy: Strategic and institutional approaches. *Academy of Management Review*, *20*(3), 571–610.

Sutz, J. (2012). Measuring innovation in developing countries: Some suggestions to achieve more accurate and useful indicators. *International Journal of Technological Learning, Innovation and Development*, *5*(1/2), 40–57.

Trojer, L. (2014). When society speaks back. Relevance issues for research in cluster contexts in low income countries. In B. Rydhagen and L. Trojer (eds.), *The role of universities in inclusive innovation: Cluster development in East Africa* (pp. 47–57). Kampala, Uganda: Nelson Mandela African Institute for Science and Technology.

UTT. (2006). *Innovation program and technology transfer: Program proposal 2006.* Cochabamba, Bolivia: UMSS.

UTT. (2015). *Innovation program and technology transfer: Annual report 2014.* Cochabamba, Bolivia: UMSS.

Vaccarezza, L. S. (2011). Ciencia, tecnología y sociedad: el estado de la cuestión en América Latina. *Ciencia & Tecnología Social, 1*(1), 42–64.

VCyT. (2011). *Potencial Científico y Tecnológico Boliviano 2011* (2nd edn). La Paz, Bolivia: Ministerio de Educación.

Wahab, S. A., Rose, R. C., and Osman, S. I. W. (2012). Defining the concepts of technology and technology transfer: A literature analysis. *International Business Research, 5*(1), 61–71.

11. The lost tiger in technological catch-up: lessons learned and implications for latecomer strategic typology

Xiao-Shan Yap and Rajah Rasiah

11.1 INTRODUCTION

Evolutionary economists have strived to examine the mechanisms behind the rapid technological catch-up of some very backward countries in East Asia. More than 50 years ago Veblen (1915) and Gerschenkron (1962) pioneered the notion of latecomer advantages. According to Gerschenkron (1962), the more backward a country is, the shorter the period it requires to catch up with the forerunners. This is because latecomers do not have to go through the same process as the forerunners in accumulating technological capabilities. Rather, latecomers can skip certain processes by strategically tapping into existing frontier technologies in various fields. The critical role of institutions to overcome latecomer disadvantages and to benefit from latecomer advantages was significantly emphasized (Gerschenkron, 1962). State intervention indeed has the ability to overcome scarcity of capital, labour skills and technological capabilities.

Two Newly Industrialized Economies (NIEs) – Korea and Taiwan – have managed to successfully catch up and upgrade their technologies in significant industries like semiconductor manufacturing. Both countries have arrived at the technological frontier through different strategies adopted by their respective governments, institutions and management leaders. To date, Korean Samsung and Taiwan Semiconductor Manufacturing Corporation (TSMC) are two giant leaders in the semiconductor industry with revenue and technological performance surpassing many forerunners in the United States of America. In comparison, the majority of Malaysian-owned semiconductor firms have thus far remained at the lower tiers of the technology ladder.

The Malaysian government set out to foster a knowledge-based nation by upgrading the country's human capital (NEAC, 2010). Unfortunately, so far this remains an unrealized vision. To encourage a supportive environment, the government has set up a number of meso-organizations, including public research institutes such as the Malaysian Institute of Microelectronic Systems (MIMOS) founded in 1985 to support the development of high-technology indigenous semiconductor firms. However, MIMOS failed to mimic the results of Taiwan due to the severe lack of a skilful management with the right strategies to manage and transfer technologies (Rasiah, 2010).

Despite the fact that the overall Malaysian semiconductor industry has not been able to catch-up with firms at the world's technological frontier, there are a few indigenous semiconductor firms that experienced high revenue growth rates in the past decade. Our study is comprised of four case studies of indigenous semiconductor firms. Two of the cases are indigenous wafer fabrication companies (one was taken over by a foreign firm in 2006), which are still at the lower ranks of the technological ladder; two others are indigenous semiconductor assembly and test firms, which experienced high growth and technological upgrading in the past decade. The purpose of this study is, thus, to examine the technological learning patterns of the indigenous semiconductor firms in Malaysia. We seek to identify the role of managerial strategies in these firms. We also attempt to identify the different roles of the local government agencies throughout the learning process of these firms. The rest of the chapter is organized as follows. Section 11.2 provides a review on the important theories relevant to this study. Section 11.3 describes our research framework and methods, whereas Section 11.4 presents our analysis and findings. Section 11.5 concludes.

11.2   LITERATURE REVIEW

11.2.1   Industrial Innovation Patterns as the Fundamental Background of Catch-Up Analysis

Innovations within industries can be broadly characterized as Schumpeter Mark I or Schumpeter Mark II models, according to Nelson and Winter (1982) and Kamien and Schwartz (1982). Schumpeter Mark I and Schumpeter Mark II industries differ in the ways innovative activities are structured and organized. 'Creative destruction' under Schumpeter Mark I is characterized by low barriers to entry into technological activities and a significant role played by new and innovative small firms or entrepreneurs. These challenge the incumbent firms and constantly disrupt the existing ways of manufacturing, organization and distribution, hence diminishing the quasi-rents attributed to earlier innovations. Schumpeter Mark II is characterized by 'creative accumulation' where large resourceful firms dominate and barriers to entry prevent the birth of new innovators. These barriers consist of the accumulated stock of technological knowledge, research and development (R&D) competencies, and the production, distribution and financial resources of established firms (Malerba and Orsenigo, 1994, 1996). The latter distinguishes firms with strong internalized R&D activities targeted at searching for new stocks of knowledge.

The Schumpeterian Mark I and Mark II patterns of innovation have also been characterized as widening and deepening respectively. A widening pattern of innovative activities is associated with continuously expanding the innovative base through the entry of new innovators and the progressive loss of competitiveness and technological dominance of established firms. A deepening pattern of innovation occurs with the concentration of a few innovators. These firms innovate from time to time through the constant accumulation of technological capabilities (Malerba and Orsenigo, 1994, 1996).

Specifically, three dimensions of Schumpeterian patterns of innovation can be identified as attributed to the technological regime, that is, the rate of concentration of innovation activities among firms, the degree of stability in the hierarchy of innovation firms, and technological entry and exit of the industry (Breschi et al., 2000). A Schumpeter Mark I industry is characterized by a large set of highly turbulent innovation firms, of which there are high technological opportunities, low appropriability and low cumulativeness within firms and a limited role of generic knowledge. These conditions result in a low concentration of innovation activities, a relatively large number of innovators, high rates of technological entry and high instability in the hierarchy of innovators (Breschi et al., 2000). A Schumpeterian Mark II industry is characterized by low opportunities, high appropriability and cumulativeness at the firm level with a strong internalized tacit and explicit knowledge base, all of which cause a high degree of concentration of innovation activities, low rates of entry and remarkable stability in the hierarchy of innovators (Breschi et al., 2000).

11.2.2   Government-Level Catch-Up Strategies

Veblen (1915) and Gerschenkron (1962) pioneered the notion of a latecomer effect. 'Latecomers' are defined as countries or firms that arrive relatively late to certain industries with a clear goal to increase their real incomes by closing the gap they have with the advanced forerunners (Mathews, 2006). In general, catching-up is analogous to the relative speed of runners racing on a path set by forerunners, while technology-building is akin to piling bricks with an undefined vertical goal (Perez and Soete, 1988). Latecomers can determine a catch-up roadmap, which allows them to access the forerunners' knowledge and technology. The governments of latecomer countries play a crucial role in determining the relevant strategies for a catch-up process, including strategies that overcome latecomer disadvantages and strategies that benefit latecomers.

In the search for what explains technological advance, institutions are referred to as the rules of the game (North, 1990). Evolutionary economists often refer to them as whatever holds and moulds the standard behavioural patterns in societies (Rasiah, 2011). The role of universities, government labs and professional societies are a few key examples of critical institutions (Nelson and Winter, 1982). South Korea and Taiwan are two major Asian examples where governments have strategically used technology to move countries from a low-income to a high-income status. For example, in South Korea the government has pursued the Schumpeter Mark II model (creative accumulation): since the 1970s the country has been characterized by a concentrated industrial structure and large conglomeration of firms in automobile manufacturing, semiconductors and telecommunications (Malerba and Nelson, 2012). To protect the successful *chaebol* – that is, diversified business groups whose size and diversity are similar to those of Japan's *keiretsu* – from the rise in oil price within 1973–1975, South Korea's government provided insulations to these large firms by expensive loans from abroad (Rasiah, 2011). The government has also strategically used performance standards as strong institutional settings to support technological catch-up in certain industries. Successful examples of this approach are Samsung, Hyundai and Pohang Steel Company (POSCO) in electronics, shipbuilding and automobiles and steel respectively (Amsden, 1989; Kim, 1997).

During the technological catch-up process of Taiwan, the local government applied the framework of sectoral system of innovations (SSI) by following the basis of the Schumpeter Mark I model (creative destruction) to support the entry of new small firms into industries like information and communication technologies (ICT), resulting in many small and medium-sized firms as well as high industrial turbulence (Malerba and Nelson, 2012). The success of Taiwan's indigenous integrated circuit firms is also attributable to the selective interventions by its government, such as the significant role of the Industrial Technology Research Institute (ITRI) (Mathews and Cho, 2000). The government focused on the development of its vertically decentralized structure, in which firms are specialized in only one particular manufacturing stage (Rasiah and Lin, 2005).

As explained above, South Korea and Taiwan have undergone industrialization in conditions that were favourable to their strategies but may no longer apply to other latecomers. Despite this, it is important to examine the strategies deployed by these countries, as we can then seek to draw implications for other latecomers. Gerschenkron's idea, originally developed for countries, can be extended to firms. Like countries, latecomer firms have accumulated knowledge used to draw plans and objectives for future products and technologies. In the integrated circuit (IC) industry, as Mathews (1997) and Brown and Linden (2009) have noted, crises have offered tremendous opportunities for latecomers to leapfrog ailing incumbents. For example, founded in 1980 the integrated circuit company UMC benefited from the technology acquisition from the financially troubled RCA by Electronics Research and Service Organization (ERSO) (Mathews and Cho, 2000).

11.2.3   Firm-Level Catch-Up Strategies in Global Value Chains

A late entry into a specific industry allows latecomer firms to strategize and access existing advanced technologies, and hence, exempts them from repeating the whole technological path advanced by the forerunners (Veblen, 1915; Gerschenkron, 1962; Abramovitz, 1956; Mathews, 2006). To further exploit latecomer advantages, firms can hasten their catch-up process by breaking the organizational inertia faced by incumbents through strategic alliances and state support (Mathews, 2006). Because latecomers strategize around the possibilities inherent in their latecomer status, it is important to specifically examine the firm-level strategies deployed by different latecomer firms in order to identify the differences that distinguish successful catch-ups from failed catch-ups.

The current stage of globalization is characterized by disaggregated global value chains (GVC) that connect activities around the world and are not generally controlled by one multinational corporation (MNC) (UNIDO, 2002/2003). These value chains, made possible by new technology, offer opportunities for latecomers to acquire the technology needed for participation and eventually to extend their role in these chains. Leading firms in advanced countries who control and provide the technology driving these chains are willing to outsource segments of these chains in order to lower costs. Latecomer firms, in addition to strengthening their technological capabilities, on the other hand are motivated by building up links with the leading firms, gaining from the latter specific organizational skills and market access. These links are referred to in the strategy literature as leverage (Prahalad and Hamel, 1990).

One of the strategies latecomer firms follow is to become subcontractors of original equipment manufacturers (OEMs). These firms not only earn revenue, but through a gradual process of embedding themselves ever more deeply into global supply chains, build and strengthen linkages that enable them to ramp up their capabilities, including technological, and as such contribute to the country's industrial development. Where production systems have not been disintegrated and no GVCs have been created, latecomers face the much more challenging task of looking for strategic equivalents or work with international agencies to create such value chains (Mathews, 2006).

The catch-up framework of Mathews (2002, 2006) contends that a latecomer firm is able to achieve its first competitive advantage because it recognizes its own weaknesses and follows a strategy that takes full account of these weaknesses. Thus, the latecomer sources its technology, knowledge and market access externally, which enables it to gain a foothold in the world's production chains. The following are important for the latecomer firm's strategic choices based on the latecomer catch-up framework of Mathews (2002, 2006): (1) through using linkages as the initial step that generates opportunities for the latecomer firm, and (2) leveraging resources to take advantage of the linkages established, then (3) out of repeated applications of linkage and leverage, learning is achieved and enables the latecomer firm to acquire dynamic capabilities.

Strategic shifts by incumbents that create linkage opportunities for latecomers (for instance, via outsourcing or OEM contracting, local sourcing, second sourcing and technology licensing in the context of high-tech industries like semiconductors and cellular telephony) provide latecomers with opportunities to leverage on and learn from more advanced firms, the so-called spillovers or externalities acquired through linkage, for example, with foreign firms (Blomstrom and Kokko, 2001). Outsourcing to a third party – e.g. OEM contracting – adds a great deal of value to the process. Specifically, based on Mathews (2002, 2006), a latecomer is likely to target those resources which are: (1) least rare; (2) most imitable (e.g. through reverse engineering); and (3) most transferable (Mathews, 2002). However, competition and complexities in ever increasing globalization indicate that a catch-up framework in the context of GVC should be constantly revised to include new dynamics such as changing characteristics in the types of resources needed.

11.3   RESEARCH METHODOLOGY

11.3.1   Analytical Framework

The analytical framework of this study is built on the basis of the catch-up theory postulated by Mathews (2002, 2006). Strategizing on finding a gateway to enter into the GVCs offers a three-staged framework of catch-up possibilities, namely linkage, leverage and learning. This forms the basis of the framework's trajectory. This learning trajectory is embedded within a broader industrial and technological environment. At each catch-up stage, different strategic elements form the sources and opportunities for latecomers to catch up (see Figure 11.1).

Therefore, the purpose of the proposed framework is to demonstrate that latecomer business strategies should be further extended from the model of Mathews (2002, 2006). Also, specializing in different segments across the supply chain and entering into the industry at different points in time require different catch-up strategies. For instance, a wafer fabrication firm requires a different catch-up approach as compared to an IC assembly and test firm. Additionally, throughout the catch-up phases, the role of institutions varies.

While Mathews (2002, 2006) identified three key characteristics of latecomers' targeted resources (i.e. least rare, most imitable and most transferable), we extend the taxonomy of latecomers' business strategies by incorporating other important facets such as strategic choices based on competition level and time allowance. We also incorporate key determinants that influence the business strategies of these latecomers, including market trend and technological regime. We also seek to emphasize that the latecomers' strategy of inserting themselves into the GVCs requires a strategic choice of business model and production stage (e.g. fabrication or assembly and test). Other key elements incorporated in the framework, such as the 'branding' strategy, IP transfer, technology trajectory and positioning strategy are identified as important elements by the interviewees. Using the proposed framework, the subsequent section maps the taxonomy and trajectory of latecomer strategies for the IC industry.

11.3.2   Data Collection and Analysis

The findings of this research are based on four focused case studies that rely on insights and information gained through a number of interviews conducted during 2012–14 with four Malaysian-owned integrated circuit firms, including two wafer fabrication companies (SilTerra and 1st Silicon,

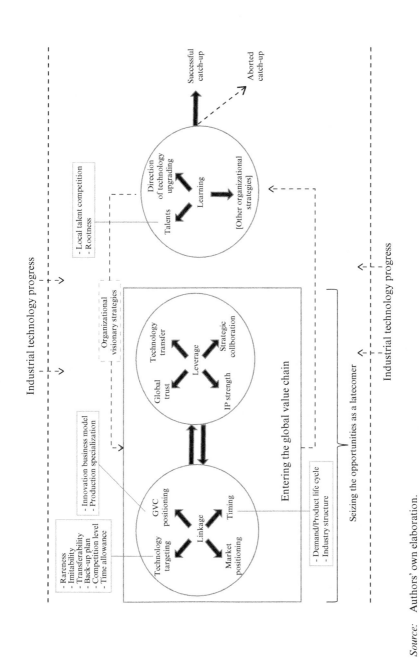

Source: Authors' own elaboration.

Figure 11.1 Latecomer strategies for technological catch-up

213

although the latter was taken over by a foreign firm in 2006); and two IC assembly and test companies (Globetronics and Inari Technology). Interview partners were mostly the CEO of these companies; in all cases, senior managers with a profound insight into the firm's strategy were interviewed. In some cases, interviews with the CEO were complemented by interviews with other senior managers. We also interviewed several relevant government agencies, which were identified by the interviewed firms as important to be included in this study. These government agencies include CREST, Usains Infotech, MIMOS, Northern Corridor Implementation Authority (NCIA), and investPenang. Three of these agencies were newly established in the 2000s. During the interviews, we sought to identify the key experiences of the four firms during their start-up phase, technological learning and growth phase, as well as their achievement over the past few years. Subsequently, we categorized those processes into start-up strategies, technological learning and growth strategies, and evaluations of achievements based on technological and economic performance, as well as industrial conditions. We also sought to ascertain from the firms whether any specific contributions were received from the identified government agencies throughout the three phases.

As a next step, we benchmarked the four Malaysian IC firms against successful catch-up Taiwanese IC firms, namely TSMC, UMC and Advanced Semiconductor Engineering (ASE), which are the largest outsourced IC assembly and test firms in the world. The purpose of benchmarking is to facilitate mapping the taxonomy and trajectory of the latecomer business strategies in our attempt to find out why Taiwanese firms have successfully caught up whereas the Malaysian cases are still struggling. Only by examining both the successful and unsuccessful cases can we identify the key determinants, strategic choices and catch-up trajectories of these latecomer firms. The key Taiwanese actors in this field were also interviewed to receive specific insights and information on institutional and firm-level business strategies.[1]

The collected data from interviews were organized using the qualitative content analysis method posited by Gläser and Laudel (2013). It extracts and processes only the relevant data or information using categories derived ex ante from the theoretical framework. Patterns in the extracted data are identified and integrated into typologies (Yin, 2011, 2014). To ensure the classifications match both theory and data, theory was modified throughout the process when needed.

11.4 LESSONS OF THE LOST TIGER AND IMPLICATIONS FOR CATCH-UP STRATEGIES

11.4.1 A Background on the Malaysian Integrated Circuit Industry

Early research on the IC industry in Malaysia argued that integrated circuit firms were perpetuating the exploitation of workers without significant upgrading (see Lim, 1978; Salih and Young, 1987). It did not examine, however, the dynamics of technology in the integrated circuit firms. Hobday (1995) presented evidence of incremental innovation in multinationals in East Asia with Malaysia as one of the examples. Rasiah (1996) and Mathews and Cho (2000) documented the upward movement of integrated circuit firms up the technology ladder. Rasiah (1994; 1996) showed that technical change and development of indigenous firms has been slow primarily due to the lack of human capital and inadequate institutional support. Rasiah (1994) and Lai and Narayanan (1999) describe the development of indigenous suppliers in Penang that have evolved largely without direct involvement of the government.

There has been a huge influx of foreign electronics firms to Malaysia since the 1970s to assemble and test electronic products for export markets after the opening of free trade zones and licensed manufacturing warehouses. However, the country still lacks an environment that supports high-tech innovations in the industry and electronics assembly has always been export-oriented. Malaysia has been reported as being trapped in middle-income level with weak infrastructures that are not conducive for high-tech innovations (Rasiah and Malakolunthu, 2009). Not only has the lack of high-tech infrastructure inhibited the local firms' ability to deepen their technological capabilities, it has also resulted in foreign firms concentrating only in labour intensive manufacturing activities borrowing the necessary technologies from their parent plants.

To encourage a supportive environment, the government has set up a number of meso-organizations. Among those are the establishments of Malaysian Institute of Microelectronic Systems (MIMOS) in 1985 with the hope to achieve national catch-up in semiconductor and related fields, the Human Resource Development Council in 1993, the Malaysian Technology Development Corporation (MTDC) in 1992, the Malaysia Industry-Government Group for High Technology (MIGHT) in 1993, the Small and Medium Industries Development Corporation (later renamed SME Corp) in 1996, and the Multimedia Development Corporation (MDeC) in 1997.

Despite all the efforts undertaken by the government, Malaysian meso-organizations failed to follow in the footsteps of some successful economies like South Korea and Taiwan. In 1997, MIMOS procured Very-Large-Scale-Integration (VLSI) Technologies in the hope of imitating the Taiwanese short-cut strategy, which is buying over foreign companies in order to acquire advanced technology. While Taiwan's ITRI proved successful in generating cutting-edge technologies, MIMOS failed to produce similar results due to the lack of skilful management and successful strategies to manage and transfer technologies (Rasiah, 1999; Rasiah 2010). After the 1997–98 Asian financial crisis, funding of these meso-organizations was cut, further curbing their ability to make a decisive difference in the catch-up process.

Subsequently, the Malaysian government strived to follow the leveraging strategy used by Singapore by offering special grants to a number of MNCs such as Intel, AMD, Motorola, Infineon, Osram, Agilent and Alterra, to enter into the wafer fabrication and design industry of the country. Only a few firms were able to engage in such activities as a result of the scarcity of qualified engineers and scientists and the lack of R&D support (Rasiah, 2010). As a result, the Malaysian government's scattered support in the local electronics industry, which does not bode well for firms' human resource and process technology capabilities, has resulted in industry players being entrenched on the lower rungs of the technology ladder (Rasiah, 2004).

The integrated circuit manufacturing industry, targeted alongside other export-oriented light manufacturing industries, for example, garments, consumer electronics and industrial electronics in the 1970s, has long been an integral component of Malaysia's manufacturing, employment and export activities (MITI, 2004). The Malaysian Institute of Microelectronics Systems (later incorporated in 1990 into the Action Plan for Industrial Technology Development (APITD)) was established to foster innovative industrial change, and closely followed by the First Industrial Master Plan (IMP1) in 1986 which emphasized integrated circuitry as a strategic industry moving forward.

Penang was presented as an operational hub for semiconductor companies, with the first firm – National Semiconductor – coming in 1971 and followed by Advanced Micro Devices (AMD), Mostek, Hewlett Packard, Monolithic Memories and Intel by 1976 (Rasiah et al., 2012). Indigenous involvement in the assembly and test arena started in the mid-1980s when Carsem, a subsidiary of the Hong Leong Group, took over operations of Carter Semiconductors. Other indigenous firms, such as Globetronics in Penang and Unisem in Ipoh, emerged subsequently. Wafer fabricating activities, on the other hand, were spearheaded by Motorola in Seremban. However, the Motorola plant ran on old transistor technology and closed down in the late 1990s. Through government efforts, other foreign firms commenced operations in Malaysia, with one of the most notable being Infineon, which started its 8-inch wafer fabrication plant in Kulim as an upstream wafer source for its front-end plant in Malacca. Samsung, on the contrary, was not convinced by the government and decided to set up operations in India in 2006.

Not all efforts by the government bore fruit. The government acquired the Very Large-Scale Integration (VLSI) company in Silicon Valley – which manufactures integrated circuits – and a wafer lab at MIMOS, only to see the labs closed down by 2001. Other initiatives of the government include creating the companies SilTerra in Kulim and 1st Silicon in Sama Jaya, with the former fabricating wafers to consumer electronics manufacturers, and the latter involved in the fabrication of application-specific integrated circuits (ASICS) of 4-inch wafers by 2007 (Rasiah et al., 2012). Multinational flagships like Intel and AMD have their local operations limited to merely improving product design, assembly and testing that consequently hindered spillover opportunities (Rasiah, 2010).

As of 2010, semiconductor products accounted for 92.7 per cent of the Malaysian total export of electronics components or 43.6 per cent of the country's total electronics exports (MIDA, 2011). Four notable wafer fabrication firms remain in the local arena – two foreign firms (Infineon and Osram), one indigenous firm (SilTerra), and one joint venture of indigenous and foreign firms (X-Fab Sarawak). Indigenous assembly and test firms are engaged in the assembly of second and third generation transistors and memory chips. Foreign firms were reported to be largely manufacturing first and second generation memories and microprocessors (Rasiah et al., 2012). Scarcity of human capital and insufficient capitalization were the reasons why at least 7 semiconductor firms, initially expressing interest in relocating their ASIC and DRAM fabrications to Malaysia, reversed their decisions after negotiations with the Malaysian Ministry of International Trade and Industry (MITI) (Rasiah et al., 2012).

Despite the challenges, a few indigenous assembly and test firms have experienced stunning growth in the past decade, including publicly listed Globetronics and Inari. Shorter product cycles and incessant miniaturization processes resemble the current nature of the industry; hence technological upgrading is crucial for successful development. Meanwhile, a number of new government agencies emerged, including Usains Infotech and the Collaborative Research in Engineering, Science & Technology Center (CREST).

11.4.2   Findings: Case Studies of Malaysian IC Firms

SilTerra. SilTerra was incubated from MIMOS as a promising firm to follow in the footsteps of successful firms like TSMC. It started manufacturing as a pure play foundry in late 2000 to fabricate 0.25 micro CMOS chips and it was the second largest fabrication house in Southeast Asia in 2006. The company was acquired by Khazanah – the government-linked investment corporation – in 2004 to provide additional capital for expansion. In 2005, SilTerra successfully fabricated 8 MB SRAM chips using 0.13 micron CMOS technology through a strategic alliance with IMEC – a Belgium-based nanotechnology research centre (Taylor, 2007).

With an award-winning 200 mm facility and design capacity of 40,000 wafers per month, the company has strived to gain a position in the global market within an extremely competitive industrial environment. The firm has moved up to rank 17 by year 2010, as one of the top 20 IC foundries worldwide. Being a 200 mm wafer foundry and despite many constraints, the corporate strategies for technology catch-up were carefully chosen in order for the firm to compete against its peers. While industry leaders like TSMC, Samsung and Global Foundries were incessantly investing in the development of 32/28 nanometer (nm) technology in 2010, the Malaysian firm was focusing on technology ranging from 180 nm to 110 nm. In fact, overall for the year 2010, the most popular nodes for 200 mm wafer foundries were 180 nm and 130 nm.[2]

SilTerra has a joint technology development project with ProMos Technologies (Taiwan) to bring SilTerra's advanced 0.13 micron and 0.11 micron High-Voltage (HV) process technology for small-panel LCD driver IC applications to ProMOS's 12-inch fabrication facilities at Taichung, Taiwan. The technology was in the pilot-run stage ready for customers' tape-out, and was on track for mass production starting in the fourth quarter of 2011. With this partnership project, technology transfer took place between the two firms and both have benefited by tapping into the fast-growing smart phone market.

The company SilTerra has also strived to work together with the country's institutions and universities. Two memoranda of understanding (MoUs) were signed between Usains Infotech Sdn Bhd (UISB) and SilTerra and MIMOS Bhd. Based on these, Usains could make use of the Multi-Project-Wafer Services and Failure Analysis Services of SilTerra, and MIMOS under the MoUs could provide a total programme management from IC design to prototyping for customers and to train graduate students in IC design.

To date, 14 US patents have been issued to SilTerra Malaysia according to the United States Patent and Trademark Office (USPTO) database. These initiatives notwithstanding, SilTerra has faced the challenge of competitors. One of the direct competitors to SilTerra Malaysia is the Vanguard International Semiconductor Corporation, which was spun off as an affiliate of the Taiwan Semiconductor Manufacturing Corporation (TSMC) by the Industrial Technology Research Institute (ITRI). Vanguard has developed driver IC technologies and has a logic technology licence with TSMC. Vanguard's primary clients include fabless firms in Taiwan such as Novatek, Himax, Orise; the company also secured contract orders from TSMC for companies like Omnivision and Richtek (Liao et al., 2011). By year 2010, Vanguard was ranked number seven worldwide among IC foundries. It is currently focusing on 8-inch technology and its most advanced technology is 0.11 um node.

A critical factor that drives Vanguard is the fact that the company's largest shareholder is the industry giant TSMC. Therefore, technology transfers take place easily between the two. Vanguard can benefit from its relationship with TSMC by accessing the company's operational efficiency know-how and strategy for improvement in wafer fabrication. Vanguard is expanding its 8-inch wafer value by increasing capacity to reach scale economies, providing half-node technology, such as 0.22 um versus 0.25 um and 0.11 um versus 0.13 um, and increasing wafer production efficiency with TSMC's recipe and equipment sharing (Liao et al., 2011).

1st Silicon (changed to X-Fab Sarawak in 2006). The state government of Sarawak invested into 1st Silicon in the late 1990s to strategically transform and foster the economic development of the state.[3] The wafer fabrication business was deemed a strategic choice to spearhead the state's entry into the high-tech and knowledge-intensive sector. The investment was aimed to create spillover effects by creating several clusters and supporting industries that work as a nucleus for growth in the domestic human talent pool and high-technology process capabilities.

The start-up of 1st Silicon was motivated by a number of reasons at that time. Among others, the communication tools industry became the largest consumer of ICs, overtaking the computing products industry in that role. Based on the interviews conducted, the demand for cellular phones was growing two times faster than the demand for personal computers. Moreover, the indigenous start-up was motivated by the scarce capacity of wafer fabrication worldwide. 1st Silicon believed that more fabs were needed to support IC industry growth. The start-up also realized the benefits that foundry can bring to fabless companies and the advantages of a 'pure-play foundry' over the traditionally capital-intensive Integrated Device Manufacturer (IDM) model.

Over the years, the investment in 1st Silicon has generally enhanced Sarawak's manufacturing expertise and global connectivity. In 2006, 1st Silicon announced the merger with X-FAB Semiconductor Foundries AG, a leading analogue/mixed-signal foundry, manufacturing silicon wafers for analogue-digital integrated circuits (mixed-signal ICs), headquartered in Erfurt, Germany. The merger was based on the strategic rationale of exploiting the significant manufacturing, technological and marketing synergies. Moreover, there was minimal overlap in terms of personnel and geographic coverage. The State of Sarawak also viewed the strategic merger and long-term partnership with X-FAB as a powerful union and as a tool to further the state's long-term goal to develop its world-class high-tech and knowledge-based sectors. The findings are categorized and summarized into three main phases. Table 11.1 shows the key highlights experienced by these two Malaysian-owned wafer fabrication firms during their start-up phase, technological learning and growth phase, as well as, during the past three years.

Globetronics. Globetronics was a humble small and medium-sized enterprise (SME) start-up in 1991. It started by serving a single customer and provided a single manufacturing service to Intel – one of the largest MNCs in Penang. As a giant MNC in Penang, Intel was a great customer, partner and trainer who initially shared critical knowledge on operations systems and set-up, equipment and tools, human resource training, skills and technology transfer with Globetronics.

Globetronics received support from MIDA, including tax incentives and financial grants to help them move up the technological value-chain. MTDC was a perfect equity partner since the second year of the start-up. There was a timely injection of resources and cash, which created a strong financial foundation for growth and expansion opportunities. Globetronics has strived to become an original design manufacturer (ODM) through co-development with its sub-contractors. There was synergistic investment and diversification into new capability and technology through customers. In the past few years, more than 15 per cent of the firm's annual revenue has been channelled back into re-investment. The firm expanded into new product and new technology market segments, including from burn-in services to plastic package assembly, to ceramics assembly, to module assembly, to customized LED and to sensor packages. Also, the firm expanded from memory devices to transistor products, to IC, to LED products, to timing devices and sensors. In terms of consumer electronics products, the firm expanded from customized products to smart phones and LED lighting products. Globetronics also collaborates with its supply chain partners to develop new materials and processes.

Inari Technology. Inari Technology was established in 2006 as a private electronics manufacturing services (EMS) provider in the IC industry, focusing on the radio frequency mobile segment, including back-end wafer processing, package assembly, and Radio Frequency (RF) testing. Its major customer was Avago Technologies.

Inari Berhad was successfully listed at Bursa Malaysia ACE Market on

Table 11.1 Key highlights experienced by Malaysian indigenous wafer-fabrication firms

Phase	Start-up	Growth	Stagnant
Silterra	• Production started in the first quarter of 2001 • Top fab of 2002 (Semiconductor International) • Located at Kulim High Tech Park • Wafer size: 200 mm; equipment capability: down to 90 nm • Designed capacity: 40,000 WSPM; installed capacity: 38,000 WSPM • Focus on HV CMOS technology	• Advanced CMOS process technologies, leading foundry-matched logic technologies, mixed-signal and high-speed RF modules, high voltage processes for display drivers • 'More than Moore' Technology. Focused on mainstream foundry technologies for 'hot' markets ranging from 180 nm to 110 nm (Digital Consumer Chipset, Display Drivers, Wireless Baseband & Connectivity, Wired/ Networking chipsets, PC Connectivity) • Cost effective migration path (0.18 um to 0.11 um) • Key growth drivers: SilTerra Display Driver IC in smart phones (rapid 2.5G to 3G migration) • Extensive partnership network to provide IP and design support, custom IP to meet specific design requirements; design solutions partner; IP verification service and turnkey service	• Ranked 17th among global pure-play foundries in 2012 • A joint technology development project with ProMOS's 12-inch fabrication facilities at Taichung, Taiwan for 0.13-micron and 0.11-micron HV process technology for small-panel LCD driver IC applications
1st Silicon (now X-Fab)	• Incorporated in January 1998, began production in the fourth quarter of 2000 • USD1 billion, first deep sub micron wafer fab in Malaysia, 30,000 WSPM • Motivated by industry drivers (communication tools); the scarce capacity worldwide; the benefits that foundry can bring to fabless firms and advantages of a 'pure-play foundry' over the IDM model	• One-stop solution for fabless design houses and IDMs (design support centre and wafer fabrication). Sharp Corporation as technology partner • Other customers comprising of fabless, IDMs, and OEMs • In 2003: 3 patents were granted by USPTO • In 2006: Merged with X-Fab. Technology by customers is transferred into X-Fab, mostly through customers' prototypes. X-Fab also develops its own prototypes • Focused on the sweet spot of mainstream production at 0.25 um	• 62,000 8-inch WSPM • X-Fab was ranked 12 in 2010 with USD317 millions revenue • Manufacturing capability is down to 130 nm • Limited privilege for R&D loan after it was taken over by X-Fab

Source: Authors' own elaboration based on the interviews held.

19 July 2011. The firm experienced stunning growth in just a few years. It carried out a series of business expansions and acquisitions. CEEDTec Sdn Bhd is a 51 per cent owned subsidiary of Inari, acquired in January 2012 with Agilent Technologies being the major customer; Inari South Keytech Sdn Bhd (ISK) was incorporated in June 2012, which is a fibre-optic division that supplies mainly to Avago. The acquisition of Amertron Global was completed in June 2013. Inari Amertron Group products are used in a wide variety of high-technology wireless telecommunications products such as smartphones, tablet computers, and wireless modems; optoelectronics, sensors and fibre optics.

During the ramping-up period of Inari, MIDA provided good support to approve another five years of Pioneer Status and continued to support the additional headcount quota to hire foreign workers. MIDA granted a matching grant of RM 18.4 million to support the technology, upgrading to lead in the latest Fine-Pitch Flip-Chip platform. If this technology were not adopted, the business would drop by half of the current performance. MIDA granted another matching grant of RM16 million to support R&D activities to bring to market more new products and services. The grants enabled a stronger business performance in the global EMS space; it allowed more businesses to be taken from Agilent and the takeover of Amertron Global, which is a bigger entity. Table 11.2 shows the key highlights experienced by these two Malaysian-owned assembly and test firms in the three phases.

11.4.3 Analysis: Industry Conditions, Firm-Level Strategies and the Role of Institutions

The Malaysian government established SilTerra and 1st Silicon as a part of technological upgrading efforts. However, the two came into the industry at a less advantageous time and the positioning of these two firms did not allow them to grow smoothly. The number of new fabs built worldwide peaked between the late 1980s and the mid-1990s, due to the emergence of the wafer fabrication industry in Taiwan. However, more fabs were being built subsequently with 11 new 300 mm fabs announced in 2002, which was a major supply factor (Dataquest, 2003). About the same time, that is, 2000–2002, SilTerra and 1st Silicon began their production with 200 mm wafer fabs. Since the early phase of SilTerra's and 1st Silicon's venture into the wafer fabrication industry, there has been an increasing trend of foundry overcapacity worldwide. In 2003, 11 per cent of worldwide foundry capacity was not occupied, whereas the rate of overcapacity increased to about 19 per cent in 2004 (Dataquest, 2003).

The key drivers for the rapid growth of Globetronics and Inari

Table 11.2   Key highlights experienced by Malaysia indigenous IC assembly and test firms

	Start-up phase	Technological learning and growth phase	Ramp-up phase
Globetronics	• A humble start-up with just two employees in 1991 • Single customer and single manufacturing service to a giant MNC – Intel • Intel – a great customer, partner and trainer as initial and critical knowledge transfer	• Focus on niche products and services – to be the best in class (identified niche) • Partnering with strategic customers (sub-con manufacturer and co-development partner) • Synergistic investment & diversification into new capability and technology by partnering customers • Continual reinventing by partnering with strategic customers (co-development with sub-contractors to move to ODM) • Collaborate with 'supply chain partners' to develop new material and processes	• Total investment in the last 5 years (51%) was higher than the total investment over the last 21 years • New business revenue over total revenue in the last 5 years had the same percentage as TSMC's • Quartz and timing products to world number 1 producer; LED products and manufacturing services to 3 of the 4 world top LED firms; sensor products to all the global smartphone and tablet brands
Inari Technology	• Established in 2006 as an EMS provider, with a focus on the radio frequency mobile segment including back-end wafer processing, package assembly, and RF testing • Major customer was Avago Technologies	• Capacity readiness – to capture growing market demand for Fine-Pitch Flip-Chip packaging products and therefore increase country export GDP • Process technology upgrading (Fine-Pitch Flip-Chip packaging) • Business expansion and acquisitions including CEEDTec, Inari South Keytech (fibre-optic division supplies mainly to Avago), and acquisition of Amertron Global • Inari Amertron Group products are used in a wide variety of high-technology wireless telecommunications products such as smartphones, tablet computers, and wireless modems; optoelectronics, sensors and fibre optics	• Listed at Bursa Malaysia ACE Market, 19 July 2011 • Boosted by growing demand of the RF semiconductor devices • Net profit increased by 62.7 per cent to RM16.5 million from RM10.1 million in 2012 • Upgrading RF Flip-Chip Assembly Technology

Source: Authors' own elaboration based on the interviews held.

Technology include their right positioning strategy and their focus on niche products. Both companies have chosen RF as one of their key technology products.[4] They have strategically used R&D grants by MIDA to upgrade the critical process technologies.

In Table 11.3, we evaluate the case studies and summarize the analysis based on the firm-level key strategies, as well as the success of these strategies when taking into consideration the industry conditions. We also summarize the role of the local institutions throughout this process in Table 11.4.

11.4.4   Towards a Typology of Latecomer Strategies

To account for a more comprehensive set of latecomer strategies, we mapped the taxonomy and trajectory by benchmarking the Malaysian cases against the successful cases in Taiwan in Table 11.5. Figure 11.2 benchmarks the technology level of Malaysian foundries against the world frontier (TSMC). It is found that the Malaysian foundries have not been able to close the technology gap with the technological frontier after years of attempting to catch-up. Moreover, the technology gap has increasingly widened in the past decade.

At the start-up stage, latecomers' target of technology is bounded by characteristics like rareness, imitability and transferability as posited by Mathews (2002). Instead, the Taiwanese first pure-play foundry chose to transfer and focus on the then non-mainstream technology (CMOS) despite also transferring the then mainstream technology (NMOS) for 'insurance' purposes. By examining the target considerations of the Taiwanese firms during the initial stage, we also found that the targeting strategies depend very much on other facets such as competition and whether the choice can buy time for the latecomer. For instance, the Taiwanese foundries began by producing the technologically obsolete chips of toys, music and timing devices. The incumbents had ceased producing these chips at that time and hence viewed the foundries as not posing any threat. TSMC enjoyed a total of seven years of no stiff competition from the incumbents and could spend time building up its capabilities.

We also found that the timing of the latecomers' entry is an important factor. Entry by latecomers at different points in time reflects the different market trends and technological regimes faced by the latecomer firms. The point of entry for the Malaysian firms was the time when the telecommunication products began to boom. The changing technological regimes of the industry had significant impacts to latecomer strategies. In this case, the industry was transitioning from Mark II to Mark I patterns of innovation after TSMC emerged as the world's first pure-play

Table 11.3 *Firm-level strategies and industry conditions*

	Start-up strategies	Technological learning and growth strategies	Technological and performance indicators
Silterra	• Both firms targeted the right products (communication tools) • However, there was scarce capacity of wafer fabrication worldwide in 2000, the year of their establishments, but not in the following few years. It was believed by 1st Silicon that more fabs were needed to support IC industry growth • Had wrong impression that the increasing fab capital costs and lower-risk way to enter the IC industry as the growth drivers	• Incremental innovations – horizontal product expansion by adding new features at each existing technology nodes ('More than Moore' Technology) • Focused on mainstream foundry technologies for 'hot' markets ranging from 180 nm to 110 nm • Cost effective migration path (0.18 um to 0.11 um) • Key growth drivers: smart phones (rapid 2.5G to 3G migration) • Joint technology development project with ProMos facilities in Taiwan (shared capacities)	• Wafer size is 200 mm, manufacturing capability is down to 90 nm • Capacity: 38,000 WSPM • Key competitor – Vanguard, an affiliate of TSMC which focuses on 8-inch technology, has developed driver IC technologies and has a logic technology licence with TSMC. It secures contract orders from TSMC • By year 2010, SilTerra was ranked 16th and Vanguard was ranked 7th worldwide among IC foundries
1st Silicon (now X-Fab)	for foundries	• Sharp Corporation as technology partner • 1st Silicon: 3 patents in year 2003 • Technology by customers is transferred into X-Fab, mostly through customers' prototypes. X-Fab develops its own prototypes too • Sweet spot of mainstream volume production at 0.25 um ('More than Moore' Technology)	• Capacity: 62,000 eight-inch WSPM • Manufacturing capability is down to 130 nm • X-Fab was ranked 12 worldwide in 2010 with USD317 million revenue

Table 11.3 (continued)

	Start-up strategies	Technological learning and growth strategies	Technological and performance indicators
Globetronics	• Single customer and single manufacturing service to a giant MNC – Intel • Intel – a great customer, partner and trainer as initial and critical knowledge transfer • MTDC – a perfect equity partner since the second year of start-up	• Focused on niche products and services – to be the best in class (identified niche) • Incremental innovations • Synergistic investment and diversification into new capability and technology by partnering customers • Strived towards the ODM model by co-development with its sub-contractors	• New business revenue over total revenue in the last 5 years had the same percentage as TSMC's • The annual turnover in 2012 was RM300 million • A 100% Malaysian-owned firm, producing for world top 20 electronics brands
Inari Technology	• Started with a focus on the RF mobile segment, include back-end wafer processing, package assembly, and RF testing • Tapping the incentives given by MITI and MIDA, which provided good support to approve the manufacturing licence, pioneer status and headcount quota to hire foreign workers	• Capacity readiness – to capture growing market demand for Fine-Pitch Flip-Chip packaging products and therefore increase country export GDP • Process technology upgrading: Fine-Pitch Flip-Chip packaging technology • Aggressive business expansion and M&A (CEEDTec Sdn Bhd, ISK, Amertron Global acquisition • Driven by Amertron Group products: high-technology wireless telecommunications products such as smartphones, tablet computers, and wireless modems; optoelectronics, sensors and fibre optics	• Revenue grew 32.6 per cent to RM62 million from RM46.8 million a year ago, boosted by growing demand from the RF semiconductor devices • Higher demand enabled the group to benefit from higher production capacity utilization and greater economies of scale • Driven by smart mobile communication devices such as smartphones and tablet computers – as it focused on the RF segment

Source: Authors' own elaboration based on the interviews held.

Table 11.4   The role of institutions and their specific contributions to firms

Government agencies	Objectives and role	Contribution to firms
CREST	To promote collaborative research between industry and academia; to accelerate university's ability to produce industry-ready researchers; to increase competitiveness of Malaysia's E&E industry	Collaborative research with SilTerra
Usains Infotech	To provide shared E&E design & development services to make it affordable for SMEs, talent development, to nurture research collaborations among academia & industry; to develop and commercialize IPs	R&D collaborations with Globetronics including LED driver development IC design collaborations with SilTerra (0.13 u & 0.18 u), MIMOS (0.35 u) and X-Fab (1.0 u high voltage)
MIMOS	To provide IC shared facilities and services to the E&E industries in Malaysia	R&D collaboration with SilTerra
MIDA	To provide R&D grants for technological upgrading projects; to assist companies that intend to invest in the manufacturing and services sectors; to facilitate the implementation of their projects	Provided tax incentives and financial grants to Globetronics to move up the value chain Provided good support to Inari to approve the manufacturing licence, Pioneer Status and headcount quota to hire foreign workers. Provided few R&D grants to Inari to upgrade their process technologies
MTDC	To be the leading integrated venture capital solutions provider; to build world-class Malaysian technology companies through strategic partnerships	The perfect equity partner to Globetronics since the second year of start-up

Source: Authors' own elaboration based on the interviews held.

foundry. Therefore, Taiwanese foundries entered into the industry in the Mark II environment whereas Malaysian foundries entered into a Mark I environment.

Importantly, all the latecomers have sought a gateway to enter the GVC. Two key considerations were the business model and the

Table 11.5 *Typology of latecomer strategies*

Catch-up stage	Latecomer strategies		IC Manufacturers			
			Wafer fabrication		Assembly and test	
			Taiwan case	Malaysia case	Taiwan case	Malaysia case
Start-up (Linkage)	Targeted technology	Rareness	Non-mainstream technology (CMOS)	Mainstream technology	Mainstream technology	Mainstream technology
		Imitability	Imitable	Imitable	Imitable	Imitable
		Transferability	Transferable	Transferable	Transferable	Transferable
		Competition level	No major incumbent in CMOS, other incumbents aborted production of toys, timing devices etc.	Major incumbents in CMOS, telecommunication products	Major incumbents exist	Major incumbents exist
	Time allowance		7 years to build capabilities	Nil	Nil	Nil
	Timing positioning in GVC	Market trend	Toys, music, watches	Telecommunication era	Toys, music, watches	Telecommunication era
		Innovation pattern	Mark II to Mark I	Mark I to Mark II	Mark II to Mark I	Mark I to Mark II
		Business model	Contract manufacturer	Contract manufacturer	Contract manufacturer	Contract manufacturer
		Production stage	High end fabrication	High end fabrication	Low end assembly and test	Low end assembly and test
	Human capital	Rootness	Indigenous engineers and R&D scientists	50% use of expatriates as engineers/scientists	Indigenous engineers and R&D scientists	More indigenous engineers
		Local competition	An appropriate size of local talent pool	No specific strategy	An appropriate size of local talent pool	No specific strategy

	'Branding'	Use of a global well-known customer	No specific strategy	Use of a global well-known customer	Use of a global well-known customer
Leverage	IP	Leveraged the customers' knowledge	Limited leveraging capacity	Leveraged the customers' knowledge	Leveraged the customers' knowledge
	Technology	Strategic alliance, virtual vertical integration	Shared capacity	Merger and acquisitions; backward and forward integration	Merger and acquisitions
Learning	Technology trajectory	Radical and incremental innovation	Only incremental (horizontal) innovation	Radical (limited) and incremental innovation	Only incremental (horizontal) innovation
	Positioning strategy	Target hot and niche segments	Target only the sweet spot (hot market)	Target hot and niche segments	Target only the sweet spot (hot market)
Successful or aborted catch-up		Successful	Aborted	Successful	Successful*

Notes: *Good economic performance. Continued to catch up with technology at the point of time this research was conducted; grey boxes indicate strategies led by institutions.

Source: Authors' own elaboration based on the interviews held.

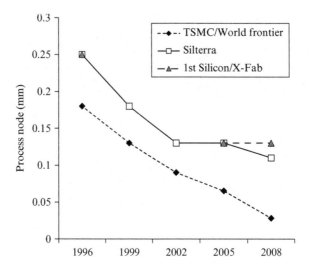

Source: Authors' own elaboration.

Figure 11.2   Malaysian IC technology not able to catch-up

production stage across the target value chain. We seek to highlight that all the latecomer firms have adopted the contract-manufacturing model. Nevertheless, this chapter shows that the choice of being a contract manufacturer is more of a unique case for the Taiwan foundries, especially TSMC.

Developing human capital is no doubt an important issue. The Taiwanese foundries used 100 per cent indigenous human capital in their R&D whereas the Malaysian foundries have 50 per cent of their engineers as expatriates due to brain drain issues. The Taiwanese government encouraged talented Taiwanese based overseas to return to their homeland in order to help build the IC industry. However, they only arranged for 10 per cent of the Taiwanese to return in order to create an adequate local talent pool. This is because an overly competitive talent pool would make the 'returns' less attractive to the Taiwanese expatriates living abroad. The role of the government and institutions in these processes are highlighted in grey boxes in Table 11.5.

How far a latecomer firm can then leverage from the linkages depends more on the role of the entrepreneurial management. Through his extensive networking experience from his previous career, Morris Chang, the founder of TSMC, managed to contact and attract Intel to become TSMC's global customer although the foundry was in its infancy. The trust of Intel in the new-born foundry has brought TSMC numerous leverages, including technology and skill transfer, as well as attracting other customers worldwide to come to the infant foundry. The Malaysian assembly and test firms used a similar strategy by beginning production for a global MNC, such as Intel for Globetronics and Avago for Inari. However, the Malaysian foundries did not do the same. Other leveraging strategies include the transfer of IP knowledge and strategic alliances with customers or vendors for vertical integration or backward and forward integration.

As latecomer firms begin to learn, they have to consider their technological trajectory and positioning strategy. Taiwanese foundries are found to have pursued both radical and incremental innovations. For instance, TSMC has pursued the miniaturization league of Moore's Law, as well as More than Moore's Law (horizontal expansion).[5] As a comparison, Malaysian Silterra and 1st Silicon were only pursuing the More than Moore's Law, which was to add functional features to each existing node instead of participating in the miniaturization race. We also find that, in terms of market positioning, TSMC and ASE have sought to target the entire market across the value chain, that is, producing all available nodes. Malaysian foundries and assembly and test firms have all targeted at the hot market, that is, producing at 130–90 nm.

11.5   CONCLUSIONS

Whereas the Malaysian owned 1st Silicon has been taken over by the German owned X-Fab, SilTerra has rather been an aborted catch-up effort in the policymaking of the nation. Nevertheless, two Malaysian-owned assembly and test firms (Globetronics and Inari Technology) have had stunning growth over the past decade. The firms' expansions have contributed to the country's technological learning by focusing on constant upgrading in process technologies. A critical role has been played by a few specific government agencies throughout the process, such as MIDA, which has contributed significant R&D grants to both indigenous firms.

This chapter has important implications based on the proposed analytical framework and the subsequently derived typology for latecomer catch-up strategies. Business perspectives have been introduced into the development context at both the institutional and organizational level. Because latecomers lack technological capabilities, they are forced to seek competitive advantages through various forms of outsourcing. That is, firms in developing countries can leverage off their temporary low-cost comparative advantage to offer complementary goods and services and capture latecomer effects (Mathews, 2002). These latecomers are thus able to overcome their disadvantages and exploit to the full their few advantages as latecomers. It makes sense for latecomers to make use of all the available resources from the advanced world that they can acquire, in return for providing services, such as low-cost manufacturing. This has been the case for the Taiwanese and Malaysian assembly and test firms.

For the above trade-off to work, latecomer firms must consciously make a strategic choice. One beneficial choice is the insertion as a player in the global economy, with the potential for upgrading, extending beyond the firm to the national level (Mathews, 2002, 2006). It needs to be recognized, however, that not all firms have that organizational capability, and that such opportunities for upgrading may not present themselves. The case of the foundry showcases this phenomenon. Despite the Malaysian government trying to mimic the Taiwanese catch-up model, unlike their Taiwanese counterparts, the Malaysian foundries have failed to catch up with the world's technological frontier. In fact, we seek to emphasize that the successful catch-up of the Taiwanese foundries should not be explained merely using the above trade-off argument. No doubt the Taiwanese foundries sought to insert themselves into the GVC by reducing its customers' cost burden. However, it was a cautious and strategic insertion. The fabless firms in the US outsourced to the first pure-play foundry (TSMC), not because of the lower cost of manufacturing, but the exemption from manufacturing at all. Rather, such a business model did not exist until the Taiwanese foundry created a path-breaking strategy to insert itself into the GVC.

Moreover, the argument of the latecomer's strategy through the insertion into a GVC emphasizes that the point of insertion faces lower technological requirements where latecomers can begin their learning and leveraging. Because the pure-play foundry is a technology- and knowledge-intensive contract-manufacturing model, introduced by TSMC into the industry, it actually requires very high technological capabilities to catch up and keep up. This explains why the Malaysian assembly and test firms managed to grow steadily whereas the Malaysian wafer fabrication firms could not. Therefore, this also indicates that the chosen production stage (fabrication or assembly and test) as a mean to insert into the GVC requires different strategies.

Some organizational structures are also more appropriate for specific environments. Different production specializations and different points in time of catch-up processes also showcase very different catch-up strategies due to evolving industrial innovation patterns. As compared to the assembly and test firms, for instance, the foundries faced a technological regime with higher cumulativeness and a higher degree of economies of scale. These two conditions have caused the foundry industry to constantly face a very stiff price war. Such conditions have also led to the fact that assembly and test firms are still able to perform well although they are not at the technological frontier. Within the foundry regime, different points in the time of entry have an important bearing on latecomer strategies, as the underlying technological conditions evolve over time.

NOTES

1. The names of the interview partners are available from the authors upon request.
2. This paragraph is based on the information received during the interviews conducted in 2012 with companies participating in this study.
3. Sarawak is a state in East Malaysia.
4. RF was introduced in the 20th century in commercial products. This technology has enabled many models of *portable gadgets* such as mobile phones and tablets in the past decade.
5. Moore's Law is a prediction made in 1965 by Gordon Moore, co-founder of Intel, which states that the number of transistors per square inch on ICs would double every year (Interviews, 2013).

REFERENCES

Abramovitz, M. (1956). Resource and output trends in the United States since 1870. *American Economic Review, 46*, 5–23.
Amsden, A. (1989). *Asia's next giant: South Korea and late industrialization*. New York: Oxford University Press.
Blomstrom, M., and Kokko, A. (2001). Foreign direct investment and spillovers of technology. *International Journal of Technology Management, 22*(5/6), 435–454.
Breschi, S., Malerba, F., and Orsenigo, L. (2000). Technological regimes and Schumpeterian patterns of innovation. *Economic Journal, 110*(463), 388–410.
Brown, C., and Linden, G. (2009). *Chips and change: How crisis reshapes the semiconductor industry*. Cambridge: The Massachusetts Institute of Technology (MIT) Press.
Dataquest. (2003). Available through Gartner Market Insights research database.
Gerschenkron, A. (1962). *Economic backwardness in historical perspective*. Harvard: The Belknap Press of Harvard University Press.
Gläser, J., and Laudel, G. (2013). Life with and without coding: Two methods for early-stage data analysis in qualitative research aiming at causal explanations. *Forum: Qualitative Social Research, 14*(2), Art. 5.
Hobday, M. (1995). *Innovation in East Asia: The challenge to Japan*. Aldershot, UK and Brookfield, VT: Edward Elgar Publishing.
Kamien, M. I., and Schwartz, N. L. (1982). *Market structure and innovation*. Cambridge: Cambridge University Press.
Kim, L. (1997). *From imitation to innovation*. Cambridge: Harvard Business School Press.
Lai, Y. W., and Narayanan, S. (1999). Technology utilization level and choice: The electronics and electrical sector in Penang, Malaysia. In K. S. Jomo, G. Felker

234   *Innovation in developing and transition countries*

and R. Rasiah (eds.), *Industrial Technology Development in Malaysia* (pp. 107–124). London: Routledge.

Liao, P., Chung, A., and Windsor, R. (2011). *Anchor Report: Asia Foundries.* Nomura Equity Research, accessed 17 April 2013 at http://www.nomuranow.com/research/globalresearchportallogin/login.aspx?ReturnUrl=%2fresearch%2fglobalresearchportal%2fDefault.aspx.

Lim, L. Y. C. (1978). *Multinational firms and manufacturing for export in less-developed countries: The case of electronics industry in Malaysia and Singapore.* Ph.D. Dissertation, Ann Arbor: University of Michigan.

Malerba, F., and Nelson, R. (2012). *Economic development as a learning process: Differences across sectoral systems.* Cheltenham, UK and Northampton, MA: Edward Elgar Publishing.

Malerba, F., and Orsenigo, L. (1994). Schumpeterian patterns of innovation. *Cambridge Journal of Economics, 19*(1), 47–66.

Malerba, F., and Orsenigo, L. (1996). Schumpeterian patterns of innovation are technology specific. *Research Policy, 25*(3), 451–478.

Mathews, J. (1997). A Silicon Valley of the East: Creating Taiwan's semiconductor industry. *California Management Review, 39,* 26–54.

Mathews, J. (2002). Competitive advantages of the latecomer firm: A resource-based account of industrial catch-up strategies. *Asia Pacific Journal of Management, 19,* 467–488.

Mathews, J. (2006). Catch-up strategies and the latecomer effect in industrial development. *New Political Economy, 11*(3), 313–335.

Mathews, J., and Cho, D. S. (2000). *Tiger technology: The creation of a semiconductor industry in East Asia.* Cambridge: Cambridge University Press.

MIDA. (2011). *Industries in Malaysia: Electrical and electronics industry,* accessed 30 October 2013 at http://www.mida.gov.my/env3/index.php?page=ee.

MITI. (2004). MIDA Annual Media Conference on the Performance of the Manufacturing Sector in 2003, accessed 30 October 2013 at http://www.miti.gov.my/cms/content.jsp?id=com.tms.cms.article.Article_15dba7ba-7f000010-5e095e09-a457c76b&curpage=tt.

NEAC. (2010). *New Economic Model for Malaysia Part 1.* Kuala Lumpur: National Economic Advisory Council.

Nelson, R., and Winter, S. (1982). *An evolutionary theory of economic change.* Cambridge: Harvard University Press.

North, D. (1990). *Institutions, institutional change, and economic performance.* Cambridge: Cambridge University Press.

Perez, C., and Soete, L. (1988). Catching up in technology: Entry barriers and windows of opportunity. In G. Dosi, C. Freeman, R. Nelson, G. Silverberg and L. Soete (eds.), *Technical change and economic theory* (pp. 458–479). London: Pinter.

Prahalad, C., and Hamel, G. (1990). The core competence of the corporation. *Harvard Business Review, 68*(3), 79–91.

Rasiah, R. (1994). Flexible production systems and local machine tool subcontracting: Electronics component transnationals. *Cambridge Journal of Economics, 18*(3), 279–298.

Rasiah, R. (1996). Institutions and innovations: Moving towards the technology frontier in the electronics industry in Malaysia. *Journal of Industry Studies, 3*(2), 79–102.

Rasiah, R. (1999). Malaysia's national innovation system. In K. S. Jomo and

G. Felker (eds.), *Technology, competitiveness, and the state: Malaysia industrial technology policies* (pp. 180–198). London: Routledge.

Rasiah, R. (2004). Technological intensities in East and Southeast Asian electronics firms: Does network strength matter? *Oxford Development Studies*, *32*(3), 433–455.

Rasiah, R. (2010). Are electronics firms in Malaysia catching up in the technology ladder? *Journal of Asia Pacific Economy*, *15*(3), 301–319.

Rasiah, R. (2011). The role of institutions and linkages in learning and innovation. *International Journal of Institutions and Economies*, *3*(2), 165–172.

Rasiah, R., and Lin, Y. (2005). Learning and innovation: The role of market, government and trust in the information hardware industry in Taiwan. *International Journal of Technology and Globalisation*, *1*(3), 400–432.

Rasiah, R., and Malakolunthu, A. (2009). Technological intensities and economic performance: A study of foreign and local electronics firms in Malaysia. *Asia Pacific Business Review*, *15*(2), 181–197.

Rasiah, R., Kong, X.-X., Lin, Y., and Song, J. (2012). Variations in the catch-up experience in the semiconductor industry in China, Korea, Malaysia and Taiwan. In F. Malerba and R. Nelson (eds.), *Economic development as a learning process: Differences across sectoral systems* (pp. 113–156). Cheltenham, UK and Northampton, MA: Edward Elgar Publishing.

Salih, K., and Young, M. L. (1987). Social forces, the state and the international division of labour: The case of Malaysia. In J. Henderson and M. Castells (eds.), *Global restructuring and territorial development* (pp.168–202). London: Sage Publications.

Taylor, C. (2007). *SilTerra teams with IMEC for 90-nm research*, accessed 30 October 2013 at http://www.edn.com/article/461933-Silterra_teams_with_IMEC_for_90_nm_rese arch.php.

UNIDO – United Nations Industrial Development Organization. (2002/2003), *Industrial Development Report* (Chapter 6).

Veblen, T. (1915). *Imperial Germany and the industrial revolution*. Reprinted by A. M. Kelley, 1964, New York.

Yin, R. (2011). *Qualitative research from start to finish*. New York: The Guilford Press.

Yin, R. (2014). *Case study research: Design and methods*. California: SAGE Publications.

12. Epilogue. Innovation systems in developing and transition countries: what is different, what is missing and what are the implications?

Alexandra Tsvetkova, Jana Schmutzler and Marcela Suarez

In this book, we set out to provide a detailed analysis of whether and how the concept of the National Innovation System (NIS) is applicable in the context of developing and transition countries. The way of studying innovation from a system perspective, which inevitably entails interdisciplinarity, is relatively young (Edquist, 1997) and as such lacks well-established concepts (Lundvall et al., 2011b). Generally, two main conceptualizations of NIS prevail in the literature: a narrow and a broad one (e.g. Lundvall, 2007). It is the latter that tends to be applied in the context of developing and transition countries (Lundvall et al., 2011b). Yet, there is no single NIS definition and some researchers cast certain doubts on the applicability of any conceptualization of an NIS – originated in the developed world – to its less developed counterpart (Arocena and Sutz, 2000). Although sometimes felt in selected chapters in this book, and definitely meriting further study, the specific limitations of the applicability of an NIS framework to the developing and transition countries and reasons for these limitations are outside of the scope of the analyses presented in this volume. Rather, the book's contributions mostly embrace an NIS approach in an attempt to understand innovation processes and their implications at both macro and micro levels. The chapters in this edited volume, taken as a whole, offer insights from the developing and transition countries on a range of issues grouped around the following questions:

- What are the challenges for innovation at the macro (system) and micro (firm) level according to the experiences of developing and transition countries?

- What is the role of public policies in the transformation of national innovation systems?
- What innovation practices successfully overcome challenges to innovation?
- What is the role of collaboration and learning in fostering innovation?

A unified approach to studying innovation in the less-developed part of the world is a natural first step for doing so and is important for several reasons. First, given the role of innovation in closing the economic gap with the developed world, and the scarcity of research on innovation systems in developing and transition countries (Lundvall et al., 2011a), NIS-focused country-level explorations build our knowledge of what propels or hinders the development and consolidation of an NIS and, thus, potentially contributes to catching-up processes. But, perhaps more importantly, the detailed analyses of NISs in the less developed part of the world are relevant for policymakers. Such studies provide the basis for international comparisons that help to identify the factors, policies and circumstances conducive to the success of an innovation agenda in an otherwise turbulent environment. Keeping this in mind, our book documents and analyses challenges and adaptive strategies taken by firms, universities, industries and governments. We provide evidence for a context-based applicability of a broad definition of an NIS where the constitution and consolidation of an innovative system needs to be seen as a path-dependent two-level process embedded in the sociocultural context, macroeconomic structures and institutions of a country. Additionally, conveying the richness of experiences from nine developing and transition countries from Africa, Asia, Europe and Latin America, we offer a strong basis for discussion that may help governments, firms and universities in their strides to successfully innovate.

We start our discussion with the macro, or system, level of analysis, presenting a variety of ways governments in diverse parts of the world, from Europe and Africa to Latin America, approach the challenge of initiating and shaping their NISs. Despite the apparent diversity of approaches, there are commonalities too obvious to ignore. Insufficient resources and limited capabilities of private actors, weak and elusive formal institutions, ephemeral protection of property rights that makes fair return on investment into knowledge less likely, poor cohesion between business and social interests together with often small internal markets define the leading role of a government in developing and supporting NIS. It is unsurprising since government is perhaps the only player able to take on a holistic approach and channel substantial resources into building an NIS and advancing innovation-based economic development within a top-down approach in such circumstances. The success of the active governmental efforts, however, is not guaranteed. Chapters in the first part of this book (and, to a lesser extent, in the second part) attest to the importance of a range of factors that are crucial for continual NIS development. Macroeconomic and political stability appears to be a basic precondition that creates fertile ground for innovation to flourish and an NIS to be established, whereas a hectic political and economic environment usually sets back the progress of building a successful NIS. Political and economic shocks may open a window of opportunity to the innovation-led development of a country, as described in Chapters 3 and 4, but beyond this they are harmful to steady growth. Equally important is the commitment of a government to creating and supporting favourable conditions for innovations and a clearly communicated will to support an innovation agenda in the country. This will and perseverance in the government support for innovations should lead to a general understanding of the final goals and the methods to achieve them, as can be observed in the case of the Brazilian healthcare sector. Coordination and dialogue are crucial here but, as Chapters 2, 3 and others show, those are the elements that usually are missing in the way governments in developing and transition countries tackle the issue of innovation promotion. As a result, governmental efforts are often fragmented with implementation scattered across various public institutions with complex and often confusing structures of subordination. The ad-hoc and disjointed actions of governments in their attempts to stimulate innovative initiatives and to build NIS lead to a wide range of suboptimal outcomes that the chapters of this book so eloquently illustrate.

To give a few examples, in Peru the steering capabilities of the Peruvian National Council of Science and Technology (CONCYTEC) founded in 1981 were gradually marginalized by handing executive political power and funding management for science and technology over to the Ministry of Production (PRODUCE). An independent agricultural innovation system further eroded CONCYTEC's duties and prevented it from consolidation of a Peruvian NIS. Duplication of numerous governmental functions and activities in the area of innovation, their incoordination and excessive red tape, hampered collaboration among governmental bodies that form the country's NIS and limited private firms' access to public resources earmarked to support innovation. In Armenia, fragmentation of public policies aimed at fostering NIS has prevented actors other than the government from shaping the innovation agenda. The resultant policies are poorly aligned with the needs of firms and universities who are integral components of any NIS and are central to its efficient development. In addition to governmental inefficiency and the waste of resources in task duplication, fragmentation and poor coordination exerts its toll on firms too. For instance, in Malaysia innovative companies surveyed by Abuduxike and Aljunid (Chapter 7) conceive such a state of affairs as a major setback for NIS functioning and express concerns about situations when public policies initiated by one governmental body are not recognized by others. Coupled with a limited understanding of the innovation companies' needs, public policies that proclaim support of innovation as their goal often do not perform to their full potential. More generally, discordant organization of NISs in developing and transition countries with weak links and interactions among its components, a lack of trust and understanding between government, universities and private actors together with missing channels to articulate all stakeholders' concerns, impair successful government–industry–academia collaboration in many countries covered in this book. This leads to misaligned policies, inefficient or sometimes non-existent implementation mechanisms and university curricula (centrally defined in many transition and developing countries) that fail to efficiently support innovative initiatives or prepare specialists equipped with skills required by innovative firms in the marketplace.

Although governments in developing and transition countries play the leading role in promoting and shaping NISs, their attempts are often uncoordinated and misaligned with market demands. There are, however, examples of deliberate governmental strategies to involve a wide range of stakeholders in the development of an innovation policy agenda or to capitalize on the economic mechanisms in place. In the case of the Brazilian healthcare sector (Chapter 5) purposeful attempts to coordinate various governmental bodies and agencies and to include a wide range of stakeholders in the goal-prioritizing process for the National Health Policy facilitate the alignment of economic (including innovation-related) and social policies in one direction with a set of social goals in mind. Instead of competing governmental institutions, Brazil seems to have achieved – at least to some extent – a functioning collaboration among governmental bodies, which strengthened the healthcare NIS of the country. Likewise, public policies in the Argentinean software sector (Chapter 6) that simultaneously supported the development of local technologies and the procurement of foreign technologies were successful because they managed to tap into synergies of the complementary nature of the internal and external innovation processes.

Not all countries are successful in tailoring their innovative policies to the needs of firms, universities and other private agents. When confronted with an unsupportive environment for innovation efforts, companies are forced to find their own ways to overcome challenges to successful innovation. In the second part of the book we present evidence of the specific challenges to innovation in transition and developing countries and the responses to those challenges adopted by companies. Building collaborations domestically and abroad, and learning through interactions with a multitude of actors are among the most widely adopted tactics, as Chapters 7 through 11 show. It appears that the central cohesion mechanisms of any NIS, collaboration and learning, become ever more important in the less-developed world as they additionally are the vehicles to overcoming barriers created by inefficient formal institutions, underdeveloped market structures and customary practices that often are not open to the global nature of technological innovation. In this light, Chapters 8 and 9 explore the prevalence of collaborations and the association between the nature of collaboration and innovation activities in two countries that differ substantially both institutionally and culturally. The conclusions, however, are remarkably consistent. Collaboration is at the heart of the innovation strategies of individual firms but their spread and intensity are rather limited. Since companies in both countries are unlikely to be a part of well-established and long-lasting business alliances, especially on an international scale, efforts to create conditions conducive to expansion, deepening and sustaining innovation-based networks among firms, appear to be a promising avenue to a consolidated NIS.

The efforts to promote more collaboration, to a great degree, should be targeted at establishing and supporting trust, an informal institution fundamental to active partnerships in any settings and an important dimension of social capital (Knack and Keefer, 1997; Nahapiet and Ghoshal, 1998), which is central to efficiently governing social relations and collaborations (Arrow, 1974; Blau, 1964; Garfinkel, 1963; Ouchi, 1980; Parsons, 1951). As several chapters show, however, it tends to be weak or missing in many contexts covered in this book. How exactly trust can be successfully promoted among economic agents in the less developed world depends on local informal institutions, culture, heritage and shared values. The country case studies of this book shed light on the specific barriers – and potential avenues to overcome these – that should be helpful for understanding the ways to consolidate their respective NIS. For instance, in Armenia – due to its soviet heritage, deeply rooted not only in the minds of people but also in the functioning of the market – multinational enterprises (MNEs) are viewed with suspicion and the fears of merciless exploitation of local resources by MNEs are deeply ingrained in societal consciousness (Chapter 3). This, together with a strategy of insider privatization implemented after the breakdown of the Soviet Union, limited the presence of foreign owners in the Armenian economy and made international collaborations in general, and integration into Global Value Chains (GVC) specifically, a rare practice. As a result, firms' ability to technologically upgrade is limited. In Hungary, on the other hand, the Soviet heritage is not a part of the country's business identity and international collaboration is perceived as an opportunity for learning (Chapter 9). Although the level of international collaboration among Hungarian small and medium enterprises remains relatively low, the overall trend is to deepen and expand collaborations, and the European policies in place offer supporting mechanisms to keep the process going.

Likewise, learning in the context of developing and transition countries is not just acquiring technical knowledge. Equally important is obtaining practical skills of communication and the sharing of ideas, needs, and perspectives; of navigating through bureaucracy and of perseverance despite volatile environments and weak formal institutions; of managing innovative business operations and business operations that are conducive to innovation; of reading market signals often distorted by the governmental involvement and arrangements and of seizing opportunities. In a sense, effective learning in developing and transition countries, especially when it comes to skills that cannot be obtained in a classroom, is potentially the most powerful engine of an innovation system within a country, a region or a sector. Given the overall low trust among actors within an NIS, learning is a communal effort that needs to be steered and nurtured. The challenge that many countries overviewed in this book face is an inflexible education system that poorly adjusts to the new realities of a globalizing world and may be an obstacle to, rather than a mechanism of, the smooth functioning of an NIS. Unable to access a pool of labour force with specific qualifications, innovative firms have to spend substantial resources on building their own human capital base capable of driving and sustaining firms' innovation activities. Closer collaboration between universities, industry and government, which often is the main source of both funding and curriculum changes, appears important for overcoming this hurdle to efficient innovation in developing and transition countries. The role of universities in advancing the innovation agenda and innovation-led development, however, is not limited to labour force training. As illustrated by the experience of Universidad Mayor de San Simón (UMSS) in Chapter 10, a university can actively shape a regional innovation system from the bottom up. By acknowledging the importance of social relations in addition to technical and scientific issues, UMSS paved the way for enabling trusting relationships among diverse actors of an emerging regional innovation system based on a mutual understanding of the needs, goals and capabilities of all actors involved. Another efficient way for companies in the less developed part of the world to build innovative competences is to leverage their natural advantages and, for example, to become a part of GVC. If this is viewed as a stage in knowledge accumulation and acquisition of technological skills, as was the case with two successful Malaysian assembly and test firms (Chapter 11), rather than the end in itself, gradual movement up the chain as the expertise is accumulated can bring indigenous firms to a new level in terms of both their innovative ability and contribution to social welfare.

In conclusion, based on a variety of experiences from different countries and sectors studied in this book, we believe that the NIS concept is a useful analytical and normative tool to study innovation in developing and transition countries, as long as it is used in a context-specific way that accounts for the two levels of an NIS and their interdependence. The chapters in this edited volume illustrate how the macro (or system) level impacts the behaviour of individual economic actors, and how well-articulated and comprehensive public policies can facilitate competency-building, learning and innovation. In contrast, deficient and fragmented public policies, competition for power and financial resources among governmental bodies, unprofessionalism, especially when it comes to evaluating merits of a research project, selective channels for the concerns of private interests to be heard and attended to, overly bureaucratic procedures, corruption and a lack of trust in the government and among economic actors, deter firms and universities from active and efficient participation in an NIS, hampering its formation and consolidation. The importance of collaboration and learning in such a milieu is paramount; these central NIS elements have the ability to enhance the innovation system and bring it to the next level. However, collaboration and learning themselves, and their potential effects, depend on the macroeconomic and political environment, on consistency of governmental efforts to promote innovation and on local culture. Despite this dependence, and a generally dominant role of governments in initiating and supporting innovation systems in developing and transition countries, active participation and private initiative may by highly fruitful, as the example of Bolivia's Universidad Mayor de San Simón suggests. A promotion of collaboration and learning, both domestically and internationally, is another area where both public and private efforts are likely to be efficient in the consolidation of an NIS and enhancing innovation-led economic growth as the cases of European public policy in Hungary and public policy in the Argentinean software sector convey. The richness of the case studies presented in this book paint a diverse picture of successes and failures in initiating and consolidating NISs in developing and transition countries. Most importantly, however, these case studies open multiple avenues for further research that may explore potential limitations in the applicability of the NIS framework, and specific modifications or new perspectives on innovative practices and their interrelations, that would help nations of the less-developed world to attain social and economic goals, capitalizing on the opportunities presented by technology and innovation.

REFERENCES

Arocena, R., and Sutz, J. (2000). Looking at national systems of innovation from the South. *Industry and Innovation, 7*(1), 55–75.

Arrow, K. J. (1974). *The limits of organization.* New York, NY: Norton.

Blau, P. (1964). *Exchange and power in social life.* New York, NY: Wiley.

Edquist, Ch. (ed.) (1997). *Systems of innovation: Technologies, institutions, and organizations.* London: Routledge Taylor and Francis.

Garfinkel, H. (1963). A conception of and experiments with "trust" as a condition of concerted stable actions. In O. J. Harvey (ed.), *Motivation and social interaction: Cognitive determinants* (pp. 187–239). New York, NY: Ronald Press.

Knack, S., and Keefer, P. (1997). Does social capital have an economic payoff? A cross-country investigation. *Quarterly Journal of Economics, 112*(4), 1251–1288.

Lundvall, B.-Å. (2007). *Innovation system research: Where it came from and where it might go.* Globelics Working Paper, No. 2007-01, accessed 15 November 2016 at https://ideas.repec.org/p/aal/glowps/2007-01.html.

Lundvall, B.-Å., Joseph, K., Chaminade, C., and Vang, J. (2011a). *Handbook of innovation systems and developing countries: Building domestic capabilities in a global setting.* Cheltenham, UK and Northampton, MA: Edward Elgar Publishing.

Lundvall, B.-Å., Vang, J., Joseph, K., and Chaminade, C. (2011b). Innovation system research and developing countries. In B.-Å. Lundvall, K. Joseph, C. Chaminade and J. Vang (eds.), *Handbook of innovation systems and developing countries: Building domestic capabilities in a global setting* (pp. 1–32). Cheltenham, UK and Northhampton, MA: Edward Elgar Publishing.

Nahapiet, J., and Ghoshal, S. (1998). Social capital, intellectual capital and the organizational advantage. *The Academy of Management Review, 23*(2), 242–266.

Ouchi, W. (1980). Markets, bureaucracies, and clans. *Administrative Science Quarterly, 25*, 129–141.

Parsons, T. (1951). *Social system.* Glencoe, Ill: Free Press.

Index

Abramovitz, M. 50
Academy of Science Malaysia (ASM)
    137
Action Plan for Science, Technology
    and Innovation (PACTI) 96
Agrarian Reform 19
Ajao, B. F. 157
alliance capitalism 173
all-out-populism 26
Altamirano, T. 27
Anand, S. 90
Andean Pact 20
Argentina software sector
    direct approach application,
        complementarity tests
        118–122
    emerging economy, application
        116–123
    industrial policy in 116–118
    sectoral performance, development
        policies and complementarities
        122–123
Argentine Technology Fund
    (FONTAR) 118
Armenian business climate 58
Arocena, R. 2, 16, 51, 193
Asia-Pacific Economic Forum (APEC)
    30
association approach 112

BioNexus status 144
BioNexus status companies 138
Biotechnology Corporation of
    Malaysia (BiotechCorp) 138
biotechnology, defined 135
Biotechnology Master Plan (BMP)
    138
Biotechnology Regional Innovation
    Centres (BRICs) 132
biotechpole of Sidi Thabet 73
Bolivian University System (SUB) 195

Bramwell, A. 193
Brazilian National Development Bank
    (BNDES) 96
Brazil Maior Plan 98
Brown, C. 210
Brundenius, C. 192, 193
Bye, B. 62

capitalization of knowledge 193
Carranza, V. 31
Cassiman, B. 118
Cassiolato, J. 17
Castells, M. 173
Cervantes, M. 158
Chamber of Information and
    Communications of Argentina
    (CICOMRA) 117
Chamber of Software and Computer
    Services of Argentina (CESSI)
    117
Cho, D. S. 215
civil society organizations 23
commercial liberalization 114
Commonwealth of Independent States
    (CIS) 56
Community Innovation Survey
    123
complementarities, innovation
    activities
    economies, developing 112–116
    theoretical arguments and empirical
        studies 110–112
correlation approach 111
Costa, L. 100
creative forgetting 53, 54
creole liberalism 19

De Althaus, J. 19
developmental university 190–203
diaspora 58
Dunning, J. H. 173

EBRD transition report 57
Economic and Industrial Health
     Complex (CEIS) 90
economic development 1, 15
economic reconstruction 28
Edquist, C. 191
Etzkowitz, H. 193
ex-ante concept 16, 51
Executive Group of the Health
     Industrial Complex (GECIS) 98

firm-level perspective 3
focus group discussion (FGD) 135, 136
forced conscriptions 26
foreign direct investment attraction 112
foreign direct investments (FDIs) 28,
     29, 56, 58, 68, 73, 78, 81, 151
foreign technology buying 112
Freeman, C. 111, 173
Free Trade Agreements (FTAs) 35
Fund for Innovation, Science and
     Technology (FINCYT) 34, 35
Fund for Research and Development
     for Competitiveness (FIDECOM)
     34
Fund for the Promotion of the
     Software Industry (FONSOFT)
     117

Gadelha, C. 100
geographical proximity 180
Gerschenkron, A. 206, 208
Gevorkyan, A. V. 58
Gläser, J. 214
Global Competitiveness Index (GCI)
     18
global financial crisis 31, 56
Global Innovation Index rank 58
global value chains (GVCs) 9, 16, 29,
     62, 210–211, 240, 241
Globetronics 220
governance system, Armenia 59
gradual territorial control 25
gross domestic expenditure on R&D
     (GERD) 177
gross domestic product (GDP) 17, 30,
     56, 57, 132
Growth Acceleration Program (PAC)
     96
Gu, Sh. 52

health biotechnology (HB), in
     Malaysia
     challenges, firms' perspective
          140–148
     economic impact of 132–133
     facts and figures 137–140
     funding issues 144–145
     government policy and regulation
          147–148
     human capital issues 145–147
     issues and challenges 131–152
     methodology 135–136
     National Health Innovation System,
          biotechnology firms 133–135
     Niche areas 147
     product development (PD) chain 150
     sector development, National
          Innovation Systems 142–144
     STI capabilities 136–137
     study design 135–136
     sustainable HB sector, development
          148–152
Herrera, A. 88
Higher Education Institutions (HEIs)
     181, 182
Higher Level Personnel Training
     Coordination (CAPES) 96
Hobday, M. 215
Hommen, L. 191
Human Capital Report 58
Hungarian small- and medium-sized
     enterprises 171–186
     innovativeness and networking,
          economy 176–178
     networking, motivations 182–184
     networks, participation 178–182
     RDI collaboration 173–175
     research methodology and sample
          175–176
hyperinflation 27, 28, 37

import-substituting industrialization
     (ISI) 19, 28
Inari Technology 220–222
inclusive development, innovation 87
Industrial Competitiveness
     Development Fund (ICDF) 73
Industrial Eco-Technological Parks
     (PITEs) 36
informal institutions 4

information and communication
technologies (ICT) 68
information technology (IT) sector
60
Innovation and Competitiveness
Programme for Peruvian
Agriculture (INCAGRO) 30
innovation system research, developing
countries 156–157
innovation via imitation process 76
innovative biotechnology firms 131
Innovative Economy Development: An
Initial Strategy 59
Institute for Industrial Technology and
Technical Norms (ITINTEC) 20,
23
Institute of Agricultural Innovation
(INIA) 31
intellectual property rights (IPR) 59
International Monetary Fund 114
interventionism 19, 26
Isola, O. O. 158

Jegede, O. O. 157, 159
Johnson, B. 53

Kamien, M. I. 207
Kitanovic, J. 63
Kitanovic's model 55
knowledge exchange (KE) 53, 70
knowledge generators 193
Korean Samsung 206
Koubaa, K. 76

Laboratory for Social and Solidarity
Economy (LabESS) 79
Lai, Y. W. 215
large-scale privatization 53
latecomer strategic typology 206–233
Laudel, G. 214
learning, Armenia 61–64
through foreign actors 63–64
through local networks 62–63
learning economy 52
liberated zones 30
Linden, G. 210
List, F. 50
low-end forgetting process 53
low-skilled labor 54
Lundvall, B.-Å. 51, 53, 191

Malaysian Institute of Microelectronic
Systems (MIMOS) 207, 215,
216
market liberalization 37, 53, 54
market–multinational enterprises
(MNEs) 240
Maskus, K. E. 194
Mathews, J. 210–212, 215, 224
micro–macro effect 114
Millennium Development Goals 6
Ministry of International Trade and
Industry (MITI) 142
Ministry of Production (PRODUCE)
34, 35, 38, 40, 41, 238
Ministry of Science, Technology and
Innovation (MOSTI) 142
Mohnen, P. 111
Morel, C. 103
Morero, H. A. 119
multilateral organizations 26

Narayanan, S. 215
National Agenda of Priorities in
Healthcare Research (ANPPS)
95, 96
National Biotechnology Policy (NBP)
138
National Competitiveness Report 61
National Council of Science and
Technology (CONCYTEC)
25–27, 29, 30, 34–36, 38, 40, 41,
238
National Fund of Science and
Technology (FONDECYT) 25
National Innovation System, of
Armenia 49–65
components 58–61
determinants, actors and networks
54–61
governance system 59
learning and 61–64
macro environment 56–58
in transition countries 50–54
National Innovation Systems (NISs)
1–4, 16, 17, 37, 236–237
macroeconomic and political
stability 238
in Armenia 49–65
in Bolivia 191–2
in Nigeria 158–159

in Peru 15–48
in transition countries 50–54
National Plan for Productive
    Diversification (PNDP) 35–36
national programme of research and
    innovation (NPRI) 78
National Research Council (CONI) 20,
    23, 37
National Sectoral Innovation System
    (NSIS) 69
national STI/H policy (PNCTIS) 95
National Strategic Plan of Science,
    Technology and Innovation
    (PENCTI) 34, 38
National Superintendency of
    Education (SUNEDU) 36
National System of Agricultural
    Innovation (SNIA) 34
National System of Science and
    Technology (NSST) 20, 23, 27, 30
National System of Science,
    Technology and Technological
    Innovation (SINACYT) 17,
    34–38, 40, 42
National University of San Marcos
    (UNMSM) 28
Nelson, R. 207
Newly Industrialized Economies
    (NIEs) 206
Nigerian mining industry 156–167
    collaboration on innovation, impact
        165–166
    linkage of actors in 163–165
    methodology 159–161
    model specification and statistical
        analysis 160–161
    prevalent types of innovation
        161–163
    sampling 159
    study variables and measurement
        159–160
Niosi, J. 134
Nussbaum, M. 90

Ohmae, K. 173
ordered probit estimation 119
Organisation for Economic Co-
    operation and Development
    (OECD) 51, 131
organizational innovation 160, 162–163

organizational learning 53
Oslo Manual 159
Oyebisi, T. O. 158
Oyewale, A. A. 158

Partnerships for Productive
    Development (PDPs) 97
Perry, M. 61
Peru's policy transitions 17
Peruvian economy 16
Peruvian National System of Science
    and Technology 17–37
    failed industrialization 19–24
    lost decade, 1981–90 25–27
    National Innovation Systems 31–37
    organizational and institutional
        foundations, resetting 27–31
    Public Funding Bonanza 31–37
    state interventionism limits 19–24
Plan Inca 20
planning system legacy 54
political violence 28
power asymmetries 15
private investment 26, 29
privatization 52, 54
process innovation 162, 166
Productive Development Policy 97
protectionism 26

Radosevic, S. 65
Rasiah, R. 215
Regional Innovation System (RIS) 50
research, development and innovation
    (RDI) 171, 184–186
resource-based view (RBV) approach
    110
Röller, L.-H. 111
Roolaht, T. 61

Sagasti, F. 25, 27, 31
Scandinavian Institute of
    Competitiveness and
    Development (SICD) 196
Schumpeterian Mark I industry 208
Schumpeterian Mark II industry 208
Schumpeter, J. A. 50
Schwachula, A. 87
Schwartz, N. L. 207
science development 59
science push innovation 61

science, technology, and innovation in
health (STI/H) 87
inclusive development 90–92
science, technology and innovation
(STI) 2, 6, 18, 34, 37, 38, 41, 86,
111
inclusive development 88–90
Sectoral Mining Innovation System
156
Sectoral Public Research Institutes
(SPRIs) 20, 25, 27, 29, 38
sectoral system of innovations (SSI)
209
Sheahan, J. 28
SilTerra 217–219
Sirius 54
Siyanbola, W. O. 158
small and medium enterprises (SMEs)
31, 73
social capital concept 51
social programmes 29
social science research 124
Soete, L. 173
Sölvell, Ö. 200
soviet heritage 52
state-owned enterprises (SOEs) 56
state policies 55
STI Framework Fund (FOMITEC) 35
STI/H, in Brazil 92–102
historical background 92–93
Ministry of Healthcare, 2004–07
95–97
Ministry of Healthcare
reinforcement, 2012–14 98–99
policy trajectories synthesis,
interactions and priority setting
99–102
policy trajectory, 2002–14 93–99
promotion of, 2002–03 93–95
strengthening of interactions,
production sub-systems 97–98
S&T indicators 30
structural economic reforms 37
structural reforms 28
structural support policy, TPIS 72–74
financial mechanisms, R&D 73–74
human capital policy, KE 74
innovation centres and collaborative
incentives 72–73
1st Silicon (X-Fab Sarawak) 219–220

Sutz, J. 2, 16, 51, 191
Synopsys 61

Taiwan Semiconductor Manufacturing
Corporation (TSMC) 206, 224,
230–232
Technological and Foreign Trade
Policy (PITCE) 96
technological catch-up of Malaysian
semiconductor firms 206–235
analytical framework 212
data collection and analysis 212–214
firm-level catch-up strategies, global
value chains 210–211
government level catch-up strategies
208–210
industrial innovation patterns
207–208
industry conditions, firm-level
strategies and institutions,
analysis 222–224
latecomer strategies, typology
224–231
Malaysian IC firms, case studies
217–222
Malaysian Integrated Circuit
Industry 215–217
research methodology 212–214
technological catch-up process 2,
206–233
technological innovation 240
Technological Innovation Centers
(CITEs) 36–38, 41
Technology-Based Enterprise
Incubator (EMBATE) 201
Teece, D. J. 110
terrorism 28, 37, 78
Tiffin, S. 157
TPIS, after Jasmine Revolution 78–80
human capital skills dilemma 79–80
institutional background change,
revolution 78–79
obstacles to innovation catch-up,
pharmaceutical companies 80
TPIS, before Jasmine Revolution 69–78
conjunctural support policy 70–72
efficiency, firm level analysis 74–78
firm-level innovation survey 75
firm-level R&D, structure and
practices 77–78

strengths and weaknesses, firm-level
perspectives 75–77
structural policy instruments 70
structural support policy 72–74
Trade-Related Intellectual Property
Rights (TRIPS) agreements 73
transition economies 52
Triple Helix model 191, 202
Trojer, L. 197
tropical infectious diseases 148
Tunisian Guarantee Company (TGC)
73
Tunisian Investment Incentive Code
(IIC) 70
Tunisian pharmaceutical innovation
system (TPIS) 69
Tunisian pharmaceutical market 70,
76

United Nations Economic Commission
for Europe (UNECE) report
60
Universidad Mayor de San Simón
(UMSS), Bolivia 190, 241, 242
context of study 194–195
mode 2 and innovation culture,
research community 201–202
National Innovation Systems
191–192

research activities background
195–196
systemic interaction approach,
cluster development 198–201
theoretical framework 191–194
universities, NISs 192–194
university technology transfer unit
and activities 196–198
university technology transfer unit
(UTT) 190, 197–199, 203

Vaccarezza, L. S. 192
VCyT report 194
Veblen, T. 206, 208
Very-Large-Scale-Integration (VLSI)
Technologies 216, 217
Veugelers, R. 118

Wahab, S. A. 194
Wald test 119
weak institutions 2
Whittaker, H. 15
Winter, S. 207
Wolfe, D. A. 193
World Bank 114
World Economic Forum report 80

Yacoub, L. 81
Yacoub, N. 75, 81